The Pragmatist's Guide to Relationships

Ruthlessly optimized strategies for dating, sex, and marriage

Simone & Malcolm Collins

http://Pragmatist.Guide
Copyright © 2020
Simone & Malcolm Collins
All rights reserved.

As with our last book, *The Pragmatist's Guide to Life*, you can get a free audio version of this book by visiting our website: Pragmatist.Guide/RelationshipsAudio

Our first crack at writing this book turned out to be so extensive that we ultimately divided our work into two separate volumes. This volume, *The Pragmatist's Guide to Relationships*, outlines strategies for securing relationships, sex, and marriage and introduces methods for maintaining positive relationships. The other volume, *The Pragmatist's Guide to Sexuality*, focuses on how our brains process sexually arousing stimuli and how pair-bonding behavior systems (aka love) can be gamed. As with all products of the Pragmatist Foundation, the proceeds from sales will go to nonprofits.

To be notified when the next Pragmatist Guide goes live, submit your email to Pragmatist.Guide/Notifications

> When putting this book together, we solicited feedback from fans of *The Pragmatist's Guide to Life* who offered to pitch in with early edits of subsequent Pragmatist's Guides. We dedicate this book to these generous and insightful editors who spent hours and days of their free time improving this book. Having such a diverse array of perspectives allowed us to create something hundreds of times better than anything we could have constructed on our own.
>
> Shout outs to some of our most stalwart help: Jacques Ronaldi, Jasmine St John, and Jake Berger.

Contents

Why Read This Book 1
The Pragmatic Model 2
How the Marketplace Affects Relationship Stability 10
Other Marketplace Considerations 14
Know What You Bring To The Table 18
The Dominance Lure 21
The Nice Lure 30
The Sexual Exploration Lure 33
The Easy Lure 38
The Love Lure 41
The Sneaky Lure 43
The Pygmalion Lure 47
The Status Lure 57
The Self-Identity Lure 59
The Friend with Benefits Lure 69
The Long-Term Relationship Lure 71
The Social Construct Lure 76
Which Lure Should I Use? 78
   Relationship Contracts 84
Implied Contract Escalation 88
Marriage Contracts 91
Constructing a Marriage Contract 99
Conflict Resolution Clauses 107

Addressing Finance Clauses in Marriage Contracts ..115
   Common Financial Configurations in Relationships 121
Addressing Marriage Contract Violations 127
Cognitive Separation 138
Cognitive Siloing 139
Cognitive Integration 144
Economic Trends to Exploit 154
Timing Considerations 163
Marriage 187
Geography 190
The Human Mating Season 192
Choosing Not to Have a Partner 193
   "Bad" Relationships 197
   Our Inefficient Biology 217
   Non-Monogamy 242
Why is Non-Monogamy Not the Norm? 245
New Relationship Energy 251
What Monogamous People Should Learn from Poly Culture 253
   Compersion 255
The Myth of Our Poly or Monogamous Past 258
   How to Train Your Partner 262
Marry Someone Who Will Work to Make You Better ..263
Partner Training Tips 265
When To Begin Training 267

- Dealing With An Ex's Training 268
- Accidental Training 272
- Maintaining a Positive Relationship 274
  - Internal Communication 282
- Effective Transference of Information 286
- Ignored Communication 291
- Self-Narratives and Communication 293
  - Rekindling Relationships 296
  - Abuse as a Concept 301
  - Attractiveness Strategies and Research 319
- The Puzzle 320
- The Solution 321
- Less Practical (But Immensely Fun) Tidbits on Attractiveness 324
- Realistic Expectation Setting 341
- Leveraging Point-Based Motivational Systems 343
- Leveraging Social Reinforcement 345
- Getting Back On the Market 346
  - Breakups: A Guide 348
- High Taxation Breakup Methods 348
- Low-Taxation Breakup Methods 351
- Breakup Traps 352
  - Conclusion 354

Appendix

How to "Get Laid" as a Young Adult 360
Engaging and Talking to People 369
Escalating Conversations 371
Flirting 373
Broaching the Topic of Sex or a Relationship 378
Moving to The Idea of Sex... 379
Getting References.. 382
Warnings 385
But I Hate Being Rejected! 387
   Securing a Long-Term Relationship 389
Male Template Strategy 390
Female Template Strategies 396
   Securing a Husband 401
Age Considerations in Husband Searches................... 401
Helpful Husband Hunting Tactics 403
   Leverage Peer Pressure... 403
   Pop the Question.. 403
   Consider Moving On After 22 Months And No Engagement 403
   Make Sacrifices... 404
Sex and Dating in a World with Social Distancing 405
But Whatever I Do, Nothing Works!....................... 413
People Who Just Don't Have a Chance...................... 413
People Who Fail Because of Who They Are................ 416

Defining Human Relationships 418
Factors Affecting Desirability 421
Physical Attractiveness.................................... 422
Kink Preference... 424
Contractual Perks or Downsides 424
Personality + Trope 425
Mental Attributes 426
Emotional, Hormonal, and Instinctual Factors 427
Availability.. 428
Chastity-Promiscuity 431
Wealth 432
Fertility.. 433
Physical Alteration 434
Children from Previous Partners..................... 435
Beliefs About the World.................................. 436
Sources of Recreation.................................... 437
Opportunity Cost 437
Status 438
Signaling 438
The Four Core Markets 440
On Citations and Studies 455
Why People Cheat Rather Than Leave a Relationship 456
What to Do When a Partner Cheats........................... 458
Other Factors Contributing to Cheating 462

Sex in a Long-Term Relationship 464
Common Marriage Contract Themes 474
Guide to Avoiding Crazy.. 479
How to Avoid Dangerous and Unstable Sexual Partners 481
How to Avoid Dangerous and Unstable Long-Term Partners 487
A Call for Introspection 497
False Red Flags 497
Hurting People in Relationships............................ 507
How To Avoid Hurting Relationship Partners 507
How To Avoid Hurting Sexual Partners 509
Abuse 513
The Control Theory 515
Abuse as a Relationship Strategy 517
Lying in Relationships 522
Intentional Misrepresentation in Relationships 522
Unintentional Misrepresentation in Relationships Due to Unanticipated Changes.. 526
Defense Against Misrepresentation 528
Attachment Styles... 531
A More Effective Way to Approach Attachment Styles 535

WHY READ THIS BOOK

People hate thinking systematically about how to optimize their relationships. It is normal to hear someone say: "I will just wait for something to happen naturally" when talking about one of the most important aspects of their life while genuinely believing that this approach has reasonable odds of success. Imagine if people said the same thing about their careers. It would sound truly bizarre for someone to expect a successful career to "just happen naturally" and yet it is entirely normalized to expect that good relationships will.

People pay tens of thousands of dollars to receive degrees in computer science, marketing, and neuroscience. They make tough sacrifices with the understanding that the skills and knowledge they build in these domains will dramatically affect their quality of life. Ironically, people spend very little time systematically examining mating strategies—despite the fact that a robust understanding of the subject can dramatically affect quality of life.

We will happily argue that your sexual and relationship skills matter *more* than your career skills. If you want to be wealthy, the fastest way to become so is to marry rich. Nothing makes happiness easier than a loving, supportive relationship, while one of the best ways to ensure you are never happy is to enter or fail to recognize and escape toxic relationships. If you want to change the world, a great partner can serve as a force multiplier. A draft horse can pull 8000 pounds, while two working together can pull *24,000 pounds*. When you have a partner with whom you can synergize, you gain reach and speed that neither you nor your partner could muster individually.

Heck, even if you are the type of person to judge your self-worth by the number of people with whom you have slept, a solid grasp of mating strategies will help you more than a lifetime of hitting the gym (and we say this with full acknowledgment that hitting the gym *absolutely* helps). A great romantic relationship will even positively impact your health (a 2018 paper in *Psychophysiology* found that the presence of a partner in a room lowered participants' blood pressure) and increase your lifespan (a 2019 paper in the journal *Health Psychology* showed individuals in happy marriages died young at a 20% lower rate).

This book presents our mental library of information on how relationships function and thus can be your guide to systematically developing a mating strategy that will optimize your ability to achieve your goals, even if those goals happen to be as straightforward as happiness and personal fulfillment.

The Pragmatic Model

Just as our first book, *The Pragmatist's Guide to Life*, shows readers how to use The Pragmatic Thought Framework to build a system for making their own decisions about how the world works, this guide uses the same framework to help our audience take a ruthless, practical, and unsentimental approach to sex, dating, and marriage.

The Pragmatic Thought Framework used in our guides is straightforward:
1) Decide what you want to achieve and why.
2) Create a plan to achieve that thing based on the type of evidence you decide has value to you.
3) Execute that plan while constantly testing it, validating it, and adjusting it as you obtain better information.

You might imagine this framework is uncontroversial. This is not the case. In a society obsessed with forming teams, identifying and labeling "bad guys," and discouraging thoughts that might hurt someone's feelings or cause distress, this model for thinking is quite iconoclastic.

All that is a rather ostentatious way for us to say that some ideas in this book will be offensive. We did not set out to write a book that won't offend people.

Offense is an emotion people feel when something credibly challenges their worldview. When an idea that challenges one's worldview is not credible, one may find it worrying, threatening, and maybe even rage-inducing, but one will *not* feel the emotion of "offense." If we have succeeded in writing a book that challenges societal norms surrounding relationships, we will have created a book that most readers will find at least a little offensive.

We personally *love* ideas that offend us. To us, offense is like the burn you get in your muscles during an intense workout; a burn that in part results from all the microtears in our muscles that ultimately lead to new growth (well that and lactic acid buildup, but that confuses the analogy, so we will ignore it). The discomfort caused by the creation of those microtears is quite literally a direct sign that ultimately we will become stronger, better people.

All that said, if any of our theories are so disagreeable to you that you feel compelled to challenge our view on the subject, we invite you to engage us in a way that leverages the types of evidence we value: Unbiased, well-designed scientific/anthropological studies and common cultural tropes. You can reach us at Hello@Pragmatist.Guide

HOW TO USE THE APPENDIX

Throughout this book, we will reference the appendix, which serves as a repository for content that will likely only be relevant to a niche audience.

Some appendix resources to get you started (these sections should be read before diving into the rest of the book if they are relevant to you):

- *How to "Get Laid" as a Young Adult,* page 360: If you are inexperienced and still trying to figure out how to easily secure a partner, we encourage you to read this section of the appendix before moving forward in this book. We wrote this section in an attempt to stifle the proliferation of techniques optimized by thirty-year-old pick-up artists for use in bars, which are hardly appropriate for safe and effective use by younger audiences (i.e. a seventeen-year-old with no experience dating). When a person is inexperienced, a dangerous cocktail of hormones and social norms can make getting laid feel like the only thing that matters, leading them to make life-altering decisions out of desperation without a source of level-headed, logical advice. We imagine a portion of the people who picked up this book fall into this demographic, so we wrote this section to help them safely and reliably date and secure a partner. If you are older than twenty-five and trying to learn how to secure a partner, even if you

are inexperienced, the advice in our chapter on lures will be more applicable to you.
- *Securing a Long-Term Relationship*, page 389: This is a crash course for those looking to find and secure a long-term partner at any stage of life.
- *Securing a Husband*, page 401: This section is an exploration of the data surrounding who is most likely to propose and when.
- *Sex and Dating in a World with Social Distancing,* page 405: This appendix chapter details adaptations that may be made to dating and sexual strategy when in-person interaction becomes limited or more dangerous—such was the case with the COVID-19 pandemic that arose during the final stages of the book's editing. This particular event can be seen as a case study revealing insights into optimal ways people might modify partner acquisition strategies as the world and technology change.
- *But Whatever I Do, Nothing Works!*, page 413: This chapter explores possible causes if all of your relationships fail or you have been totally unable to secure a partner no matter what you try. It will also help you troubleshoot your situation.
- *Defining Human Relationships*, page 418: This is a short section that can help you think through how to define the concept of a relationship and how the various aspects of the concept interact with each other. This is not a section we would recommend for the casual reader. This philosophical odyssey is intended for those trying to get a more holistic understanding of our perspective on the topic and how that perspective may color our advice.

- *The Four Core Markets*, page 440: Here we discuss the differences between "The Sex Market," "The Dating Market," "The Long-Term Relationship Market," and "The Non-Monogamy Market." The key takeaway is this: One's value on the various markets differs dramatically, with women typically having a statistical advantage in markets oriented around short-term relationships and men having an advantage in markets oriented around long-term relationships. Do not assume that because you perform well in one market (like the sex market), you will perform well in another (like the long-term relationship market) or that the skills/public image you build to appeal to people on short-term markets will transfer to long-term markets. In other words, learning how to secure high-quality sex partners is not a skill set that will necessarily increase your odds of securing a spouse.
- *On Citations and Studies,* page 455: This chapter addresses our stylistic choice to only occasionally cite studies, the short answer being that we think citations lend false weight to tenuous claims and promote dangerous mental shortcuts. Cases in which we do not cite sources will nevertheless contain sufficient information enabling you to open a search engine, search for, find, and explore the research in question personally (which is our strong preference).

Other appendix chapters will be referenced at relevant locations throughout *The Pragmatist's Guide to Relationships*; they offer a deeper dive on subjects only lightly addressed in the main body of the book.

THE MARKETPLACE

The realms of dating, marriage, and sex are all marketplaces, and we are the products. Some may bristle at the idea of people as products on a marketplace, but this is an incredibly prevalent dynamic. Consider the labor marketplace, where people are also the product. Just as in the labor marketplace, one party makes an offer to another, and based on the terms of this offer, the other person can choose to accept it or walk. What makes the dating market so interesting is that the products we are marketing, selling, buying, and exchanging are essentially our identities and lives.

As with all marketplaces, every item in stock has a value, and that value is determined by its desirability. However, the desirability of a product isn't a fixed thing—the desirability of umbrellas increases in areas where it is currently raining while the desirability of a specific drug may increase to a specific individual if it can cure an illness their child has, even if its wider desirability on the market has not changed.

In the world of dating, the two types of desirability we care about most are:
1) Aggregate Desirability: What the average demand within an open marketplace would be for a relationship with a particular person.
2) Individual Desirability: What the desirability of a relationship with an individual is from the perspective of a specific other individual.

Imagine you are at a fish market and deciding whether or not to buy a specific fish:
1) Aggregate desirability = The fish's market price that day
2) Individual desirability = What you are willing to pay for the fish

Aggregate desirability is something our society enthusiastically emphasizes, with concepts like "leagues." Whether these are revealed through crude statements like, "that guy's an 8," or more politically correct comments such as, "I believe she may be out of your league," there is a tacit acknowledgment by society that every individual has an aggregate value on the public dating market, and that value can be judged at a glance. When what we have to trade on the dating market is often ourselves, that means that on average, we are going to end up in relationships with people with an aggregate value roughly equal to our own (i.e., individuals "within our league"). Statistically speaking, leagues are a real phenomenon that affects dating patterns. Using data from dating websites, the University of Michigan found that when you sort online daters by desirability, they seem to know "their place." People on online dating sites almost never send a message to someone less desirable than them, and on average they reach out to prospects only 25% more desirable than themselves.

The great thing about these markets is how often the average desirability of a person to *others* is wildly different than their desirability to *you*. This gives you the opportunity to play arbitrage with traits that other people don't like, but you either like or don't mind. For example, while society may prefer women who are not overweight, a specific individual within the marketplace may prefer obese women, or even more interestingly may have no preference. If a guy doesn't care whether his partner is slim or obese, then he should specifically target obese women, as obesity lowers desirability on the open marketplace, but not from his perspective, giving him access to women who are of higher value to him than those he could secure within an open market.

When trying to make an arbitrage play, do not be confused by what society implies that people want and by what people *actually* want. For example, society pretends that both nerdy males and females have low value in most markets, when in reality, once you are out of high school (and sometimes well before), the nerdy archetype has one of the highest values on the marketplace, meaning that targeting otherwise traditionally attractive nerds is a terrible arbitrage play for someone who is indifferent about the archetype.

How the Marketplace Affects Relationship Stability

Individual Desirability / Aggregate Desirability = Your Desirability Ratio

The higher a relationship's Desirability Ratio, the more stable a relationship will be. If a relationship's Desirability Ratio drops below one for either partner, the relationship becomes very likely to dissolve.

To put that in other words: When your partner is much more desirable to you than their "league" would suggest, and when this dynamic is mutual (i.e., each partner values the other more than society on average values that other partner), your relationship will be uniquely stable. However, if either partner values the other *less* than that person would be valued on an open market, the relationship becomes unstable.

Imagine a famous video game streamer who has little interest in the outdoors in a relationship with a world-class competitive fly fisher who has little interest in gaming. Each partner in this relationship has extremely high aggregate desirability in certain markets (essentially being gods in the gaming/fly fishing worlds), but perhaps only middling individual desirability (you can imagine the fly fisher being occasionally fed up with how much time the gamer spends "behind that goddamn computer screen" and vice versa). Intuitively, you will see this relationship as not particularly strong, but perhaps not contextualize that instability as resulting from an unfavorable Desirability Ratio.

While keeping a close eye on Desirability Ratios seems like common sense to us, we have never heard anyone in the relationship industry highlight this dynamic. This is odd because the effects of this on the dating and marriage markets are extreme. This is one of the many reasons why celebrity relationships are so short-lived and fraught with conflict—celebrities essentially have maxed-out aggregate desirability, making it virtually impossible for their individual desirability to their partner to stably stay above their aggregate desirability.

Desirability Ratio also has enormous value as a concept to the average person. If you are looking for a uniquely stable relationship, seek targets who have more value to you than to the average person, and look for those who see value in you that the average person would overlook.

The great thing about one's relationship stability rating is it is not something that requires much effort to maintain so long as their relationship is stable.

Our biology and culture naturally strengthen relationships over time. The longer we are in a (good) relationship, the more we find ourselves emotionally attracted to the individual with whom we are in that relationship, which raises each partner's desirability to the other partner.[1] Individual desirability of each partner also increases over time, due to genuine social, financial, and logistical entanglement as well as due to the sunk cost fallacy[2]. This increase in individual desirability over time in a relationship is not a small or insignificant effect. Even just the social stigma of leaving someone you have been dating for ten years is quite high—to the extent that social pressure alone could cause you to stay with a long-term, ungrateful partner who physically let themselves go instead of going after the kind, supportive,

---

[1] This is true for all relationships except those created by Dominance Lures—another reason why those relationships are so unstable and the communities that use them feel so threatened by the concept of hypergamy.

[2] Sunk Cost Fallacy: When an individual invests in something, not because they see it as a good investment, but because they do not want to write off investments they have already made in that thing.

and attractive person you see on your commute who keeps making passes at you. The individual desirability of a partner isn't just a conglomeration of positive pressures pushing you into a relationship with them but negative pressures pushing you away from leaving them.

Note for Context:
- There are many choices an individual can make that will alter their desirability on the market to specific sub-populations. For example, dressing like a hipster is going to increase your attractiveness to a specific profile of a partner and could be a useful strategy to filter for partners with specific characteristics you are looking for. In *The Pragmatist's Guide to Sexuality,* we broke down a number of factors and looked at how they correlated with arousal patterns. One of the most interesting associations from the perspective of this topic was related to cat and dog ownership. For example, when compared to men who prefer a partner with a *cat*, those who prefer a partner with a *dog* were significantly more likely to be turned on by acting dominant during sex—thus if your goal is to attract a dominant guy, you could better filter for them by choosing to own a dog instead of a cat. This is probably not the best way to determine what kind of pet you choose—but hey, it's interesting. For a more detailed breakdown of this, see *The Pragmatist's Guide to Sexuality.*

Appendix: *To gain a full understanding of how various factors affect your desirability, see Factors Affecting Desirability on page 421 in the appendix. This section will* *be particularly useful in helping you build strategies around arbitrage opportunities for yourself in the dating, marriage, or sex markets. In this section, we explore factors affecting individual and aggregate desirability, such as how kink preference or a preference for monogamous vs. polyamorous lifestyles may affect one's desirability across markets and how such preferences can be effectively signaled. We also address concepts related to the fluctuations of aggregate desirability between subcultures and discuss how these fluctuations can be leveraged to one's advantage (e.g., the aggregate desirability of a naturally pale person will be higher within the goth subculture than within Western society in general, even though that subculture is contained within Western society).*

Other Marketplace Considerations

Misjudgments of Aggregate Desirability

An individual who misjudges their own aggregate desirability in a marketplace is often doomed to an unhappy life while any partner they have is doomed to a less-than-ideal relationship. A person with an inaccurate understanding of their market value will have a difficult time finding a partner who is willing to date them, concede to their desires, and meet their expectations. Once in a relationship, this misguided individual will be more likely to not appreciate what they have.

Poor assessments of market value present a serious problem in a society that seems to actively encourage people to develop inflated perceptions of their aggregate desirability. It is ultimately quite harmful to tell someone: "Guuuurl—you are a goddess; you are perfect just the way you are, and you deserve a great guy!"

You, like all people, are not perfect. There is plenty of work you could do to raise your value on the open market. Those who allow themselves to have friends who discourage them from improving themselves are less likely to improve themselves enough to secure a "great girl" or "great guy."

Another glaring issue associated with aggregate desirability misjudgments stems from a failure to understand that aggregate desirability on one market does not equal aggregate desirability on another market. For example, a person can have a very high value on the sex market, but a very low value on the long-term relationship market. We talk about this in detail within the appendix section titled The Four Core Marketplaces on page 440, so we will not elucidate this point further here.

Aggregate desirability evolves over time. A young man who was captain of his high school football team may fail to internalize that even though he was in the top 1% of his market in high school, his aggregate desirability will plummet to the bottom 5% if he puts on weight in college and/or fails to secure a well-paying or prestigious job upon graduation. A young woman may not internalize that, while she may have an easy time finding male partners willing to commit to a long-term relationship with her when she is in her early and mid-twenties, a period of peak attractiveness and minimal attachments, she will have a much harder time finding a high-quality, long-term partner once she is in her thirties and especially if she has a child from a previous partner. If either of these individuals still conceptualizes their aggregate desirability as being what it was at the highest point in their lives, relationships with them will be . . . unpleasant.

Your Value Off the Market

A measure of increasing relevance in many societies is "individual off-market value." This is the value a person gains from not being in any relationship at all.

A number of factors can drive off-market value very high:
- The feeling of freedom and independence some gain from not being in a relationship.
- The value an individual places on their own time; this is uniquely true during career-building periods of life given the heavy time investment required for dating.
- An individual may positively modify their off-market value as part of their self-image—in other words, when an individual thinks being single makes them a better person.
- A strong negative association with those to whom an individual is most attracted, such as a heterosexual woman who looks down on men, a heterosexual man who looks down on women, or a gay person who looks down on gay people.

Off-market value becomes uniquely important when it rises above the value of a relationship with someone in one's league. This dynamic may result from someone having very high off-market value or relatively low value in their chosen relationship markets. For example, someone may love the freedom of being single so much a relationship with anyone isn't worth it, or someone may be very unattractive and not value a relationship enough to be in one with the type of person who would be willing to date them. In such cases, an individual will put no effort into dating and have their views on the subject of relationships continually reinforced by not being in one.

Uneven Relationships

While rare, there is one type of relationship in which both partners value each other more than they would be valued in the open market, and despite this, the relationship is still systematically unstable. These are uneven relationships: Relationships in which one partner has a way higher individual desirability to the other than the other does to them (i.e., one party in a relationship may be absolutely infatuated with the other, but this infatuation is not shared).

How this affects a relationship can vary widely, as some individuals actually *prefer* to be in a relationship in which they have less to lose by leaving than their partner, while others strongly prefer to be in a relationship in which each partner benefits equally.

Generally, the "best" inequality in a relationship is one in which both partners believe they have secured the better deal. These relationships are far more common than you may believe and typically exist whenever individuals each see the other through "rose-tinted glasses." Relationships in which both partners believe they are getting the better deal are extremely stable.

Know What You Bring To The Table

In the context of all the things that a person might look for in a partner, it is critical to know what *you* bring to the table. What differentiates you on the open market? What makes you uniquely worth attention? What value do you present?

Knowing your worth on the market plays a key role in not falling prey to exploitative partners. It is almost unheard of for someone leagues above another to pursue them. In fact, if someone who is obviously much higher value than you expresses interest in you, it means one of two things:
1) Something about you fulfills a niche desire of theirs. You may, for example, remind them of someone important to them. Or perhaps you unknowingly activate one of their kinks. For more detail on how that works, see: *The Pragmatist's Guide to Sexuality*.
2) The high-value person does not intend to have a monogamous relationship with you (this gets more complicated if you are polyamorous). It doesn't really matter to them if a partner is far below them in value if that partner does not preclude them from continuing to search for someone who is of equal value to them. Low-value partners can make for splendid placeholders for those still looking for a long-term match.

RELATIONSHIP LURES AND THEIR RESULTING RELATIONSHIP DYNAMICS

A lure is a type of value proposition presented to a potential partner. The type of lure used to establish a relationship will set the tone for that relationship going forward, meaning your choice of lures has significant short and long-term consequences.

The types of lures fishermen choose to use can heavily influence the types of fish they catch. Two fishermen fishing from the same spot may find themselves catching entirely different types of fish if they are using different lures. Similarly, when you are "fishing" for a relationship, the lure that you use can completely alter the type of relationship you "catch." In fact, one lure used to attract a target may yield a relationship dynamic that is entirely different from the relationship dynamic that would have emerged were a different lure used on that same target.

If Mike convinces a woman to date him because he is dominant, the resulting relationship will be entirely different than if he had inspired this same woman to date him by convincing her that, through dating him, she could improve herself (though such dynamics might be ameliorated through therapy).

One of the core reasons why people either end up in one bad relationship after another—or come to believe that all members of a certain gender have very constrained behavior patterns—is that they do not understand how different lures function (in male communities, this often manifests in the saying "AWALT," which stands for "all women are like that"). These people do not realize that the lure they are using is *creating* those relationship dynamics and/or constrained behavior patterns.

Talking with individuals who say guys or girls always act like X or Y feels like talking to a fisherman who insists that all fish have whiskers. When you point out that all the lures in his tackle box are designed specifically to only catch catfish, he just turns and gives you a quizzical look saying, "what's your point?"

To attract long-term partners in a manner that yields a relationship dynamic that will work over the long term, it helps to be aware of common lures used, the manner in which they may affect relationships, and appropriate times to leverage each.

These common lures include:
- The Dominance Lure
- The Nice Lure
- The Sexual Exploration Lure
- The Easy Lure
- The Love Lure
- The Sneaky Lure
- The Pygmalion Lure
- The Status Lure
- The Self-Identity Lure
- The Friend With Benefits Lure
- The Long-Term Relationship Lure
- The Social Construct Lure

Before you dig in, please note:

- Most partner acquisition strategies involve the use of multiple lures simultaneously. While this is the case, it is also the case that, in most of these, one lure is used predominantly and is "flavored" by others. Regardless, use your best judgment to attempt to predict how the combination of lures you choose to use will determine which types of relationships you are able to "catch."
- When discussing lures, we refer to the person being attracted by a lure as the "target" and the person utilizing a lure as the "pursuer." This is only for convenience, as we had to find some way to linguistically separate the two positions when describing how a specific lure is implemented. Nevertheless, every relationship is a two-way street. Just as one person will use one of these lures to secure a partner, that partner is using a lure to secure that person. Each lure used will heavily color the resulting relationship. There is no such thing as a relationship with only one pursuer and only one target—no matter how active one party is compared to another.

The Dominance Lure

The Dominance Lure is the default human mating lure. It can almost be thought of as the "traditional human mating display." It entails asserting physical and mental dominance in a very "traditional way" to attract those who are looking to surrender and/or indulge in that aspect of the human condition.

To get an idea of what the Dominance Lure looks like, consider the protective bad boy from a campy romance novel. This character is likely a muscular, confident man who unflinchingly sets rules and dictates how things will be in a way that borderline suspends a target's agency.

The Dominance Lure is extremely common among pick up artist communities (groups that develop concerted strategies designed to secure sex), but it can also be learned from one's childhood family dynamics. Dominance is typically thought of as a male-only lure; however, it can also work for females.

Dominance Lures are so effective because they involve the pursuer taking initiative and granting the targeted party the luxury of doing very little. Humans, being the inherently lazy creatures they are, *adore* not having to think. The proposition of just "going along for the ride" with someone who seems to know what they are doing can be immensely attractive.

Dominance Lures have extra appeal to targets with low social intelligence, low confidence, or a strong desire to be submissive in a relationship. The Dominance Lure is also significantly more effective on targets who are inexperienced in the BDSM scene or too traditional to be comfortable exploring the BDSM scene. Relationships with intentionally constructed, consensually agreed-upon power imbalances put in place for sexual gratification are not "Dominance Lure" relationships and instead are "Sexual Exploration Lure" relationships, as they have very little in common with relationships founded through subconscious implementation of dominance displays (in other words, dom-sub relationships are not Dominance Lure relationships).

Dominance can work on almost any target except those who have a self-image that would punish them severely for submitting to another human (these individuals include some of the following: people in the polyamorous scene, doms, Red Pillers, MGTOWers, those who ascribe to certain schools of feminism, etc.). Various studies back up the broad effectiveness of the Dominance Lure—including a 2018 study out of the University of Göttingen, which demonstrated that dominance predicted mating success for males even more than physical attractiveness.

Dominance displays can be easily amplified through behavior and posture changes. Studies have found women on average find men who smile less and strike brooding or swaggering poses more attractive, perhaps because smiling is a sign of submission in primates. Conversely, men in the aggregate prefer women who smile and find women less attractive when they look proud or confident—more on why dominance displays are effective for women in spite of this later. In addition, more dominant individuals make decisions faster. This is one of the reasons it is considered "unattractive" when a man takes a long time deciding at a restaurant.

One of the more frustrating aspects of dominance displays is that they are usually associated with communicating with one's target as . . . well, kind of a dick. Frustratingly, ample research suggests that this technique is objectively effective at getting replies from women on dating websites. Studies have even shown that not only do women respond less to positively worded messages on dating platforms but also that the more desirable a woman is, the fewer positively worded messages she will receive (See: "Aspirational pursuit of mates in online dating markets" in the journal *Science Advances*—we are citing our source here, as we expect a lot of our readers to be uniquely surprised by this and it would be hard to Google).

Relationships founded using a Dominance Lure require a constant assertion of dominance by the dominant party (communities that use this strategy often call this "maintaining frame"). This can be prohibitively exhausting in long-term relationships and is one of the core drawbacks of this lure.

Relationships founded through this strategy also fail to build a unique attachment among partners over time (at least not as much as other types of relationships), and thus they engender less fidelity. **In other words, in the case of most relationship dynamics, partners like each other more as they spend more time together. This is less common among relationships established around a Dominance Lure.** This is the critical difference between Dominance Lure relationships and intentional power exchange relationships, like dom-sub relationships, in which fondness and fidelity typically do appreciate over time.

Why does dominance build trust and fondness in intentional power exchange relationships but not Dominance Lure relationships? This building of fondness happens in intentional power exchange relationships because dominance is exercised as a "gift" to the submissive partner to elicit an emotional reaction in them that they have requested. Both partners in intentional power exchange relationships are aware of this often-taxing gift exchange. To put it in other words, in an intentional power exchange relationship, confidently giving humiliating instructions to a partner that are tailored to their arousal pathways is the same as taking time to wake someone up with breakfast in bed in a traditional relationship. Dominance in intentional power exchange relationships takes time and effort to organize and is obviously meant as a gesture of care whereas in a Dominance Lure relationship, the act would not be a gift exchange but instead one primarily motivated to maintain an imposed perception of the dominant partner.

There are other reasons why Dominance Lure relationships do not increase in quality over time like almost all other relationship types: The cognitive dissonance and social cost associated with leaving a Dominance Lure relationship do not increase over time due to the negative stigma society associates with these arrangements. The social cost of cheating is also much lower within Dominance Lure Relationships—among both parties. Dominant partners in relationships built around a Dominance Lure are less likely to feel guilt upon cheating, due to an inherent lack of respect for and emotional attachment to the target (a perspective often cultivated by practitioners of the Dominance Lure to make it easier to maintain dominance). Submissive partners in Dominance Lure relationships feel little guilt upon cheating because the relationship's primary value to them involves a specific emotional set elicited by the dominant partner—not the dominant partner themselves.

A fascinating aspect of the Dominance Lure involves routine boundary tests initiated by the target, which are commonly referred to online as "shit tests." In a shit test, the target challenges the prospective partner's dominance to ensure it is still high. Essentially, if someone attracts a target by displaying dominance, their value to the target is those displays, thus the target will regularly trigger dominance displays by testing the dominance of their partner and pushing boundaries.

While some common relationship-related questions asked by a target of their pursuer, such as "How many girls have you slept with?" are potential drama-riddled bombs in the context of a Dominance Lure relationship, they are completely innocuous in other types of relationships. For example, if a question regarding sexual partner count came up within the context of a Sexual Experimentation Lure-based relationship, the target is likely just attempting to determine if you need to share your papers proving your STD status and in such a context, you should be perfectly open and honest. On the other hand, if a target in a Dominance Lure-based relationship asks this, they really want an indication of the pursuer's sexual prowess and dominance. A target may even be testing whether or not the dominant pursuer will deign to answer. After all, if a target can force their supposedly dominant pursuer to answer them, this would signal that they hold some control over the pursuer, making the pursuer less dominant, and therefore less attractive.

That "shit tests" are not universal may sound questionable to those who have only used dominance-based or power exchange lures to secure their partners, but **shit tests are not normal adult behavior**. When Malcolm was looking for a wife, he had a quota of five dates a week for years, and on those hundreds of dates, he only experienced something that could be counted as a shit test six to eight times—though before that, when he experimented with Dominance Lures for low effort sex, he received shit tests constantly. Shit tests are a specific and rational reaction to the value proposition of a Dominance Lure. If someone is selling you a car, you'll want to make sure it operates and handles well. If someone is selling you dominance, you'll want to make sure they can properly dominate.

We have little information on how Dominance Lure strategies work for females, as females who prefer to maintain a constantly dominant position in a relationship are already a little sexually atypical, and thus it is usually easiest for these women to express their dominance through BDSM communities and relationships ignited under complementary BDSM interests (which, as we have noted, operate with totally different dynamics than those of Dominance Lure relationships). That said, we can hypothesize that a female employing a Dominance Lure would be even more effective than a male employing it, as this rare occurrence would make them high-value market commodities (even if demand is low, the supply of this type of woman is even lower). Contrary to conventional wisdom, some studies have found that men, on average, have a slight preference for being submissive, whereas women have a *strong* preference for being submissive, statistically speaking. In a study on arousal pathways and sexual preferences we ran through the Pragmatist Foundation, we found that while

75% of women get at least somewhat aroused by seeing a partner act dominant, a hearty 49% of men are aroused by partners acting dominant as well. While fewer men than women are aroused by dominant partners, this does not negate the finding that almost half of men are aroused by dominance. Should a non-trivial proportion of men really somewhat prefer submission, women who prefer (or are even *just OK with*) dominance will have a distinct advantage, as our stats show the majority of women on various dating markets are simply not comfortable being anything but the submissive partner.

See *The Pragmatist's Guide to Sexuality* for more statistics and analysis related to dominance and submission preferences—it is full of fascinating data. One of our findings relevant to this discussion is that while 45% of women responding to a survey we conducted reported finding the naked male form to be very arousing and 48% reported finding the sight of a penis to be very arousing, a heftier 53% reported finding a partner acting dominant in a sexual context to be very arousing. Dominance is literally more likely to be "very arousing" to the average female than naked men or penises and thus the average woman has more of a "dominance-focused" sexuality than a "male-focused" sexuality.

Another interesting tidbit that emerged from The Pragmatist Foundation's study on sexuality was a correlation in women between (1) arousal from being dominant and (2) perceiving oneself as being attractive. In other words, if a female survey respondent reported herself as being attractive, she was much more likely to also report that she felt turned on by acting dominant.

This likely means attractive, confident women are less likely to be lured into a relationship by dominance.

Males who leverage Dominance Lures often find success at securing sexual partners and sometimes can even leverage this lure to secure a partner for a socially traditional (sometimes known as TradCon-style) marriage, in which their spouse's core contributions are sex, home-keeping, and child-rearing. That said, this strategy is only of optimal utility (i.e., the best of all available lures to use) among middle-aged males with little sexual experience who are primarily looking for sex or young men who lack the social intelligence to leverage other lures. Despite its limited utility and the low quality of relationships it generates, the Dominance Lure is of genuine value to those two groups. In fact, among lower-value males in those groups with low social intelligence, the Dominance Lure may genuinely present their only real shot at experiencing sex they don't pay for.

Of all the lures we have investigated, the Dominance Lure is the only one that people specifically train themselves to look out for in potential partners and avoid. Unfortunately, people unfamiliar with how the lure actually is meant to work just memorize a few classic Dominance Lure strategies like "negging" and then look for them as red flags on dates. Negging, for the uninitiated, involves an individual belittling or lightly insulting a target in an attempt to establish dominance and manipulate the target into wanting to impress them.

By categorizing negging as a red flag and sign to end a date, many filter out otherwise strong candidates who were *not* actually implementing a Dominance Lure strategy. Do not confuse all challenges to your logic, your lifestyle, and your opinions, with negging. Also, do not conflate negging with statements that make you uncomfortable. A number of the other lures use challenging questions as a legitimate filter or expectation-setting tool. A statement like: "Do you like X political figure? Because I won't date you if you do" is not a neg; it is a useful question for filtering out potentially bad matches.

A personal anecdote here might help: On our first date, Malcolm told me: "I am not looking to date; I am looking for a wife and expect to find her in a few months at Stanford, due to its large pool of pre-vetted candidates." This could have been a neg if he were employing a Dominance Lure strategy, but within the strategy he was employing, this blunt statement was simply a courtesy expectation setter to prevent me from wasting time on a lead that may not fit what I was looking for in a relationship. A good rule of thumb for sorting out an intentionally employed "neg" from a normal challenging question or statement is to look for such challenging statements being deployed in a flirtatious voice (as they are deployed with a Dominance Lure) instead of a matter-of-fact tone (as they would be when implementing the Pygmalion Lure) or conscientious tone (common in normal human conversation).

The Nice Lure

The Nice Lure is almost completely ineffective at actually securing what people want in a relationship, but it is so commonly used that we would be remiss not to describe it. Those deploying the Nice Lure offer submission—signaled through niceness—and accommodation in hopes that they might receive either sex or a relationship in return. It is the standard "nice guy/good girl" strategy—also known in some circles as "beta" behavior. The core idea of this strategy is that if the pursuer is really, *really* "nice" to someone and does everything the target asks, the target may be willing to date and might even have sex with them. Those who proclaim in frustration: "Why can't I get a date/sex??? I am such a nice guy/girl..." are using the Nice Lure.

While we call this the Nice Lure, there is nothing particularly nice about it. We refer to this lure as "nice" because displays of submission can easily be misinterpreted as niceness both by the pursuer and the target. What is really happening in these displays is an individual is subconsciously signaling to their target that they are willing to be a submissive partner and give their target power over them in exchange for sexual access. Since submission displays—such as offering to do someone's homework for them, smiling (a submission display in most primates), giving them your stuff, politeness, or carrying things for them—can look like "just being nice" and can be played off that way, it is often hard for a target to identify the intended payout the pursuer expects from these displays. This can cause significant consternation to the pursuer when the target constantly accepts their submission displays but still denies sexual access. In some cases, repeatedly rejected pursuers leveraging the Nice Lure become aggressively submissive, a signal to any potential partner that their genes are hot garbage and a hard turn off for both most men and women.

To be clear here—the Nice Lure is almost always performed subconsciously. A person does not actively think, "how do I get X target to breed with me? Oh, I know: Be oppressively obsequious all the time!" A deeply primitive part of their brain only sees two paths to sex, dominance, or submission, and it has determined they are not dominant enough to take a dominance display path. (We should take a moment here to also draw attention to the fact that, historically speaking, the Dominance Lure was also a primarily subconscious pathway, but one that was eventually co-opted by individuals who saw how effective it was, codified it, and trained themselves in it. It is still a pathway that occurs naturally, just at a very low frequency when contrasted with its artificial variant.)

While a Nice Lure is almost never effective at igniting sexual interest in a target, it can be successful at securing a relationship when a target feels that they can exploit the submissive nature of their pursuer. In such cases, the pursuer may even be granted sexual access in exchange for continued submission. In this sense, the Nice Lure and Dominance Lure are the only lures that involve "shit tests." In a Dominance Lure relationship, shit tests exist to ensure the partner is still dominant, whereas in Nice Lure relationships, shit tests are of utility to ensure the prospective partner is still submissive and thus can still be used as an informal servant.

The Nice Lure does not work for any gender at securing healthy long-term relationships. While the Nice Lure can be used to obtain sex, it is not even very effective at that. The core reason this strategy is so ineffective is it signals to targets that the pursuer has nothing to exchange for a relationship except their dignity, which apparently has little value anyway. Having to resort to the Nice Lure proves an individual's lack of value on the wider marketplace.

The Sexual Exploration Lure

We outlined the use of Sexual Exploration Lures in the appendix section of this book as a viable strategy for young people just looking for sex. Sex feels good and the vast majority of the population wants to have it. There are many people out there who want to explore new and interesting ways of experiencing sex with someone just like you (well . . . *maybe*—more on that soon).

The Sexual Exploration Lure is peculiar in that it manifests very differently in youth than it does in adults. Amid teenagers, this lure can be effective on pretty much anyone and is generically implementable in the sense that sexual experimentation for someone who is inexperienced can just be kissing, holding hands, or sex. In youth, fooling around in any capacity can be experimental and exciting. However, once a person becomes an adult and sex is no longer interesting or difficult to secure, this lure typically requires becoming involved with one of two categories of adult communities interested in sexual exploitation.

These categories are, roughly:
1) Communities oriented around openly sexually exploring a number of new partners (e.g., the branch of the polyamorous community that is big

into sexual exploration, swingers, etc.): For those whose sexual tastes are vanilla in nature, there are lots of communities out there that merely revolve around having sex.
2) Kink communities (e.g., BDSM, hot wifers, Gor, Kinbaku, TPE, etc.): Should you genuinely be interested in sexual exploration from the perspective of someone who would like to explore new ways of having sex, there is a vibrant rainbow of kink communities at your disposal. Involvement in these communities may require a significant investment of time (e.g., a four-week course on safe bondage practices) and money (e.g., thousands of dollars on specific outfits or equipment). A good way to meet these communities is to look for local "munches." (If you are interested in getting an entertaining, sweet introduction to lifestyles in which kink hobbies play a key role, we heartily recommend Sunstone: A free and beautifully illustrated comic series by Stjepan Sejic available online.) IMPORTANT: The first time you approach one of these communities, do so non-sexually and without pretense. DO NOT walk up to one of these communities for the first time saying that you are a "master" or something like that.

Should you decide to leverage the sexual exploration lure as an adult, especially if you become intimate with a large number of sexual partners, build a habit of being regularly tested for STDs, keep your latest test results handy (scans on your phone that you can quickly send to a prospective partner are a must), study your local sex/kink community's consent rules in great detail, resign yourself to always maxing out the protection you are using, and put earnest and genuine effort into skillfully pleasing your partners. Word gets around in these communities rapidly, seeing as so many of their members are sleeping together. If you act like an asshole or refuse to play by the rules, you will be expelled.

The biggest downside to utilizing sexual exploration communities for sex is that many (but not all) will expel members who neglect to submit their worldviews to the group's chosen ideology (usually some form of sex-positive liberal feminist perspective, though conservative iterations of the groups do exist). Surprisingly, the Sexual Exploration Lure tends to form strong long-term relationships and may be the single strongest lure available to the majority of females over thirty hunting for a committed relationship (not that it's uniquely great for women in this demographic; women over thirty just have so few other options available to them due in large part to high-quality men leaving relationships and returning to the dating market at lower rates than high-quality women).[3]

---

[3] Specifically, we would point to 70% of divorces being initiated by women. It seems to be that when women get dissatisfied with their partners, they are more likely to leave them. This implies that if a person has a bad personality that reveals itself after a few years—or had their life spiral out of control between their 20s and 30s—they are more likely to be spit back onto the dating market if they are male. Obviously, marital dissatisfaction is not the only motivation for divorce, but this subtle skew in behavior increases the extent to which the mature dating market is disproportionately populated by the cream of the female population and the dregs of the male population.

With regard to this lure's perhaps counterintuitive tendency to generate long-term relationships, we hypothesize that five factors are at play:
1) Survivorship bias: Sex and kink communities are pretty quick to kick out jerks and police the relationships within them in said relationships' early stages. This policing is not ironclad, but as with many tight-knit communities composed of groups of people who share a common interest, members usually have a non-trivial amount of emotional investment in other members, have more-efficient-than-average means to learn about problems, and have more motivation to intervene when they see a toxic relationship forming.
2) Selection bias: To interact effectively with these communities, a person probably has a stronger idea of who they are and what they want than an average person off the street. Accurate awareness of one's self and one's actual desires are astoundingly low in most dating/relationship/sex markets, which leads to many poor matches.
3) Lower risk of making illogical, hormone-based decisions: If the studies indicating that promiscuous individuals experience lower levels of oxytocin release are correct, those in this community may be less likely to enter a long-term relationship with someone just because a wash of hormones have made them feel deeply in love and bonded to their partner. Those who maintain a lower sexual partner count experience significant exposure to the risk of blinding love. (We talk about this phenomenon and the

associated studies later in the book, see page 217.)
4) Maturity: Individuals in this community have often intentionally chosen to stay single until a later age (this puts them in stark contrast to adults who are single because they have failed to secure or maintain a healthy long-term relationship). Thus, these individuals on average are often more emotionally stable than those still single available in the general mid-life dating market.
5) Clear intention and communication: Relationships formed as a product of this lure are more likely to have super specific relationship contracts (especially around definitions of things like infidelity and consent), which decreases conflict.

Common Mistakes to Avoid:
- Keep in mind that the Sexual Exploration Lure is not the "I am Great at Sex" lure. The "I Am Great at Sex" approach to seduction is completely ineffective at securing high-value partners. Sure, a person may be able to secure sex with someone a few leagues below them because they signaled their availability and desperation, but this strategy is ineffective for people in the same league. Why? Because the "I am Great at Sex" lure comes off as desperate and makes a person seem emotionally unstable, leading many targets to conclude that the person is not worth the risky lay. This is true for both men and women.
- Also, remember that sexual exploration is *just* sexual exploration—it is not about imposing one's sexuality on someone else. A person randomly emailing someone with what they want to do to

them sexually is not sexual exploration; that's just non-consensual cybersex. Think of it this way: If you are putting together a game of baseball, you need to first get to know people, understand the rules, determine what you want the specific rules to be for that game, schedule a day and time to meet up and play, etc. Baseball does not really come up as the core of the interaction until the game itself begins. Emailing someone with how hot you think they are is like running up to them while flailing a baseball bat and screaming "baseball now," then bemoaning the fact that everyone runs from you screaming and calls the cops when you try to play baseball with them.

The Easy Lure

The Easy Lure entails signaling that one would gladly have sex with, date, or get married to a specific individual for next to no cost (in terms of time or money). This is not a lure that a huge number of people consciously choose; however, it is often accidentally adopted as a habit that does, admittedly, enable one to secure sex and can lead to the ignition of relationships.

This strategy is much more effective for females than it is for males. We have to wrack our brains to come up with even hypothetical situations in which The Easy Lure is an effective strategy for males if their targets are under thirty.

In the 1980s, some experiments were conducted in which both men and women approached strangers and invited these strangers to sleep with them or come back to their apartment. While men agreed to these propositions over half the time, not a single woman took a strange male up on his offer (it should be noted that only attractive men and women were presenting these propositions). Even in instances in which researchers controlled for fear of violence by asking women if they would sleep with their best friend if given such a proposal, women still said yes at much lower rates than men (though if you torturously massage the data, it is possible to make the numbers just about even . . . But that is the case with almost any data set). However you look at it, a woman can realistically—though not safely—approach strangers on the street, ask for sex, and frequently secure it whereas a male cannot. Should you want to read more about these studies and the follow-up work in more detail, refer to the section on Sexual Marketplaces in the appendix on page 440.

A person not realizing that they are attracting prospective partners with an Easy Lure can be dangerous. It is common for some young women to not recognize that the attention they are getting stems from the fact that they are inadvertently signaling that sex with them will be low cost. It is difficult not to get hooked on the positive emotions the attention makes a person feel—especially if they are blithely unaware that said attention is being hurled their way because those giving it think they are a low investment target for sex or dating. Such attention can easily subconsciously train some young women to signal that they are sexually available when doing so is far from their intention.

While any young woman will have some susceptibility to this, those with histrionic personality disorder, borderline personality disorder, and in manic stages of bipolar disorder, are uniquely susceptible to this subconscious conditioning, and it affects them more severely.

When I (Simone) was younger, I fell prey to this to an extent until Malcolm pointed out what was happening. I was incredibly friendly and wore a lot of wacky and somewhat revealing clothing that caused people to look down on me—but also shower me with compliments. Those who looked down on me did not mention or clearly indicate their condescension, but those giving me compliments were very vocal.

The damaging effects of this subconscious training can extend to behavioral patterns much more damaging than mere revealing clothing. Specifically, a woman acting a little mentally unstable or not very bright can signal to guys that sex with her will involve low investment, which may cause this behavior to be positively reinforced. This is highly damaging at a societal level.

Humans are remarkably easy to subconsciously train by consistently verbally rewarding a specific behavior or rewarding it through attention.

While we discuss this lure in the context of its subconscious negative effects on some young women, this lure is also sometimes intentionally implemented—even by adults. One study found that 23% of adults still ask their friends to signal to a target that they would be willing to romantically engage them if the target made a pass (i.e., that it will be a low investment, low-risk effort to obtain sex and/or a relationship with them).

While Easy Lures can hypothetically enable one to secure easy sex, they have few (ethical) real-world uses and expose one to non-trivial danger. Specifically, some people interpret Easy Lure signaling (especially when combined with a request to spend time alone with them) as a tacit consent to sex. These individuals can become angry and belligerent upon discovering this isn't the case. Thus, even if a person is just looking for sex, the Sexual Experimentation Lure is unflinchingly superior to the Easy Lure: It requires almost as little effort, is just as effective, works for all genders, and doesn't carry as much additional risk (although, every sexual encounter carries some risk).

The Love Lure

The Love Lure mirrors the Easy Lure in many respects; however, instead of offering sex with low investment from the target, the pursuer offers love (i.e., "You should sleep with / choose / marry me because I will love you more than he / she does"). This is probably the single least effective lure we will discuss, but for some reason, it is one of the lures people most actively attempt to deploy. People think because they feel love towards someone, they are doing that person a favor. Perhaps more bizarrely, many are under the impression that love alone can be traded for a relationship.

The love you feel is a feeling inside *you*. This love is not a feeling within your target. Your target cannot profit from or be sustained by your love. By loving someone, you are using them or the idea of them to masturbate the aspect of your cognition that produces the positive feelings that come from love. Thinking that someone will want to be with you because "you love them" is like thinking that someone will want to be with you because you masturbate while looking at a picture of them.

People's beliefs about the value and power of love disgust and horrify your gentle authors. Our society sees love as magical fairy dust instead of an emotion that is activated by specific environmental stimuli. If a genuinely lucid person just wanted something to love them, they would get a dog and not waste time, money, and heartache on a pathetic hairless ape.

People only value the love they feel for you. The love you have for others is only valuable to them if it helps *them* in some way, such as your affection making it easier for them to extract resources from you (and we assume that is not the type of relationship you want), or your affection indicating broadly to them that they "are loved," which may reinforce an important part of their desired self-identities.

You may think to yourself: "I get it, but I am super lovable!" We find that almost every human who thinks this about themselves has really only become good at loving themselves. These people are completely useless to others from a relationship standpoint.

The only way to become actually "lovable" in a way that allows a person to secure relationships with new partners is to practice making people fall in love with them and study the science associated with the topic. Love can be systematically and reliably induced. We discuss methods for inducing the emotion of love in detail in *The Pragmatist's Guide to Sexuality*.

The Sneaky Lure

The Sneaky Lure is the last of the ineffective lures we will discuss at length.

While we find it dumb, the Sneaky Lure strategy is remarkably common among adolescent males. This strategy entails progressing towards a sexual interaction with a target while doing everything one can to prevent rejection by attempting to occlude the fact that the goal is sex.

Deployment of the Sneaky Lure commonly proceeds along lines like:
- Come back to my place, I don't want you to risk going home drunk.
- Let's just sit next to each other and watch shows together.
- Let's wrestle a bit!

When questioned as to whether the pursuer thinks their actions are leading to sex, sneaky strategists will strongly imply they don't. Either they don't really have a plan for when they reveal their true intentions or their plan is to have their target conclude: "Well, we have gone this far, let's just get this over with."

This strategy can also be utilized over a period of time in which the prospective partner tries to get as close to dating their target as they can while avoiding anything that makes the relationship official because doing so would give their target a chance to concretely reject them. Essentially, the pursuer prefers the imprisonment of a "Schrodinger's Relationship" to even a chance of rejection.

The worst-case scenario with this strategy involves investing an enormous amount of time and energy in befriending a target with the expectation that this will lower the barriers that must be overcome for one's target to agree to sex or a relationship, only to be turned down in the end. When this happens, implementers of this strategy often have the gall to actually get angry at their targets. This is one of the many origin points of the "nice guy" cliché—pursuers who get angry at their targets for their own poorly thought-through strategies involving enormous upfront investment without a guaranteed payout.

Why do people adopt this strategy if it is both ineffective and likely to lead to a terrible outcome? Simply put, because being rejected hurts.

Those who make some initial forays into the dating world quickly learn that in the majority of cases, when they make their intentions clear, they get rejected. They may also notice that rejection does not arise when they *do not* make their intentions clear. These individuals may come to be subconsciously trained to believe that strategies involving a direct approach simply do not work, whereas strategies involving an indirect—sneaky—

approach *might* work. They may even delude themselves into thinking that various "subtle cues," such as body language, hints dropped in jokes, and innuendo act as sufficient notice of their intentions to their targets. (For the record, they do not).

The Sneaky Lure strategy is also sometimes used by individuals on the casual dating market, leading to the classic "friend zone" failure scenario in which prospective partners waste months or even years building a friendship with targets they really only wanted to date.

Recognizing when you are implementing the Sneaky Lure strategy is as easy as thinking through your romantic and sexual interests and asking yourself if you have explicitly shared them with your target(s). If not, why not? Are you obscuring your intentions because you think your target won't be friends with you if they know? Do you not share your intentions because you believe they will be met with rejection? Make sure you actually have evidence substantiating your fears, as it is likely that you merely fear rejection and not a loss of your target's friendship. It is fairly easy to remain friends with someone after clearly stating there is no sexual interest as long as said someone does not keep pushing for escalation . . . well, ish—when a person turns another down, they often lose respect for them.

Sneaky Copulation and Female Mimicry

A specific method of utilizing The Sneaky Lure reflects a set of behavior patterns similar to those observed in other species, known as sneaky copulation and female mimicry. Among some species that exhibit sexual dimorphism, a certain percentage of males may transform themselves to look like females. For example, among bluehead wrasses, a species of fish featuring territorial males that are typically much larger and differently colored than females, some males "choose" to be smaller and colored like a female, then use this disguise to slip under the nose of the more masculine males and get close to females who wouldn't have anything to do with them were they privy to their ultimate goal—breeding with them.

Sexual mimicry most often occurs among species whose females, when given a choice, will choose larger, ultra-masculine males. Among such species, only the largest, most masculine men will get to breed and pass on their genes—unless, of course, some males figure out how to disguise themselves as females, infiltrate female groups, and occasionally covertly inseminate (rape or pressure into sex) their female compatriots.

Some human males attempt to exploit a similar strategy. These men typically adopt "white knight" personalities and loudly yet submissively signal how pro-woman they are in a subconscious attempt to infiltrate protected spaces where they feel they will face less competition from other men.

Now let's be clear, we are not saying all men who exhibit "white knight" behavior are leveraging a sneaky copulation strategy. Most white knight types are genuinely trying to help people. What we assert instead is that a certain small portion of white knight types are indeed leveraging this strategy. We know of some women who were victims of this strategy personally, so we can say for a fact that it does happen.

Fortunately, these individuals are often easy to spot. When a person believes something because of a logical thought process, they will likely have a number of areas in which their view deviates from the party line. When someone is using their ideology as a sexual strategy, they will almost always adhere to the party line to the letter and change their views to match group consensus as said consensus evolves. This is because they aren't really fighting for their own beliefs—rather, they are making an effort to signal beliefs they think will gain them sexual access to a community that would otherwise expel individuals like them.

The Pygmalion Lure

The desirability of a pursuer who leverages a Pygmalion Lure stems less from who they are and more from their capacity to transform their target. We have a strong bias in favor of this lure, as it is the one that initiated our relationship.

Targets choose pursuers utilizing the Pygmalion Lure because the target believes that they can become better people themselves (or people more closely aligned with their ideal selves) through a relationship with said pursuers. Because the Pygmalion Lure offers, quite literally, a shot at one's greatest ambitions, this is arguably the best lure for creating an effective long-term relationship.

Pygmalion Lures typically yield one of two types of relationships:
- **One-Way Pygmalion Relationships:** In these relationships, one partner leverages the Pygmalion Lure while the other presents the Power Surrender Lure. The surrendering partner is drawn to the relationship because the Pygmalion partner made them / is making them into someone they want to be, while the Pygmalion partner has affection for the surrendering partner because the Pygmalion partner is able to craft their perfect mate. These relationships are less stable than Two-Way Pygmalion Relationships because if the partner improving the other fails to actively improve themselves at the same time, they may reach a point at which they have improved their partner as much as they can (it is hard for you to craft someone better than yourself). Should this point be reached, the relationship loses value to the individual looking to improve.
- **Two-Way Pygmalion Relationships:** These are relationships in which both partners use the Pygmalion Lure to secure each other. Both parties believe the primary value of the other individual is that that person improves them. One-Way Pygmalion Relationships can smoothly evolve into Two-Way Pygmalion relationships so long as the person shaping the other has their ego in check enough to realize when their creation has surpassed them. In other words, it is entirely possible to transform someone far weaker than you into someone even stronger than you, who is capable of helping you, in turn, become even better. Two-Way Pygmalion Relationships are one

of the most stable relationship structures for long-term, fulfilling, and beneficial relationships.

While relationships based on a Pygmalion Lure require significantly more maintenance than relationships created through most other lures (in the sense that one is acting not only as a romantic partner, but also a life coach, career coach, image consultant, and advisor) that maintenance typically benefits both parties' careers, personalities, and identities. We would argue the results make the effort well worth the hassle. Pygmalion Relationships only lose their stability if one partner decides that they no longer need to improve or when partners come to disagree about who they ought to become (a partner trying to transform a person into someone they do *not* want to be is not only of no value, but it is also something most people would want to avoid—no matter how amazing they are, the target would be better off staying single than being with them).

The core downside of the Pygmalion lure is that to use it, the pursuer must simultaneously be a genuinely accomplished person—at least accomplished enough to command the respect of their targets—and capable of providing genuinely good counsel. If I (Simone) did not desperately want to be more like Malcolm from the moment I first met him, his offer to help transform me into my ideal self would have lacked allure. If his initial advice to me hadn't made a huge positive impact on my life, I would not have continued our relationship.

Another large downside to the Pygmalion Lure is that while it creates good relationships when a person finds a target who is genuinely compelled by the idea, finding such a target requires a huge throughput of potential candidates, as few people are looking for a relationship in which constant self-improvement is an expectation and most are uncomfortable with the idea of a partner who wants them to be better than they are right now. Those using the Pygmalion Lure should expect to be turned down far more often than those only looking for companionship and sex.

In addition, Pygmalion relationships require partners to disregard many classic relationship red flags. When Malcolm told me he was excited to work with me to rewrite my personality, overhaul my wardrobe, change my accent, pick new friends, change my habits down to what I ate/drank, and transform every aspect of who I was, I became excited by the vision we had for my potential and was flattered to learn he believed I had the cognitive capacity and work ethic to become the person both he and I dreamed I might become.

Today's prevailing wisdom marks such propositions as hostile and possibly even abusive. It is considered inappropriate to tell someone you love they can improve themselves through hard work and personal sacrifice, to not accept one's partner "for who they are," and to actively encourage them to change significant aspects of themselves. When I met Malcolm, I was a social media manager living with crippling social anxiety that prevented me from interacting with the outside world, I couldn't even leave my house to eat at restaurants. Within a few years of meeting Malcolm, I had become the CEO of a portfolio of international businesses that do over a hundred million dollars in sales a year, I was traveling between countries/continents every month, I regularly lectured at top universities (including Stanford, Harvard, and Carnegie Mellon), and I had picked up a graduate degree from Cambridge along the way—not to mention levels of calm, self-confidence, and contentedness that before I could not have fathomed possible. Without Malcolm's intervention, and without transforming myself into someone I wanted to be, I would have plateaued and lived as I did for the rest of my adult life. **To many, the key sacrifice of a Pygmalion-Lure-generated relationship is that, by definition, your partner does not love you "for who you are," but rather for the potential of who you have the capacity to become.**

How to Use the Pygmalion Lure

The steps necessary to seduce someone using the Pygmalion Lure are neither as self-evident as many of the other lures nor delineated in other books, so we believe they warrant a walkthrough.

To use the Pygmalion Lure, engage the target in questions about who they want to be and why, then talk them through the process of developing a strategy and goals that will get them where they want to be. If interested, the target will implement the strategies they crafted over the course of discussions you had with them on dates. If the strategy is working, on their own time, you will see them individually, refining even more ideas and bringing them to you for discussion. If your target finds these conversations help them improve—and they are the type of person who craves continued improvement—they will naturally move toward a closer relationship with you.

Deployment of the Pygmalion Lure does not start around questions of self-betterment like cliché self-help systems do. Instead, the first few dates should be entirely focused around discovering the target's values and working with them to parse out how those values tie to their long-term goals. If the target says something vague or generic that indicates they have never really thought through what they value (common responses indicating this include proclaimed desires to be happy, fulfilled, or "make the world a better place"), encourage them to dig deeper. If the target desires happiness or fulfillment, for example, ask them how they came to conclude that their entire life should be devoted to optimizing a particular emotional state. In *The Pragmatist's Guide to Life,* we call this value, the thing(s) one is trying to maximize with one's life, a person's "objective function."

Once an objective function has been established, help the target develop a plan for maximizing that objective function, focusing on both granular, immediate tasks, and a larger game plan. At no point is it necessary to tell a target: "I will help you realize your goals." The very nature of these interactions should make that apparent. In fact, at no point should a pursuer using the Pygmalion Lure even be telling their partner what to strive for or how to see their objective function realized. Pygmalion relationships are not about you imposing your values and goals on another person. Instead, your primary purpose when deploying a Pygmalion Lure should be to help the target think through their own values and goals—and to stick to plans they independently develop.

While this process can be difficult to execute, our first book, *The Pragmatist's Guide to Life,* provides a step-by-step walkthrough, featuring the tools necessary to holistically discuss all the things a potential partner might choose to establish as core values and reasons to live. Refer to *The Pragmatist's Guide to Life* if you are having trouble developing a framework that allows you to talk through questions of values and goals in a way that doesn't just push a target toward your own belief set. Pushing a partner toward your own goals or belief set instead of helping them unfurl their own will backfire on those hoping to deploy the Pygmalion Lure; the moment a target feels like their pursuer, rather than they themselves, are dictating who they become, the pursuer has lost any chance at a successful relationship.

The Dangers of False Pygmalion Relationships

Two categories of relationship can look very similar to a Pygmalion Lure relationship but are not. In one False Pygmalion Relationship type, a Damsel in Distress Lure is used to attract a target who, through "saving" this prospective partner, is able to fulfill a certain desired sense of self (which we will talk about shortly). In this relationship type, the core value of the relationship to the pursuer is getting to feel like a hero, not unlocking the target's raw potential. In another False Pygmalion Relationship type, one partner essentially acts as the other's service submissive and emotional support, a form of the Love Lure in which a prospective partner does whatever is asked in service to their target's goals while supporting them in moments of emotional weakness. These False Pygmalion Relationship categories are worth noting as they are quite different in the dynamics and the risks they create when contrasted with true Pygmalion Lure generated relationships.

In both of the above relationship types, a target "trading up" for a better partner once they achieve the toe hold in life they were searching for is common, whereas when the Pygmalion Lure is used, trading up is a rare occurrence. Essentially, targets in the above scenarios are more likely to see the pursuer as a disposable source of free labor, resources, and emotional support while they move toward their goals, as opposed to seeing their pursuer as the architect of their identities and success.

The easiest way to tell these two types of relationships apart is the specific type of self-improvement being attempted. In these False Pygmalion Relationships, the pursued partner is often attempting to either pull themselves up from rock bottom (get out of a bad situation, get off drugs, etc.) or they are using their partner to achieve a specific goal (get into and through grad school, get a specific promotion, etc.). This is critically different from a Pygmalion Lure Relationship in which similar goals may very well exist but are ultimately secondary to rewriting one's core identity.

A good example of this difference would be what is expected when Partner A comes home crying after failing to achieve some aspect of A's goal for themselves. In a False Pygmalion Relationship, Partner B will be expected to give emotional support and remind Partner A they are still loved. On the other hand, in a Pygmalion Lure Relationship, such a reaction would be seen as enabling weakness and a major violation of trust. Instead, Partner A would expect Partner B to gently ask them what they gain from their current emotional state and to refocus them on the correct next steps without rewarding negative emotional reactions with attention, which will only make such unproductive emotional reactions harder to control in the future. In a Pygmalion Relationship, the thing a pursuer's partner loves about them is their ideal selves. Indulging an emotional outburst from one's current, less-than-ideal self is more likely than not going to hamper the emergence of one's ideal self, of the person one's partner actually loves and cares about.

Subconsciously, people want attention more than they want happiness, so by rewarding negative emotional states with attention, you can actually train a person to be *more* unhappy in the long run or enter states of unhappiness with a smaller triggering event—especially when in the presence of their partner. One key difference in Pygmalion Relationships involves valuing your partner's long-term mental wellbeing over the immediate catharsis and support of consoling them—and more importantly, having your partner recognize and appreciate those decisions.

This sort of behavior pattern would only be seen as a positive reaction to one's partner being emotionally distressed in a Pygmalion Relationship and would be a negative behavior pattern in constructive relationships formed by other lures (hence you should not expect the above response in all positive relationships—just this one type). If your partner expects you to recognize and appreciate your long-term wellbeing over your short-term emotional caprices, you know what type of relationship you are in. In other relationship types, one would be better off comforting one's partner. In this moment, one has a choice between being a source of emotional support for a partner and strengthening one's relationship with them, but at the cost of subtly conditioning them to associate negative emotional states with a positive outcome (attention). The optimal reaction depends on one's desired relationship type.

It is not unheard of for people to "trade up" from even Two-Way Pygmalion relationships. People trade up from Pygmalion relationships in very specific circumstances, which are easy to avoid. In False Pygmalion Relationships, an individual may trade up for someone who is more arousing, more prestigious, or more successful. In a Pygmalion relationship, trade-ups really only happen consistently when there is a perception that one party has stopped trying to improve themselves/their partner, or that the goals each party is striving have shifted or might never have been the same to begin with. For example, one partner may decide to become a stay-at-home dad and this decision does not align with his partner's perception of his potential. This can be avoided so long as partners take time to ensure the alignment of their goals and values.

The stability in Pygmalion Relationships stems from the belief that one has attached themselves to an appreciating asset. From the perspective of a Pygmalion Lure relationship, the concept of people leaving their current relationships in the name of hypergamy is preposterous (hypergamy is the act of choosing to leave one's current partner for another of superior status). This is because even if Pygmalion-bonded partners were to meet better prospective partners, they could not trust that those partners would continue to improve, whereas they have already proven to each other that both of them are committed to constant improvement. Hypergamy is only a threat to partners who are stagnant, which is why it presents such a threat to individuals who lean on Dominance Lure tactics.

All that said, Pygmalion Lures have some glaring downsides, many of which we have already addressed, but which should be highlighted again.

Specifically, Pygmalion Relationships:
1. Require more effort to maintain than other relationships.
2. Are only accessible to people who have their shit together to a degree that others find enviable, as that envy fuels the early stages of the relationship.
3. Require more confidence to effectively execute than any other relationship type
4. Require a huge throughput of potential candidates to find a person who may genuinely be interested.
5. May lead to more damage if terminated (vis a vis typical relationship termination), especially if one or more partner begins to see another as critical to their self-improvement.

The Status Lure

The Status Lure is the closest thing that exists to a "Happiness Lure." Desire for happiness is not a strong enough drive in humans to make it effective as a lure on its own. People talk up happiness, but consistently fail to make the hard choices necessary to chase it, because at the end of the day, our instinctual laziness is stronger, and happiness just doesn't feel as good as we pretend it does. You cannot convince a person to date you just by saying that they will be happier through doing so. On the other hand, even just a *shot* at increased status is something over which people would gladly bludgeon their happiness with a lead candlestick and bury it in the backyard.

To leverage the Status Lure, signal to your target that you will increase their status in exchange for a relationship.

This lure can be utilized by a huge range of people: Celebrities, individuals from notable families, extremely attractive people, wealthy people, drummers in local rock bands, proud Bugatti owners, award-winning competitive archers, accomplished academics, or even just average Joes who made a cameo appearance in the latest trendy movie or TV series. What matters is what the target believes has value. The only thing necessary is that the prospective partner is able to sell to the target that, through a romantic or sexual interaction with them, some of their "status magic" will rub off on the target. Perceived status is the prospective partners' primary value.

This dating strategy is not very effective at securing sex—or at least a lot less effective than you may think (even many famous and super-wealthy individuals struggle to get laid). Even when executed by a local celebrity, Dominance Lures crush Status Lures in their effectiveness at securing sex.

That said, Status Lures can be helpful in casual dating markets and with securing long-term relationships.

Unfortunately, after thoroughly assimilating into whatever status you offer, your partner may eventually climb high enough in status themselves to leave you for someone with even *higher* status—unless you have done something to significantly increase the value you provide to your partner that is unique to you, perhaps by having kids with your target, providing them with some other lure, or increasing your status at a rate faster than that of your target. Be especially wary of if the status that is attracting the target is tied to an intrinsically decreasing asset. This scenario tragically comes into play among individuals who were married for the status associated with their looks. These individuals ultimately get left by their targets for younger, better models as soon as they age and lose that aesthetic value.

Remember: Everyone is both a pursuer and the target, so in the above scenario, both parties may have been using the Status Lure. Problems result when one partner's status depreciates in value over time (athletic prowess, looks, fertility) while the other partner's status appreciates (wealth, job title). A relationship in which one partner is primarily valued for their looks and the other is primarily valued for their wealth is almost guaranteed to fail in the long term because looks decrease over time while wealth typically increases.

The Self-Identity Lure

The Self-Identity Lure revolves around convincing the target that not dating or having sex with the pursuer will somehow violate their self-identity or otherwise give rise to cognitive dissonance (e.g., "If you will not sleep with me, everything you believe to be true about yourself and your character is a lie—you are not the X that you claim to be"). It is depressing how effective this lure can be when executed competently.

This is not to say that someone with low social intelligence attempting this lure will not comically crash and burn. Failed deployment of the Self-Identity Lure classically features a jilted prospective partner wailing at their target: "What—are you gay/racist/homophobic or something???" in hopes that some deep-seated insecurity will lead the target to conclude their only recourse is to sleep with their accuser.

The Self-Identity Lure has nevertheless been effectively used by particularly cunning individuals for centuries. For example, there are recorded incidents in the courts of famous European royals where pious and chaste young women were convinced to sleep with high-status individuals out of wedlock through being convinced it was the most pious thing to do and that to not have sex would be an act of impropriety and self-indulgence (with the pursuer arguing family fealty stands above social conventions).

There are two approaches one might take to deploying this lure:
- Attacking the Target's Identity
- Cultivating Cognitive Dissonance in the Target

Attacking the Target's Identity

The pursuer identifies something incredibly important to the way the target sees themselves, then builds a compelling argument that not sleeping with or dating them would violate that treasured element of the target's identity. These days this often manifests as responding to rejection from a self-identified "good, tolerant, open-minded person" with an accusation of racism, sizeism, transphobia, misogyny, or some other form of bigotry and intolerance. Many people who want to see themselves as socially conscious operate on autopilot and would rather date or have sex with someone they found repulsive than genuinely see themselves as a racist/sexist/transphobic bigot.

There are a number of other paths that follow this same basic strategy. For example, if a target sees themselves as rebellious or as the type of person who breaks societal conventions, a pursuer can leverage that aspect of their identity subtly to push past points on a date at which the target might otherwise turn them down—in this case, by implying that continuing past the target's comfort zone is the "rebellious choice," meaning that playing it safe would clash with the target's identity.

Cultivating Cognitive Dissonance in the Target

Rather than looking for something important to the target's identity, a pursuer may encourage them to clarify things they believe about the world, then leverage those beliefs to create cognitive dissonance.

The Pursuer may, for example, get a target to agree to a statement like: "Any action that makes all parties involved feel good is a good action." Next, they would escalate that logical pathway by getting the target to admit that they would find sex with the pursuer pleasurable—or at least that it would be very unlikely to be unpleasant. After clarifying these two statements (things that make people feel good = good, and sex makes people feel good), a decision to not have sex with the pursuer will likely create cognitive dissonance in the target. Most people would rather sleep with someone, even someone they are not attracted to, than experience cognitive dissonance. If the target still does not want to sleep with or date the pursuer, the pursuer gets them to list explicitly why not, then attempts to create cognitive dissonance against each of these pillars using a similar strategy.

Once you accept that most humans are just blindly stumbling through life trying to fulfill some vision of who they are, you will begin to notice how easy it is to manipulate this vision to get them to do what you want. After you gain a clear understanding of what this vision is for one of these autopilot humans, you can lead them around like a dog on a leash. This is doubly true if you are confident, non-hideous, non-threatening, not desperate, and comfortable being you. Unfortunately, failing at any of these things can set off an internal warning system in people's brains, telling them to be suspicious of your intentions and to look down on you.

While these strategies are unnervingly effective against people living on autopilot, they are completely ineffective against people who have a deep philosophical framework behind what they want from their lives (see: *The Pragmatist's Guide to Life*). These tactics are also only effective on people who are less intelligent than you, though not so stupid that they are below autopilot level. People at below autopilot levels of intelligence cannot hold a train of thought and are more influenced by biological impulses than their autopilot, which is trying to maximize a certain image of who they are. This method is completely ineffective on people in this category, though dominance-based strategies should work extremely well.

Essentially, the pursuer is looking for targets with strongly held, complex convictions—but convictions they adopted not because of the logic behind them, but because of the way these convictions make them feel about themselves.

Self-Identity Lure strategies are great for short-term dating and sex (they completely smoke dominance-based lures in terms of effectiveness when applied to higher-value targets), but are not very useful in securing high-quality, long-term relationships unless you want a pet more than a partner—and if you do, you are probably on autopilot trying to make yourself feel powerful or earn the admiration of others and thus will be unable to effectively execute this strategy. To say it another way, most people using this strategy have learned to use it through subtle subconscious training (e.g., "I notice that if I claim people are transphobic/fatphobic/racist when they turn me down, I am more likely to get laid; I like getting laid, so I shall increase the behavior that leads to the reward.").

The Damsel in Distress Lure Variant of the Self-Identity Lure

The Damsel in Distress Lure is a passive form of the Self-Identity Lure. Essentially, the prospective partner exhibits (or feigns) a need for the target. This need thereby attracts the target, as it presents an opportunity to reinforce a "heroic" part of that target's self-identity ("I am a good person / I help those in need").

The most common manifestation of this dynamic involves a stable individual dating a distressed individual because doing so reinforces their own magnanimous and heroic self-image: Visualize the stable, rich guy who dates the poor, unstable gal because giving her stability and helping her get her life on track reinforces his image of himself as a good person. That said, you can frame yourself as the necessary yin to whatever yang your target may need to "complete" their self-identity. Is your target an academic? Be the acolyte who desperately wants and needs their guidance as you work to continue their legacy. Is your target the Magician? Be the Lovely Assistant.

Relationships of this nature can be powerful for casual daters as both parties typically benefit greatly—at least when the prospective partner's need for the target is real. Specifically, the hero gets to feel great about helping someone and the damsel (gender-neutral in this case) gets to be helped and get through a rough time in his or her life.

However, relationships originating from Damsel-in-Distress lures do not make for good long-term relationships because either:
- The hero (the target) successfully and resoundingly saves the damsel (the prospective partner), and now that there is nothing to fix, the hero no longer gains much value from a

continued relationship (or the damsel, being saved, moves on). In this case, the hero often moves on to focus their attention on other partners or projects.
- The hero repeatedly fails at helping the damsel due to persistent relapses on the part of the damsel, causing the hero to lose any cognitive reward gained from helping the prospective partner and ends the relationship—or perhaps worse still, the couple falls into a stable but toxic codependent relationship.

These relationships are fine for someone just learning to date and can be beneficial to both parties in scenarios in which one appreciates their partner for what they do to help them while the other appreciates their partner for helping them reinforce a desired self-image.

As we mentioned before, these relationships are easy to mistake for Pygmalion Lure relationships and are critically different.

If you are unsure whether you are just someone's "hero" or the pursuer in a Pygmalion Lure relationship, ask yourself:
1) Does the target think of me more like their crutch (that helps support them so they can live a normal life) or more like their home gym (that improves them through challenge and work)? A crutch is disposable once a person has healed; a gym is not—so long as one wants to keep improving.
2) Is my primary value to the target (in their eyes) my advice, labor, money, security, or emotional support? If your value to your partner consists of

anything other than your advice, you are just their "hero." If you still aren't sure, think through how often they seek your advice and how often they take it.
3) If my partner were feeling emotionally vulnerable, would it improve their trust in me more were I to (a) calmly point out their lapse of emotional control and help them regain their composure or (b) comfort them? A person who sees your comforting them as a betrayal of trust demonstrates that, to them, you are a tool for constant self-improvement more than an interchangeable emotional security blanket.

The Admiration Lure Variant of the Self-Identity Lure

The Admiration Lure simply entails demonstrating a high amount of admiration for one's target. The target then dates the pursuer because they like the feeling of being admired. This tactic is often employed alongside other lures and is uniquely effective at securing dominant partners. We might go so far as to say admiration plays a critical role within any mate acquisition strategy targeting an individual that tends towards the dominant end of the sexuality spectrum. Dominant individuals often experience strong cognitive dissonance when they feel a partner does not actively admire them.

The Admiration Lure differs somewhat from other lures as it is a necessary component of almost any strategy when targeting a specific personality type, naturally dominant individuals. Failure to properly deploy it lies at the core of a huge number of failed mate acquisition strategies. This is particularly true among heterosexual and bisexual women, who (statistically speaking) are more likely than other groups to be hunting exclusively for actively dominant partners (this is not conjecture, but rather based on a large volume of data, see *The Pragmatist's Guide to Sexuality* for more detail—bisexual women actually become aroused by acting submissive in a sexual context at a rate of 80%, the highest of any demographic).

The most common mistake people make when trying to secure a dominant partner involves an attempt to raise one's stature in a partner's eyes by dismissing something about them as unimpressive (be it an achievement, a personal characteristic, a meaningful possession, distinct knowledge, an important milestone reached, etc.). While this kind of play MAY sometimes be effective at asserting dominance in purely social contexts, deflating a target's ego in an effort to increase one's own perceived value is instant death to a strategy designed to secure a dominant partner.

We have also observed individuals with a strong preference for a dominant partner who, for whatever reason, see it as demeaning to express frequent admiration toward another person. Typically this takes the form of someone with a superficially high and fragile ego they fear might be damaged through any display of admiration. We have yet to see such an individual maintain a high-value dominant partner in a stable, happy relationship.

Discomfort with expressing admiration presents one reason why professionally successful women who still want a dominant partner have so much trouble securing one. When a person is objectively smarter and further along in their career than their partner and intelligence and career status comprise the things they value most in life, how can they honestly show admiration for that 'lesser' partner? If they are someone who is objectively highly successful in the domain they value most, yet they still yearn for a happy relationship with a dominant partner, we strongly recommend that they explore admiring different domains of achievement, specifically domains in which they are weak.

The Admiration Lure is fairly useless if not deployed with genuine conviction. Feigning admiration will not get a person far. We recommend finding something the pursuer truly admires about a target and digging into that when speaking with the target about the manifold ways in which the target impresses them.

Expressing genuine admiration for a partner has near-zero downside risk—other than the fact that admiration alone is unlikely to secure a partner. While a willingness to express admiration is a near prerequisite for securing a dominant partner, expressing admiration toward a submissive or neutral partner in an attempt to augment one's appeal is still effective and necessary in many cases (just not as often a prerequisite). Learning how to admire other people and believably show that admiration is far more useful than getting good at something like sex if a person wants to secure a healthy relationship with a high-quality partner. Almost every emotionally healthy person gets a strong sense of validation from knowing they are admired and likes to surround themselves with people who yield that validation.

The one caveat of the Admiration Lure may be this: If at some point the pursuer turns *off* that addictive IV drip of admiration and validation, that action may cause their relationship to take a nosedive. This becomes a genuine risk when the core and only thing the pursuer admires about a person is temporally locked (e.g., good looks or being captain of the football team). Given how hard admiration is to believably fake, we would therefore advise avoiding relationships in which the source of one's admiration has a clear expiration date.

The Friend with Benefits Lure

Most people have a general idea of how the Friend with Benefits sexual strategy works: A person targets a partner with whom they are already friends and leverage that friendship so the transition into a sexual relationship will not involve a significant escalation of the existing relationship. While we call this the "Friend with Benefits Lure," it just as often transitions directly into a dating relationship as a friends-with-benefits-style one. The core strategy behind this lure is to make the transition from friendship to a dating or sexual relationship only require a tiny nudge because the target is already someone with whom the pursuer has a strong non-sexual relationship.

This strategy comes very close to the Sneaky Lure and can easily be interpreted as such by the target. The core difference between the two is that, in this strategy, they are friends because they both *want* to be friends and the escalation of the relationship is a bonus, whereas with the Sneaky Lure, all investment put into the friendship was made with the ultimate goal of securing a sexual relationship.

The Friends with Benefits Lure is a dangerous lure to intentionally use. Close friendships feature significant prior investment and are typically riddled with externalities (a larger friend group that could be disrupted through romantic entanglement). Failure to escalate a friendship to a sexual level can easily lead to resentment and a perception that the pursuer was attempting a Sneaky Lure all along (e.g., they were only faking friendship in an effort to secure sex and/or a relationship).

On the other hand, when executed successfully, the Friends with Benefits strategy can form strong, long-term relationships. When the strategy yields a relationship, and that relationship forms a solid foundation, the pursuer will enjoy one of the best outcomes possible. Consider leveraging this lure if you have strong evidence suggesting your target is interested and if you wish to create a long-term relationship with this person. Do not waste a valuable friendship on this potentially ruinous tactic just for sex or casual dating.

One limitation of relationships formed through this lure is that, given the couple's history as just friends, it can be very difficult to implement a hierarchy once they are in a committed relationship. This limits the categories of relationship contracts and conflict resolution mechanisms available to such a relationship. We will explore this in detail in the next chapter on relationship contracts. Fortunately, even this one limitation can be avoided if both partners are able to transition from seeing themselves first as friends and secondarily as partners to first as partners with some form of joint purpose that dwarfs their friendship.

Note from the Research:
- One study found that heterosexual men on average prefer opposite-sex friends to whom they are attracted, whereas this is not an important trait when heterosexual women choose friends of the opposite sex. In other words, straight guys prefer their female friends to be hot, whereas straight women don't care how hot their male friends are. Perhaps males secretly hope the odd female friend might become a friend with benefits and thus preferentially cultivate relationships with individuals to whom they are attracted.

The Long-Term Relationship Lure

Prospective partners deploying the Long-Term Relationship Lure are transparent about looking primarily for a long-term relationship and seek targets who leverage the same lure. Those using this lure believe they are better off in a long-term relationship than they are single or casually dating—the relationship dynamic itself is the goal.

This can either be a fairly effective lure, or it can be the symptom of a lack of appropriate planning.

Sometimes the Long-Term Relationship Lure is implemented by people sleepwalking through life who one day wake up and realize they have passed the age at which they "were supposed to be married." This is essentially the musical chairs game of choosing a life partner. Those playing this game end with whoever they happen to be with when the music stops or rush around trying to throw other people off chairs. In this game, the music often stops with a sudden realization that the window one gave themselves to find a long-term partner was too short within their life plan (e.g., thinking "I won't start looking for a husband until I am established in my career, but I also want multiple kids that are biologically mine" doesn't grant a realistic window of time to find an optimal spouse for most people, as one is usually not established in their career until their mid to late thirties and securing an optimal spouse takes around seven years of work on average).

People in this position often end up in suboptimal relationships for a plethora of reasons. Often their sad outcomes result from living in an extreme state of autopilot, just taking life one day at a time, meaning they haven't really thought through what they want from life outside of fulfilling some generic vision of a good life. Upon realizing the utter vapidness of this generic vision, these victims of society's default settings end up having that clockwork meltdown in what our society calls a midlife crisis.

That said, this lure can and does often lead to positive long-term relationships. How to implement the Long-Term Relationship Lure to ensure it does end in a positive relationship depends heavily on an individual's age and gender.

If you want to try to systematically implement this lure before your late twenties, regardless of your gender, it can be one of the more effective lures out there. The only downside is that if you want to use this lure while you are still young, you are likely to get odd looks, as people don't expect younger individuals to be transparent about a goal like this. You also may find yourself limited to more conservative partner choices, which can be problematic if a liberal ideology is important to your life goals.

To implement the Long-Term Relationship Lure in your twenties, simply clarify very early on dates that you are looking for a long-term partner and speak with your target about what they are looking for in a long-term partner. People love talking about this sort of thing in a group context, as it can be very juicy and gossipy. This gives you a chance to signal your desires to a larger group. Regardless of your gender, you will have to be aggressive and not rely on innuendo when signaling to a target. People in their early twenties often choose to believe others think the worst of them rather than just read between the lines, so you will need to assume your targets are doing this. Be warned that this lure requires a lot more time and effort (around a couple years) before getting a payout when contrasted with others, as you are asking for a much larger emotional and time commitment with someone than you are when merely offering sex or dating.

As one gets older, optimal deployment of the Long-Term Relationship Lure shifts. For men, it will always be fairly straightforward and will become easier to use as time progresses. As we discuss in subsequent chapters on timing and marketplaces after the age of 30 or so, there are fewer high-quality men looking for long-term relationships than there are women, and there are copious statistics to support this that we will dig into. However, even though women are disadvantaged when looking for a long-term relationship, simply being direct about it can still be one of the best strategies available to them with a few caveats.

The key to successfully implementing this strategy as a woman in your late twenties and over is the internalization that your relative value within the marketplace has shifted (more on the specifics of what causes this in this book's discussions of timing). Women approaching and beyond age 30 must accept that their position has shifted from gatekeeper to active pursuer. This shift in dynamics can leave one feeling hopeless, but there are actually a lot of decent guys out there waiting for a woman to pursue them. The key words here are **"decent guys"** and **"waiting for a woman to pursue them."**

Decent guys: A woman implementing this strategy will have the most success if she remembers that a male of average attractiveness is liked by only 1 out of 115 women on Tinder. An average man should expect less than a 1% interest rate on the dating market. Half of men are below average in appearance. On dating sites, men below the top 10% in terms of physical attractiveness receive very little outreach from women, *even though attractiveness is not often considered to be one of the most critical factors in the success of a long-term relationship*. We refer to Tinder as the dating app plays host to some of the most robust and practical studies on this market dynamic that have been performed, but when implementing this strategy, one should not rely heavily on Tinder and other hookup and casual-dating-oriented apps; instead, focus on apps that guys generally only use when looking for a long-term relationship (such as Match or eHarmony).

Waiting for a woman to pursue them: Statistically speaking, most heterosexual women want a man who will pursue her. Realistically speaking, most decent men who actively pursue women and want a long-term relationship have been filtered out of the market by their mid-twenties, as a significant proportion of these proactive men get locked down by partners—but this is not the only reason. Statistically speaking, men who are dissatisfied with a relationship leave at much lower rates than women, meaning good guys leave bad partners more slowly than good girls do (more on this later).

Fortunately, this does not mean a woman using this strategy will never again get to savor male pursuit; women using this strategy need only "activate" this pursuit through some pursuit of their own, initiating contact and letting the targets know explicitly they will not be rejected if they take the emotional risk of pursuit—which unfortunately comes with the cost that men are used to bearing: That the guy will tell the woman he isn't interested and change how he sees her. Sometimes life sucks. We refuse to lie to our readers and imply that they can secure a partner when in a disadvantaged state without significant personal tribulation. Such feel good assurances are the bread and butter of grifters looking to sell you something.

The Social Construct Lure

This lure entails the use of a structured social construct, such as an arranged marriage or structured matchmaking market, to create a relationship. We could easily write an entire book on the various social constructs used to produce relationships and their varying efficacy, but since this book is primarily written for those searching for relationships and sex within modern Western markets, such information would be of little utility to the reader.

It is difficult to make overarching statements about relationships born from these systems given their vast diversity. Typically, they are on the higher end of relationship quality given the intentionality that often goes into designing these social constructs and the emphasis they often place on a combined mission for the couple (as opposed to encouraging couples to obsess over how in love they are). However, as most of these systems developed a long time ago, social-construct-generated relationships almost always feature strong patriarchal overtones that are distasteful to the modern Western palate.

Some of the most common Social Construct Lures are those based around matchmaking specialists like the Jewish Shadchan, Egyptian Khatba, or the Hindu Astrologer. In these systems, a third-party relationship expert will find and match two individuals or sanctify a parent's choice of an arranged marriage partner, making it harder for hesitant assigned partners to object.

Another type of Social Construct Lure involves a matchmaking community and/or location. This can be seen among the Church of Jesus Christ of Latter-day Saints' Singles Wards or the structured social dances that are still common throughout the world (such as square dancing and contra dancing in frontier North America or the Ceilidh dances of Scotland). These systems enable youth from cultures in which premarital relations are discouraged to meet and mingle in supervised contexts with plenty of rules and chaperones. These controlled interactions are quite effective, but they can create social unrest in that they tend to visually reinforce strong gender discrepancies in terms of market availability. It is common for either males or females to leave these cultures at disproportionate levels—or a portion of a gender's population is discounted due to a social requirement for matchmaking (land ownership, virginity, devoutness, etc.). In other words, this matchmaking system can make it depressingly obvious there are far more single men than women or vice versa when a person arrives at a matchmaking event with twice as many individuals of one gender.

Many matchmaking systems are far more complex. At the Shanghai marriage market, parents write down details such as the age, height, job, income, education, family values, Chinese zodiac sign, and personality details of their children on a sheet of paper and hang up said paper on strings. These pieces of paper act as advertisements to other parents looking for a match for their child.

Social constructs designed to form relationships can become significantly more formalized and even state run, as can be seen with Singapore's Social Development Unit (SDU), which offers a combination of professional counsel and dating system technology. While we may see long-term pair-bonding as a totally personal responsibility, across cultures and history these decisions have more often been facilitated by either a person's family unit, religious subculture, or the state in an effort to maintain and propagate social order, cultural values, and/or stability.

With dropping birth rates around the world beginning to threaten the extinction of certain cultures (Japanese and Korean being the first—but not only—cultures on the list) and seriously damage the world economy, we anticipate we may see these government-run systems become more formalized and aggressive within our lifetime.

Which Lure Should I Use?

It is easy to read through the above section and think: "Well . . . Damn, there are not many good options." This is true. To speak honestly, society has not handled its transition to sexual freedom and individual autonomy, as well as we like to pretend it has. We discuss this and the associated statistics in detail at the end of *The Pragmatist's Guide to Sexuality*.

That said, every person still has a lure that is optimal for them, given their current goals, gender, and stats (intelligence, attractiveness, age, wealth, etc.).

To help you out, we will quickly recap the major lures, dividing them into three categories:
- Can be effective
- Extremely situational
- Almost never effective

We will discuss each of these three categories in the context of lures effective at securing either sex or healthy, long-term relationships, as most people reading a guide like this are looking for one of those two things.

Long-Term Relationships
- **Can be Effective**
    - The Pygmalion Lure: This is the king of lures for creating effective, long-term relationships; however, it requires more work to secure and maintain a relationship than other lures. The Pygmalion Lure also necessitates a very high level of initiative, persistence, and self-awareness that many lack.
    - The Long-Term Relationship Lure: This is a good lure to implement when young and is still fairly effective as one ages, so long as you are willing to be the active pursuer.
    - The Sexual Exploration Lure: This is the only lure on both lists, as while it is effective at obtaining sex, it is also one of the best options available for women over thirty looking for a long-term relationship. The greatest caveat to this lure is that you must be comfortable with your sexuality to use it. Another catch: To implement this lure, you

must deal with communities highly intolerant to conservative worldviews.
- The Social Construct Lure: Despite the shade our society casts on things like arranged marriages, they are often more effective than the other strategies available to our generation. Significant drawbacks of this lure include required membership in a community that has the infrastructure to support a social construct lure, the often-misogynistic cultures of these communities, and the non-trivial risk that any third party handling your matchmaking might have interests that are poorly aligned with your own.

- **Extremely Situational**
  - The Friend with Benefits Lure: This lure should only be used to create long-term relationships and carries a high risk. However, when it is successfully deployed, the Friend with Benefits Lure can lead to stable, productive relationships.
  - The Status Lure: Luring targets with some sort of status is effective when the status bump you offer is immutably connected to who you are (or is at least very secure). That said, this lure is very dangerous when the status you offer is temporary (e.g., status associated with attractiveness, youth, or a temporary position of leadership).
  - The Admiration Lure: This is a solid lure and a near necessity for securing dominant

partners. However, mere admiration is rarely effective on its own.

- **Almost Never Effective**
    - The Damsel in Distress Lure: While this lure may be mutually beneficial for short-term dating, it is dangerous for forming long-term relationships.
    - The Love Lure: As we said before, thinking that someone will want to be with you because "you love them" is like thinking that someone will want to be with you because you masturbate while looking at a picture of them.
    - The Nice Lure: This is the "nice guy/girl" strategy and is largely ineffective in all circumstances. Do not attempt to obtain a partner by behaving like an over-eager fan/servant. If that type of role in a relationship excites you, find someone looking for that particular flavor in what is called a "service submissive" within the BDSM community using the Sexual Exploration Lure.

Sex

- **Can be Effective**
    - The Sexual Exploration Lure: This is hands down the best strategy to implement when you first decide to start exploring your sexuality. The two core drawbacks are that it requires a medium to high level of social intelligence to implement, especially for men.

- The Self-Identity Based Lure: This lure is uniquely effective at securing targets who are living life on autopilot and the best lure for casual dating and casual sex (assuming you don't need to respect your partner). The major drawback is the type of people looking to have sex or casually date people they don't respect are rarely self-aware enough or have the social intelligence to competently implement the lure.

- **Extremely Situational**
  - The Dominance Lure: Dominance presents a very useful lure for any gender with low social intelligence that is only looking for sex. While understanding the mechanics behind the Dominance Lure can have utility for those of above-average intelligence, there is virtually no value in practicing it, as other strategies are strictly better, lower effort, and less risky. Under no circumstances do we recommend using dominance as a lure to obtain anything more than casual sex.

- **Almost never effective**
  - The Sneaky Lure: While the sneaky lure is effective at preventing explicit rejection, it sucks at most everything else and features high risks.
  - The Easy Lure: This is one of those lures from which nothing good can come. Even though it may help women attain low-effort

sex, it has a high probability of putting them in a dangerous situation.

RELATIONSHIP CONTRACTS

There is no such thing as a relationship without a contract. All relationships are governed by contracts, be they implied or explicit. Relationship contracts are not legal contracts, though sometimes societal expectations of relationships get worked into law (this can come into play in situations like divorce as well as the legal establishment and relinquishment of paternity).

The society in which you grew up provided you with a set of template contracts to which you implicitly agree whenever you enter a relationship, even a non-sexual one. For example, a common clause of many societal template contracts among friends involves agreeing to not sleep with a friend's recent ex. While you may never explicitly agree to not sleep with a friend's ex, your friend will absolutely feel violated if they discover that you shacked up with the person who dumped them just a week earlier.

Essentially, these social contracts tell an individual when they have "permission" to have specific emotional reactions. While this may not seem that impactful, these default standards can have a significant impact on one's life. For example, in the above reaction, a friend who just got angry out of the blue at a member of their social group would be ostracized by others within the group while a friend who became angry while citing the "they slept with my ex" contract violation may receive social support from the friend group and internally feel more justified in their retaliatory action. To ferret out the contractual aspects of relationships in which you currently participate, think through something a member of that relationship might do that would have you feeling justifiably violated, *even though* they never explicitly agreed to never take such action.

This societal system of template contracts may have worked in a culturally and technologically homogenous world without frequent travel, but within the modern world, assumed template contracts cause copious problems.

These template contracts are not always well-communicated and differ between social groups. This can lead to unintentional contract violations and the breakdown of otherwise healthy relationships. For example, within some template contracts, flirting with someone is considered infidelity, while in others, an individual may not think twice about it. Assuming your partner is going to be operating on the same template contracts as you will set you up for disaster.

Let's take a moment to look at the stats so that we can better appreciate why these mismatches are so common. One study showed that ten percent of the US population considers watching porn to be a form of cheating. What if your partner is among that ten percent and you are not? If you consume porn, you would therefore think you are golden within your relationship contract, whereas your partner would see it as you committing a clear violation—you could easily end up cheating in their eyes without ever intending to.

But wait—it gets messier. Thirty-six percent of college-age women and thirty-nine percent of college-age men said that oral contact with another person's genitals counted as sex when the question was framed as them doing it, but when the question was framed as their partner doing it, sixty-two percent of women and sixty-three percent of men counted it as sex (the sample size of this study was robust as well, at 839). As you can see, when people don't explicitly delineate contract terms and definitions, people will subconsciously define the expected norms of the contract in their favor—especially after they have broken an aspect of a contract they may have known was an expectation. This is a product of the phenomenon called the actor-observer effect. This cognitive bias allows one to give oneself the benefit of the doubt to maintain a positive self-image ("It was a one-time thing, and I was drunk, so it doesn't count"), but it does not extend this courtesy to others.

Another larger problem is that these template contracts were written into the fabric of society centuries ago—before birth control, before it was common for women to have jobs, before online dating, and when people's life spans were much shorter. Even if we just focus on one of these points, how is a template for marriage, written in an age in which it was expected that a woman would not have a job, supposed to practically apply to a modern relationship?

The template contracts society gives us simply do not produce effective, happy relationships for people living in the twenty-first century. The good news is that this problem is very easy to fix: Just be explicit with your partners about the ways a relationship contract with you differentiates from common templates—or better yet, choose a specific and optimal position to take on every element of relationships that matters, building a custom contract from the ground up.

Even when just casually dating someone, there are a few points that should be explicitly clarified. Specifically, be sure to:
1) Define infidelity: In implied societal contracts, definitions of infidelity range from sleeping with someone else without first gaining one's partner's consent to merely holding hands with someone of another gender, so it is crucial to clarify what infidelity will be within your relationship. For example, is sleeping in the same bed with someone of a gender an individual is attracted to (with clothing on) cheating?
2) Define your Cost Sharing Strategy: Who pays for what in various circumstances? This changes dramatically between template contracts and can be quite the sore spot for some. For example, do you keep track of expenses in any way? What is the maximum price allowable for surprise gifts? (This one can be a big differentiator in template contracts, as some will see an expensive surprise gift than cannot be returned as a way for an individual to non-consensually force relationship escalation.)
3) Define Your Transparency Policy: When does your partner need to tell you what they are doing? Is it OK to go on a two-week vacation without informing your partner? Is it expected that you will share your locations with each other using smartphone apps or things like Google Maps'

location-sharing feature? Do you expect them to give you their email and phone password as your relationship escalates?

Not clarifying these points and then trying to define them in your favor after a "transgression" will not work to your benefit. Telling someone you never clarified that your relationship was supposed to be monogamous, so it is okay you were sleeping with other people is transparently manipulative. You may be able to convince yourself that you did nothing wrong, but you won't be able to convince most partners of such. Everyone knows the default boyfriend-girlfriend contract in the Western world involves monogamy. If you want to alter this template, there is nothing wrong with that, but you must do so explicitly and with your partner's consent or expect your partner and their social circle to be angry.

Implied Contract Escalation

There are many ways to inadvertently and unknowingly demonstrate consent to society's default relationship contracts. Entering these contracts is not always as simple as verbally agreeing to be someone's boyfriend or girlfriend. For example, according to most Western society default templates, after a certain number of dates, after having sex, or after having spent a certain period of time dating, a portion of the population will begin to assume you have entered into a relationship. At this point, your partner, their friends, and your own friends may become angry at you if they find out you have been sleeping with or dating other people. Even though you never explicitly agreed to a relationship or monogamy, most of society will assume you implicitly accepted these terms through your actions because you did not explicitly opt out.

Bear in mind that:
1) The implied escalation points of default social contracts differ widely between individuals and many individuals don't have them at all. This is yet another reason to not presume that you and your partner are running off the same template. Research on people in the US found men don't typically think of themselves as dating until four to six dates have passed, while women consider themselves dating after between two and three dates on average.
2) Even though many people do not operate using societal default contracts and only allow themselves to assume a relationship has escalated after an explicit conversation, a relationship guide would be woefully incomplete if it did not mention that some people will nevertheless be operating under these assumptions. In the same way, it is worth guarding yourself against STIs even though not every partner has them, it is worth avoiding mismatched expectations among those with whom you regularly interact.
3) Even if the person you are dating/having sex with is not one of those people who thinks relationships can escalate without an explicit conversation, that does not mean that others in your lives will hold this belief. For example, a sex partner's parent believing that you are seriously dating can cause a big fuss when they see you with someone else at a supermarket. Again, it sucks that society

works this way and that people don't mind their own business, but someone not minding their own business can still negatively impact your life—you should still look both ways before crossing the street even at a red light.

The most catastrophic instances of implied relationship escalation are "common law marriage" conditions, which can functionally and legally marry two people who have been dating and living together for various periods of time within specific geographies. However, these are much rarer and more restrictive than you might imagine.

Fortunately, outside of the odd "common law marriage" and honor killings in regions where this book is almost certainly not going to circulate, there are no catastrophic repercussions for breaking one of these accidentally entered into societal template contracts. Nevertheless, breaking these contracts can come with a social cost to you and to your reputation.

In violating a societal template contract, you run the risk of making people doubt whether they can trust other implicit contracts they might assume they have with you, which lowers your reputation. Peers may also attempt to shame you as a way to reinforce the importance of social order.

It is easy to avoid misunderstandings caused by perceived tacit agreement to a contract. Simply communicate your intentions to your partner. If you do not want to deal with the terms of a "casual dating" relationship, just make sure that within the first few dates, you have told your partner explicitly that either you do not consider yourself to be dating them or that you expect the relationship to have terms that differ from the societal template, and consider putting this notification in writing after delivering it in person to create a clear record of your societal default contract amendment. Do this while being aware that nosy friends and family members might still make assumptions that lead to undesired consequences.

If you fail to communicate your desired relationship terms to your partner because you fear they will not agree to them, then you know for a fact you are deceiving your partner through omission. While this can be an effective strategy in the short term, it is not recommended. Such deception typically ends in discovery within three months or so and has a fairly high probability of leading to retaliatory reactions that can meaningfully impact your life (calling your boss, keying your car, destroying prized positions, spreading rumors, etc.). Failure to communicate clear intentions is rarely worth the risk when there are probably plenty of people out there willing to agree to the relationship contract you want, assuming your desired terms are not completely unreasonable and one-sided, in which case, it's not so much a contract as it is a plan to screw your partner over.

Marriage Contracts

While casual relationships can usually get by using slightly modified societal template contracts, marriage contracts typically need to be rewritten completely.

Marriage presents by far the single most important social contract into which people enter during their lifetimes. Modeling your personal marriage contract off a societal template is completely mental. Worse, if you don't explicitly alter the societal template, some elements of that societal template *will be legally applied to your relationship and life*. If society thinks you should share income or women should raise the children, and you haven't negotiated something else, tough luck: You could be legally forced down that path in the event of a divorce (and you might be forced down that path even if you have negotiated something else, depending on the country in which you live). Unlike a normal relationship contract, a marriage contract should always be written from the ground up to ensure every aspect of it yields the type of relationship you want.

Appendix: *If you are looking for a place to start when designing a marriage contract, it can be helpful to design the contract around achieving a specific "theme," such as mutual happiness, fighting for a common ideological goal, raising children, self-improvement, etc. If you want help thinking through this, we created a list of common themes in the appendix under the Common Marriage Contract Themes section on page 474.*

Download a Contract Template: We created a downloadable contract template that can help you out. You can find it at Pragmatist.Guide/MarriageContract

Clauses to Avoid in Marriage Contracts

Clauses Making Impossible Demands

Despite the fact that nearly every Western marriage ceremony includes the couple making some sort of promise to always love their partner as long as they live, we strongly recommend against including such impractical, impossible clauses in a marriage contract.

Humans cannot control feelings of love or sexual attraction (especially when they cannot control the way their partners age and change behaviorally). Imagine someone said, "love me or I will kill you." or maybe "find me attractive or I will kill you." You know very well you wouldn't be able to force yourself to feel those things—the best you could do is lie about it.

Leave clauses that promise you will feel a certain emotion out of your marriage contract. They belong on the pages of romance novels, not amid social contract clauses that affect the overall happiness and productivity of your short existence.

Clauses Leading to Asset Depreciation

Optimal relationship dynamics naturally improve each partner's individual desirability and aggregate desirability over time. Avoid building any dynamic into a marriage contract that would lead to any partner losing individual value over time, essentially dooming the future of your alliance. In other words, do not tie an appreciating asset to a depreciating asset, and do not create contracts with clauses that cause assets to depreciate.

This dynamic is most often inadvertently woven into relationship contracts when partners agree to have one partner sacrifice their future in exchange for a desirable short-term state. Such sacrifices appear most commonly in relationship contracts that permit one partner to forego a career to become a dedicated, young, and attractive sexual partner (i.e., trophy wife) or gestational carrier, childcare provider, and housekeeper (i.e., stay-at-home mom/dad).

Once the partner who foregoes a career to assume a short-term role no longer provides value in said role (e.g., the partner ages, loses beauty, becomes infertile, becomes an empty nester, hires house cleaning help, etc.), their value in the relationship plummets. It is common at this time for the partner to become resentful, having, for the most part, surrendered the chance of building a meaningful career and being capable of earning significant income. In some cases, the sacrificing partner also feels entitled ("I spent the best years of my life on this relationship—you owe me!") and expects to be rewarded as though they are still bringing value to the relationship, *even if* they become a net drain.

Relationships that require these dynamics are only safe for the sacrificing party if said individual can be absolutely sure their partner will not leave them out of faith in certain aspects of their partner's personality (not generally a safe bet to make) or if their contract includes clauses that cover the sacrificing party's support later in life. In the case of a TradCon relationship (a traditional conservative relationship), a husband would need to promise to not divorce his wife and trade her in for a younger model as soon as the kids go off to college and/or if/when the wife becomes unattractive.

Unfortunately, even fairly strong legal contracts are not ironclad and not able to consistently hold people to such promises, leaving such contracts dependent on other strong negative consequences to be even plausibly effective. These consequences might include the mostly extinct traditions of social shaming by one's community or fear that the jilted partner's family will literally kill any jilting partner. This is why TradCon like relationships are becoming increasingly uncommon outside of the few remaining pockets that consistently apply these punishments, such as strict religious groups and very conservative geographic regions.

Before you pass through this discussion visualizing heartless men abandoning post-youth women, let us set the record straight when it comes to the gender more likely to terminate a marriage. Women initiate divorce in all relationship types, including TradCon relationships, much more often, with about 70% of divorces initiated by women. We discuss the economic pressures that lead to this later.

Everyone suffers in these relationships.

"Wait," some might think: "It is really the one who keeps their job who gets screwed. They have half of everything they earned for the past few decades robbed from them to pay off someone who did a job that a minimum wage employee could have done, and worse, a court can overturn any prenup the couple had in place and force the primary breadwinner to pay a huge chunk of their income for the rest of their lives to someone they hate. What if they want to retire or leave their job for something that they are more passionate about? Tough luck, because a judge won't let them (in many Western countries, it is illegal to leave your current job for a lower-paying position if you are paying child support or alimony). Essentially, these people may become an indentured servant to the state. Heck, some Western countries have even come to define the denial of money to a spouse as abuse! Aren't the breadwinners really the partners who got more screwed? Aren't they the partners who need more protection!?"

This is one way of looking at the dynamic. We aren't choosing sides in this fight; we don't care who the "victim" is. We merely observe that the system doesn't work optimally and that people on both sides of this problem need to understand the real risk they take when they enter a long-term relationship with an individual whose income isn't scaling in parity with theirs, especially when one individual is making major life choices with the assumption of continued joint access to communal income.

"Hold on," you may be thinking; "If TradCons represent the manner in which relationships have always been structured, how could they be so flawed?"

While TradCons can be thought of as people cosplaying what they think the "historical" style of marriage was like in the "good old days," it is important to note that the style of marriage they emulate was relatively short-lived—a kind of wacky fad or social experiment. A nuclear family living together in one house with a dominant male breadwinner and 2.5 kids who stay at home with one parent only really began to exist as a "thing" in the early 1900s when male wage labor started to become common. The model largely died out in the 1970s when female wage labor got big and the "dual earner" family model came to dominate. The only reason we think of this TradCon family structure as "traditional" is that its heyday just happens to coincide with the early days of cinema and the childhoods of the people who wrote the most popular sitcoms. In reality, this relationship structure presents quite the historical anathema.

Personally, we have a predilection for a historical model of marriage called the corporate family.[4] A corporate family exists as a social unit organized around a family business. Historically, corporate families consist of 7.5 children, unmarried family members, and live-in staff. Unlike with other models, children were integrated into the lives of the adults rather than being raised by a corporation, the state, or single parent. Another peculiar feature is that staff of the family are often thought of as part of the family unit/household. Finally, unlike other relationship models, the husband and wife act as a single unit and present themselves to society that way.

Steven Ruggles, a professor of history and population studies at the University of Minnesota, estimates this alternate model to have been the way 90% of American families were structured in 1800. For those who don't read many historical books in which corporate families are featured, two good examples of a corporate (or NeoCorp) family model, would be popular media

---

[4] We do not favor this approach because it is traditional per se—things are not better because they are old—but rather note its historical roots to highlight the irony of TradCon relationships being framed as traditional.

depictions of mob families and (outside of only having two children) the fictional Addams Family.

The great thing about the corporate model when contrasted with the TradCon model is that both partners' careers advance at the same rate, removing a key vulnerability contributing to the collapse of many TradCon relationships. The downside to the corporate family model is that the career paths available to the couple become incredibly limited (we would be able to make a lot more money if we didn't always insist on working together).

Still, with the rise of the gig economy, we expect a "neo-corporate family" iteration of the model to come into vogue, with the NeoCorp iteration of the corporate family model being different in that it exists within a society featuring new innovations in child rearing and more fluid norms related to gender roles.

Defining features of the NeoCorp model:
- The couple acts as a single unit and not as kings of isolated domains of life—though they may choose one partner to be the "face" of a project for convenience.
- The couple identifies as a couple first and as individuals second.
- The model typically includes a unified family business, non-profit, or series of enterprises. This "corporation" is indistinguishable from the family unit. Thus, the name "corporate family."
- When possible, children are taught through direct involvement in the family business and daily lives

of their parents (though this aspect is highly variable).
- Individuals who work in the family business are treated as family (and sometimes live with or date family members). In this way, inclusion in the family unit is more about fighting for a common goal and competence than it is about genetic relation.
- Family wealth and power are centralized in the corporation. Contrast this with a close-knit group of related TradCon families, among which a windfall might be expected to be divvied, whereas in a NeoCorp, any windfall would be stored and grown within a centralized vehicle (such as family businesses, family foundations, family land, etc., which in turn would employ down-and-out family members).

Constructing a Marriage Contract

A shocking number of people get married without first realizing that one partner can't live a life *with* children while the other can't live one *without* them. The process of constructing a marriage contract prevents such oversights from slipping through by anticipating disagreements that may occur in the future, and pre-negotiating each potential disagreement before it becomes a heated issue.

This process enables partners to create optimal solutions outside of the heat of the moment and establish policies that might not be required for years (or may never be needed, but are nevertheless good to have around, like a lifeboat or fire extinguisher). Negotiating all these terms at once also enables partners to trade favors on points that would otherwise not be traded (for example, while the disagreements tied to thermostat control and child naming will happen years apart, a tradeoff can be made in which a partner agrees to a lower normative temperature in exchange for more control over child naming). More importantly, this process allows you to isolate and identify intractable differences before you have invested years into a marriage.

Observe what does and does not work in other relationships to build a contract that details the expected terms of your relationship and each partner's expected responses to stressors and potential points of conflict as they arise. Interview every old person willing to be open about their relationship struggles (both those who had failed marriages and successful ones). Also, peruse online threads (such as those in r/relationships and r/deadbedrooms on reddit) detailing conflicts in relationships.

It will be impossible to anticipate everything before marriage, so this contract must be a living document that will change as the relationship and its partners evolve. Prepare a process for adding both level-headed and contentious amendments. Just as good legal contracts have clauses addressing arbitration and legal jurisdiction should conflicts arise, a robust marriage contract will feature clauses outlining a thoughtful, organized process for negotiating contract alterations in a level-headed manner. Keep in mind that all marriages have unexpected complications—be they infertility or one partner getting an ambassadorship in Mongolia.

Partners in any relationship will need a way to deal with these complications as they arise.

Delineate how consent from both parties should be granted before changes are implemented. List circumstances in which a partner may not be allowed to propose changes before a cooling-off period (e.g., when they are drunk, injured, overly emotional, high, etc.). The whim of an emotional or otherwise-compromised state does not provide an effective compass for making decisions. Humans are naturally more willing to compromise their better judgment when they see someone they love in pain. Be extremely careful about allowing contract changes to be made when one partner is visibly suffering (emotionally *or* physically).

Altering Marriage Contracts to Manage Individual Desirability

Probably the most undervalued aspect of a relationship contract is that they can be updated in a manner that improves your individual desirability to a specific partner—especially after that individual desirability, for whatever reason, takes a hit or is relatively unbalanced at the outset.

Some relationships are made sustainable by favorable clauses in a relationship contract. In cases in which a very wealthy, powerful, or famous individual is marrying someone who is not, it is common for the person they are marrying to trade an expectation of fidelity in their contract to secure the partner. Essentially, one partner acknowledges that they bring less to the table in the relationship, but mollifies that fact by letting their partner sleep with whomever they choose (normally this is modulated by both a requirement for discreteness and strict controls on how much money the philandering partner can divert toward extramarital partners—note that we do not say "poly" as polyamorous communities typically exclude relationships instigated through this type of coercion/tradeoff).

Adjusting a relationship contract to modulate a partner's individual desirability becomes very interesting when the contract of an already existing long-term relationship is altered after one partner's value to the other plummets. Many circumstances can trigger these changes, but the most common are:
- One partner is caught breaking the contract's fidelity clause.
- One partner loses their libido or attraction toward the other partner.
- One partner objectively becomes less attractive either through a lack of maintenance (e.g., they stop showering regularly) or a medical issue (e.g., their face gets burned off).
- One partner loses access to something that was expected when the relationship was initiated (e.g., a relationship in which both partners were expected to work turns into a relationship in which one partner is working, and the other is a stay-at-home partner).
- One partner is discovered to be infertile.

A decline in personal desirability need not doom your relationship so long as you are willing to renegotiate your relationship contract in a way that ensures its aggregate value to everyone involved is better than the value proposed by available alternatives. Because such acts of relationship salvage require a level of pragmatic emotional maturity beyond the reach of most humans, these renegotiations are uncommon. Most drastic drops in one partner's individual desirability end in relationship dissolution.

These failures stem from an unwillingness to accept that, even though a partner's value decreased through no fault of their own, they will now have to find means (through self-sacrifice) of increasing their value to the relationship in order to maintain it. Most modern societies teach us to expect the world to be a fair place; hence we become angry when it isn't. Such reactions are objectively harmful to a person's ability to thrive in the real world.

Keep in mind that the part of the human mind that reacts aversively to "unfair" scenarios does not represent more evolved, higher-order thought, but rather lower-order instincts shared with our ape relatives. If you have a moment, look up the capuchin fairness experiments on YouTube. You'll see a monkey is happy to get cucumbers in exchange for work until he observes another monkey getting grapes for the same task—at which point he loses it and throws his cucumbers back at the researchers.

We advise against letting your monkey brain overwhelm the part of you that is human. Accept that sometimes life is unfair and build strategies to navigate the obstacles life throws at you. There is little to gain from airing grievances before a reality that frankly doesn't care what is and is not fair.

Accept that sometimes relationship contracts need to be renegotiated. If both you and your partner wanted kids that are biologically yours, yet you later find out one of you is infertile, some sort of compromise will need to be made to keep the relationship stable. If sex with people to whom you are attracted to is important to both of you, yet one of you loses their attraction to the other, some form of renegotiation will be needed.

The two most common clauses designed to manage these types of events in a relationship contract before they come into play are the "sex clause" and the "hot clause."

It is fairly typical for monogamous relationships to have a sex clause, even if it is only informally implied (e.g., "After we get married, we are still going to have sex at least once a week, right?" or "Let's only have sex when both parties are interested"). This clause is often explicitly negotiated by the party that believes they will have a higher libido going forward and often includes optional remedies (in the event that regular sex ceases being desirable to one partner) allowing the relationship to stay together even if the commitment is broken.

The "hot clause" is typically an agreement to not "let oneself go" after marriage and is virtually ubiquitous in younger marriages, though such agreements have not always been so common. We hypothesize that the popularity of this clause was spurred by younger generations' discomfort with older generations' tendency to stop investing in self-improvement after marriage. This clause can be anything from a "fat clause" to an "intellectual curiosity clause" depending on the value set of the couple and what they find "hot" or otherwise stimulating and is paired with potential remedies when breached.

Important: Should you plan to have an open marriage in any way, we cannot stress strongly enough that you pre-negotiate terms around how much money can be spent on these other partners and the level of discretion expected in each partner's interaction with them.

Varying Levels of Contract Clause Risk

There are three broad categories of clauses, each carrying with it a different level of risk:
1. Clauses about which both partners agree (e.g., "We both love minimalism and agree to hold quarterly purges of non-essential items.").
2. Clauses about which both partners agree in principle, but one partner struggles with emotionally (e.g., "We both agree to have a policy against drug use to reduce the risk of addiction and financial/legal problems . . . but oh my God I am going to miss cocaine.").
3. Clauses about which the partners disagree, but one partner concedes to the other's demands (e.g., "I want to have sex with other people, but that makes you uncomfortable. Since I really want to marry, I'll forego having sex with other people.").

The strongest relationship contracts are composed almost entirely of clauses in the first category—clauses that each partner neither wants nor feels compelled to break. Despite being clauses that are easy to adhere to, they still warrant discussion with any potential long-term partner, as it is easy for someone to poorly signal their actual preferences early in a relationship. For example, Partner A may assume that Partner B likes to live frugally and minimalistically only to later find Partner B had always assumed their lifestyle would scale up as Partner A's earning power increased—a difference in preferences that could create major conflict later in a relationship.

Clauses falling into the second category, while potentially dicey, can also be incredibly beneficial, especially for the individual making the concession. For many people suffering from addiction or involved in other potentially dangerous hobbies (e.g., base jumping, bull riding, cheerleading, racing motorcycles, etc.), the presence of a partner who cares about them enough to want them to drop that dangerous behavior is the only thing standing between them and death / serious injury.

On the other hand, an addicted individual may grow resentful of a partner who stands between them and their addiction, even if, logically, they would prefer to overcome that addiction. With such matters, it is best for the conceding party—the partner giving something up—to be the one to decide to include these clauses and write them into the contract. This partner must establish very explicit laws governing themselves, clarifying thresholds that should not be crossed, as well as responses to violations of those boundaries.

Clauses in the third category—concessions one partner would strongly prefer to exclude from the contract that are nevertheless admitted after the other partner frames them as non-negotiable—should be avoided entirely. While plenty of marriages have survived for lifetimes with partners making major ideological and value-based concessions, we see such concessions as too risky for something as life-defining as marriage.

Before terminating a relationship due to a failure to reconcile with a partner's values or deep-set needs and preferences, think long and hard about whether opposition to their non-negotiable preference is truly non-negotiable. Many supposedly non-negotiable terms, such as monogamy and religion, are more flexible than one might assume, being more a product of societal defaults than one's own values. It is best to think long, hard, and independently about one's core identity, one's top values, and the things one wants to maximize in life before drawing a hard line in the sand on difficult concessions in a marriage contract. Be uniquely suspicious of your non-negotiables if you think that they are positions on which society or your family would enthusiastically back you, as those are the stances we as humans question the least. Such "non-negotiables" may not ultimately matter that much to you, as an individual.

Conflict Resolution Clauses

No matter how well-researched and constructed your contract may be, you will inevitably run into disagreements you had not anticipated. Such hiccups can be easily dealt with so long as your contract features a conflict resolution clause dictating how the relationship responds to impasses.

Common mechanisms used to resolve conflict include:
- Compromise
- Hierarchy
- Third-Party Arbitration
- Votes

The point of conflict resolution is to come to the "correct" solution, where "correct" is defined as the solution that best serves the relationship and maximizes the objective functions of each partner (i.e., the values and life goals of each partner). With regard to this point, some methods are decidedly better than others.

On Resolving Conflict with Compromise

There is an old saying that has led to the death of hundreds of relationships: "Relationships are built on compromise." We consider "compromise" to be a toxic conflict resolution mechanism. Why? Suppose you want ten and your partner wants twenty. You will be motivated to tell your partner you want zero with the expectation that if they say they want twenty, the compromise will be ten. Similarly, your partner will be motivated to represent what they want forty—or more!

Compromise incentivizes parties to misrepresent what they really want. To make matters worse, prolonged, and repeated compromising can trick us into thinking our false, exaggerated views are our true views, which exacerbates conflict. Even the most honest person under the influence of a heightened emotional state will subconsciously adopt a more extreme position than what they really want when compromise is being used as a conflict resolution model.

Furthermore, compromise incentivizes people to tie unrelated conflicts together and exaggerate the importance and emotions tied to conflicts. For example, if a couple trade a compromise in which Terry allows Sam to adopt a dog in exchange for Terry being granted final say on baby names, it behooves Terry to pretend to care more about dog ownership and thus escalate an unnecessary conflict.

Compromise may even encourage people to create conflicts that don't exist. Let us say Sam wants the toilet paper roll pointed a certain way. Sam may get this concession from Terry by claiming to be upset about a car the couple is planning to buy—even if Sam is perfectly happy about that car choice. Worse, in pretending to be upset about the car choice, Sam may become genuinely emotionally attached to this feigned position, leading everyone to be less satisfied than they would have been had they not chosen to compromise.

Finally, compromise rewards those who act emotional and unreasonable, and it punishes those who work toward resolving conflict. In every relationship we have observed in which compromise is used as a conflict resolution method, the more unreasonable member gets their way more frequently—occasionally leading the reasonable member to dramatically snap after years of succumbing to these frustrating, unfair negotiations.

Compromise is a caustic element that turns small fissures into gaping wounds over time.

On Resolving Conflict with Hierarchy

Rather than subject yourself to the minefield that is compromise, we advocate for a hierarchical approach to conflict resolution, in which one partner is granted the right to make a final call about some or all domains related to the relationship. For example, one partner may have complete dominion over all decisions related to the couple's finances while another makes the final call on decisions related to the couple's social life.

Though domain-specific hierarchy can help to protect delicate egos, we find it most elegant to provide one party unilateral final decision-making power, meaning that one party has the final say in all disagreements not already negotiated in the contract. Unilateral hierarchy prevents tit-for-tat and retaliation problems emerging from domain-specific hierarchy (i.e., "You decided against my preference that we would go to Paris on our next vacation, so I am going to paint the living room that aubergine color you detest."). Any mechanism that yields rewards for creating conflict in a relationship is toxic.

Per the unilateral hierarchical model, whenever there is a point of disagreement, the subordinate partner alerts the dominant partner and asks them to make a call on behalf of their combined good. Surprisingly, in a healthy relationship, this method of conflict resolution actually leads to the subordinate partner getting "their way" more often than the dominant partner. Why does this happen? By giving all the power to one person, you are forcing them to take a step back from what they want and consider the conflict from a third-party perspective.

For example, suppose you stand at the top of your relationship's hierarchy, and you and your partner have a disagreement about room temperature (and you somehow forgot to include a room temperature clause in your contract . . . like a madman). Instead of thinking: "I want the room colder. How do I convince my spouse to make the room colder?" you will likely think: "I want the room colder because X, but my spouse, the person I love, wants it warmer because Y—what is an equitable solution to this that is in both of our best interests?"

Because most people in long-term relationships love their partners, the dominant partner will typically err in a partner's favor, improving their own happiness by making those they love happier as opposed to taking advantage of their position. Moreover, dominant partners must make decisions not just for those they love, but specifically for those who trusted them enough to give them the power to make final calls on their behalf—further making it difficult for a decent human to abuse such a position.

In moments of disagreement, this conflict resolution method forces both individuals to remember the commitment that they made to each other and the trust that they put in each other. This dynamic often removes the negative emotions from conflicts on both sides. If a subordinate comes to the dominant partner in anger or is acting unreasonably, they are unlikely to engender the compassion necessary to get the outcome they want.

Concurrently, the dominant partner has to take ownership for the way in which any conflict was resolved and be aware that a poor decision can literally doom the relationship, which encourages them to think logically and behave justly—instead of just arguing for a position that benefits themselves.

If you do not trust your partner enough to give them that level of control over your life, your relationship is not necessarily doomed, but we would estimate lower than 50% odds that it continues for any long period of time as a constructive, mutually beneficial relationship. By entering a long-term, committed relationship with others, you grant them immense influence over your personal success and happiness—regardless of which conflict resolution method you implement. If you cannot trust someone to sacrifice their personal best interest in favor of your combined best interest, the odds of you enjoying a successful long-term partnership together are quite low. Thus the final (and perhaps best) benefit of this conflict resolution method is that it accelerates the termination of bad marriages, an outcome we consider quite favorable in comparison to a life wasted on a bad match.

This dominant-subordinate partner method only works if the dominant partner was voluntarily given their final call power by the subordinate partner, thanks to the subordinate partner's trust in the dominant partner's prudence, wisdom, generosity, and impartiality. If the dominant partner believes they have the role because God gave it to them, because of the "natural superiority" of their gender, because the other party gave it to them as a trade (e.g., "I will let you be the dominant partner if I don't have to work"), or because they took that position by force, they will be very likely to abuse that position—as they may feel they owe the subordinate partner nothing.

On Resolving Conflict with a Third-Party Arbitrator

The dominant-subordinate partner method of conflict resolution is designed for relationships that are optimized for quality and therefore can afford to fail. If failure is not an option and you need to optimize your relationship for staying power over quality, we recommend using a third-party arbitrator for conflict resolution instead of the hierarchical model. In this model, conflicts are arbitrated by a neutral third party who acts as the deciding "vote" in a disagreement. This third party is typically a religious figure (e.g., a priest or a rabbi), a family elder, a lawyer, or a marriage counselor.

The key to writing a third-party arbitration clause into your contract is finding a way to reliably replace an arbitrator when the one with whom you start is no longer available (e.g., you have moved, they die, etc.). Should you not have a clear succession plan in place, you may reach a stalemate in which each party refuses to accept an arbitrator who does not show a clear bias in their favor.

An arbitrator is not meant to take each person's side in equal portions, but to ensure the common good of the couple in how he/she votes. An arbitrator who always sides with one party may still be doing a perfect job.

If you want to build this into your relationship contract or an exciting relationship and don't trust the above listed third-party arbiters but like our approach to thinking through things, we may be able to help out. Email Hello@Pragmatist.Guide and we can work together to come up with a procedure.

On Resolving Conflict with Votes

Should you be drawn to third-party arbitration as a conflict resolution method but not want a fixed arbitrator, you might use one or more people to act as a tiebreaker in votes. In some cases, a third/fourth member of a polyamorous triad or quad will make that final vote, or the vote might be supplemented by an agreed-upon friend group or the relationship's children. The only requirement is that the total voting body, between the relationship's partners and any outside voting party, must be odd to ensure there are no ties.

We strongly recommend against this solution. While not as inevitably toxic as compromise, votes lead to bitterness and social politicking while giving swing voters an undue amount of power in the family.

As a final note on conflict resolution in general: Conflict resolution should not be designed to grant each partner an even number of "turns" in which they get their way. Doing so actually encourages conflict, as it allows a partner to create "fake issues," then concede to them. Worse, this model does not internalize that in many relationships, one partner is almost always in the wrong when there is a conflict (perhaps because they have a greater tendency to see problems from their personal perspective, while the other partner looks at problems from the perspective of the relationship's greater goals and values). This can be very destructive to the fabric of a relationship if the habitually wrong partner is unwilling to accept that a conflict arbitration method that almost never works in their favor isn't necessarily biased or not functioning as designed.

Addressing Finance Clauses in Marriage Contracts

Because the default marriage contracts society provides do not explicitly spell out how finances should be handled, special attention must be paid to this topic. This lack of clarity on a "standard system" for handling finances has caused the most common subject of argument within a relationship to be finances (statistically speaking). If your marriage is going to fail, chances are a major component of its downfall will stem from how finances were handled. You will find it difficult to get *too* into the weeds when establishing definitions, standards, rules, and procedures with your partner(s) around finances.

Key subjects of discussion when negotiating financial clauses in general include:
- Which expenses count as joint versus personal
- Which joint expenses require discussion and joint approval
- Which personal expenses require discussion and joint approval
- How to approach budgeting

- How to approach debt (When is it OK to take out debt?)
- How to approach third-party requests for money (What will be the policy regarding friends asking for loans, elderly parents requesting support, etc.?)
- How to approach retirement (Should partners save for retirement or prioritize other present-term goals? Should each partner commit to saving, or should it be an independent decision? Should savings be pooled or individual? Is one partner expected to support another in retirement if one partner neglected to save and needs help?)

Partners typically adopt one of the following financial strategies in marriages:
- Complete Financial Separation with Agreed-Upon Individual or Shared Payments
- Complete Financial Separation with An Allowance
- Shared Pool with Discretionary Income Allowances
- Shared Pool with Pocket Money

We will go through each of these strategies in detail below. Before selecting a particular strategy, verify whether those involved have any debt, and do a credit score check all around. A partner with an abysmal credit score may not only hamper all partners' abilities to take out loans in the future, but also suffer from behavioral issues that could put the relationship at risk (i.e., it may come up that Partner B has an addiction to gambling, drugs, or a penchant for expensive products and services). It should go without saying that if one partner has an abysmal credit score, a large amount of debt, or no savings for retirement, they should allow their more financially secure and likely more responsible partner to dictate the financial terms of their relationship contract. A partner who won't take responsibility for a bad credit score, outside of cases of identity theft, presents a GIANT red flag.

Other Financial Strategy Considerations

Luxury Accessories

We often see those trying to secure wealthy partners in a traditional relationship (i.e., one in which the wealthy partner supports them) intentionally display obviously expensive accessories, such as cars, cosmetic procedures, clothing, and jewelry. This is an absurd strategy, as most wealthy individuals are good enough with money to have the sense to filter out potential partners who are going to have high ongoing expenses, even when only looking for potential trophy wives/husbands.

Expensive accessories present one of the best ways to signal you make bad financial decisions. Even targets who would not be worried by the high maintenance costs signaled by a potential partner's pricey accessories may be less interested in such people, as it would be far easier to surprise and delight a partner who lacks such fancy things (i.e., Where's the fun or feasibility in pleasing the individual who supposedly has everything?).

Expensive accessories exist to signal dominance to other peers of the same gender when a person has nothing else to recommend themselves, not to establish value to potential partners. Besides, expensive accessories make for a terrible store of value.

Mismatched Expected Lifestyles

Humans do not need much money to feel fulfilled, though some normalize to higher burn rates than others, and each partner's desired burn rate can profoundly affect both partners' ultimate happiness. It is, therefore, crucial when selecting a long-term partner to assess the lifestyle and monthly spend level this partner requires to be happy.

We know two men of similar age (semi-retired, US-based). Both love to travel and explore the world. Ironically, the wealthier man travels less than the more middle-class man and comes across as significantly less fulfilled, frequently expressing his regret that he cannot travel more because it is so prohibitively expensive. How can this be?

The lifestyles to which each man and their respective partners have normalized make all the difference in the world. The middle-class man and his partner are willing to fly coach and stay in bare-bones hotels and Airbnbs, whereas the wealthier man and his partner must fly in business or first class, rent luxury cars, and stay in luxury accommodations. Even with his generous savings, the wealthier man simply cannot afford to constantly travel in his semi-retirement.

A household's burn rate—monthly spend for both partners combined—typically is determined by the burn rate of the partner who defaults to more expensive things to achieve a baseline level of comfort. This is because the person who defaults to nicer restaurants, hotels, and houses when given the choice determines the spend rate of both partners (i.e., if Malcolm is happy staying at a cheap Airbnb, but Simone couldn't be happy anywhere below the quality of the Ritz, then both Malcolm and Simone will be spending money at the Ritz). **A family's burn rate can affect its lifestyle and financial freedom dramatically—more than the wealth each partner brings to the table.**

When a person is financially constrained, they will only live up to the quality they can afford. Nevertheless, as people get wealthier, most reach a point at which they stop wanting to increase the luxury within which they live. For example, Warren Buffet has a net worth of $84 billion dollars but still lives in a house he bought for $31,000 in 1958, doesn't have a computer at his desk, doesn't carry a cell phone, and drives himself in a car he bought for $45,000 in 2014—plus in his spare time, he plays bridge with friends. This behavior is not unique to Warren Buffet; most financially successful people reach, over the course of their lives, a point at which they "max out" their luxuries.

Do everything possible to avoid a partner if it looks as though there is a large mismatch in ideal lifestyle and "necessary" monthly spend. Failure to do this may lead to a life spent treading water, no matter how much each partner earns. Many partners work punishing hours late into life at jobs that don't inspire them, foregoing lives with more time for leisure, family, hobbies, and passions (albeit less money) because their spouses require a relatively expensive lifestyle to be happy. Plenty of ultra-wealthy celebrities are barely staying afloat financially because they never hit their personal stopping point.

The best way to assess this in an individual is to just talk through it. Get their opinion on various luxuries: Would they work six extra hours each week if it meant that whenever they fly, it would be in business class? Were money no object, how many bedrooms and bathrooms would they have in a house? If they could make clothing appear out of thin air, what clothing would they materialize, and how often would they materialize more? Would they take on a night/weekend job if it meant that they could always drive around in a nicer car? If they had a choice, would they feel more content in a cheap house with low taxes in the suburbs, or would they prefer one apartment in the center of an expensive city even after having kids?

We really can't stress enough how much this will matter to your life and how thoroughly you need to vet this in potential partners.

You have three lives available to you:
1) If the water rises faster than you can swim, you will live your life underwater, panicking while you hopelessly gasp for air.
2) If the water rises in pace with your swimming speed, you will spend your life treading water—every day feeling like a pointless struggle.
3) If the water stops rising and you swim fast enough, then you can break free and live with the birds—only then will you understand what freedom feels like.

Asceticism is as valuable a trait in a partner as earning potential.

Note from the Research:
- Studies have repeatedly shown that people who buy less "stuff" show higher mental wellbeing, fulfillment, happiness, decreased psychological disorders, and decreased psychological distress. You might be inclined to think this may be due to some related effect and not just pure asceticism increasing happiness as the writers of *Materialist values, financial and pro-environmental behaviors, and well-being* did. They tried to determine if it was actually the self-knowledge that these individuals were being environmentally conscious that lead to the positive mental effects of asceticism, but instead found that asceticism driven by the goal of helping the environment did not have the positive effects of asceticism for its own sake.

Common Financial Configurations in Relationships

Complete Financial Separation with Agreed-Upon Individual or Shared Payments

Partners who feel uncomfortable pooling finances and commingling assets may choose to adopt a strategy in which each partner's finances are completely separate (Partner A never sees Partner B's income, has no access to their bank account, etc.). Each partner assumes individual or shared responsibility for different communally enjoyed expenses.

For example, Partner A may choose to buy a house and pay for the house as well as annual property taxes independently. Whereas Partner B pitches in by paying for water, electricity, internet, and streaming entertainment subscriptions. Together Partner A and B share health insurance and childcare costs.

Should you choose to adopt this strategy, be explicit in your financial management clauses about which expenses are expected to be shared and what is to be done when one partner decides that it is no longer worth spending money on something (usually this means that product/service goes away entirely if the other partner does not wish to independently shoulder the financial burden).

For example, what if the individual who was paying for streaming services just decides to stop? Their partner, not wanting to lose access to this joint resource, might assume this financial responsibility. Through this process, more and more financial responsibility can quietly shift to one partner, creating a system that feels deeply unfair and builds resentment.

The adverse effects of this strategy include the distinct signaling of a lack of trust and misaligned incentives (e.g., if Partner A's income will go up 300% if the couple moves, whereas Partner B's income will drop 30% with relocation, Partner A will likely resent Partner B if the couple does not move, and Partner B will likely resent Partner A if they *do* move).

Nevertheless, this strategy is optimal for relationships that are not expected to last, especially for those with an individual who has earned or will earn an amount of money that is disproportionately higher than their partner. Avoiding the comingling of assets is essential if you are the wealthier partner in a relationship and are keen to avoid the financial damage associated with a divorce.

This strategy is also optimal for relationships in which one partner is irresponsible with money or has problems with an addiction of some sort, as well as relationships in which a partner has anxiety tied to money and finances—quite the common neurosis.

Partners incorporating this approach into their marriage contract must be sure to address:
- Whether one partner will ever receive an allowance from another partner (which may be necessary if one partner earns significantly more than the other partner yet wants to maintain a parity of lifestyles).
- Which products and services purchased by each partner individually may be used by the other partner (e.g., If Partner B buys an expensive car, is Partner A allowed to drive it?).
- What happens when one partner decides to stop paying for something on which the other relied (e.g., heating or Netflix).
- Whether each partner is entitled to know how much money the other partner has or not (e.g., is Partner A entitled to know that Partner B has no retirement savings? This is the only financial model in which it is possible to enter into a relationship without a full understanding of your partner's finances).

- How the relationship will function in retirement and during times of hardship (If Partner A has a retirement fund and Partner B has nothing saved, is Partner A expected to support Partner B in retirement, enjoying a lower quality of life than expected due to Partner B's lack of savings?).

Shared Pool with Discretionary Income Allowances

Couples who wish to work on some financial activities jointly but manage other activities personally benefit most by funneling all of their income into a joint account, but splitting off an agreed-upon percentage or amount of income into private discretionary spending accounts.

This strategy gives individuals privacy and freedom with finances while also keeping incentives aligned, as in most cases, discretionary income is equally distributed and therefore each partner is incentivized to maximize the relationship's overall income rather than just their personal income.

Perhaps, one partner is keen to build up a retirement fund, whereas the other inherited wealth sufficient to act as a retirement fund and wishes instead to invest newly received income in startups. Or maybe each partner has a guilty pleasure or hobby on which they like to spend money and would rather do so without judgment from the other partner. Consider also partners who wish to purchase surprise gifts for each other without the other partner necessarily learning about the purchased item early when reviewing a credit card statement. In all of these scenarios, a strategy involving pooled income with private discretionary income allowances is optimal.

Those adopting this strategy must create very clear policies around the following things:
- How the amount of discretionary income is calculated. Is it whatever is left after all agreed-upon shared expenses divided by two? Is it a fixed amount each month?
- Whether each partner receives the same amount of discretionary income. What if one partner has a very easy job that earns only a small amount, whereas the other partner works 60+ hours a week and finds their work very stressful?
- Which expenses may come out of the relationship's joint account, and which expenses are to come out of each partner's discretionary income? How are vacations funded? How is food paid for, especially if one partner consumes a lot of expensive organic food or alcohol and the other does not?
- Whether and how funds in the shared pool will be further subdivided into accounts/funds that are intended for specific purposes, such as an emergency fund, a fund dedicated to childcare costs, a fund dedicated to home improvements, a fund dedicated to saving up for vacations, a fund dedicated to discretionary income for the couple (e.g., luxuries that all partners want but aren't necessary for survival), etc.

Single Pool With Pocket Money

Partners who expect a lifelong relationship and minimum administrative burden often opt to pool all of their finances into a joint account and pay for all expenses from joint accounts. This strategy usually involves some form of joint discussion and agreement that must be made and reached before expenses above a certain threshold are approved (e.g., buying a boat or house).

While this approach is simple, it can lead to bitterness and resentment when one partner racks up more small personal expenses than another or when partners reach an impasse regarding a significant expense, which, in any other scenario would be resolved by purchasing the non-jointly desired product or service using personal or discretionary funds.

Those who adopt this strategy must negotiate clear clauses delineating:
- The minimum threshold for joint discussion and agreement for an expense. Do expenses under $100 require approval? What about expenses over $300?
- An approval process for expenses above the agreed-upon threshold. How will agreements be documented? How can misunderstandings (i.e., "I thought you said it was fine when I asked you at 3:00 a.m. last night") be avoided?
- The procedure to be followed when the couple reaches an impasse on an expense that is desired by one partner but rejected by another. Does each partner have an annual amount of joint funds they may spend despite disapproval?
- The procedure to be followed when one partner feels the other partner is spending above what is permissible on products and services that disproportionately benefit only them.

- As with the shared-pool-with-discretionary-income strategy, whether funds in the shared pool will be further subdivided into accounts/funds that are intended for specific purposes.

Keep in mind that if one partner expects to financially exploit another partner, this will be the strategy they are most likely to advocate. The best way to avoid financial exploitation by another partner is to maintain entirely separate finances and allocate an allowance to the partner if it is clear that they wish to financially exploit you or are flagrantly irresponsible with money.

One final financial relationship tip: Don't forget to both share your ideal future living situation with your partner and have them share theirs with you. These differ widely between people. Comic Johnny Beehner has a routine in which he describes his wife turning to him a few weeks after their marriage and saying, "I can't wait until we can settle down on our little farm," to which he replies: "Our little *what?!*" People often assume their retirement dreams are universal. This is far from a reality.

Addressing Marriage Contract Violations

Each possible contract violation should be matched with an appropriate consequence of which all involved parties are aware.

The default **theoretical** response to contract violation among most template marriage contracts granted by society is: DIVORCE!!

Did she cheat? Divorce!

Did he become a lazy deadbeat? Divorce!

People like to say they will leave their partner when wronged while their responses to being wronged in practice typically vary from angry outbursts to retaliatory contract violations.

Unenforced contract terms are extremely dangerous to an entire contract's integrity. It is better to leave out terms that will not be enforced than to leave them in and allow them to train others that violations will go unpunished.

If someone tells their partner: "If you do X, I will leave you," then fails to leave their partner once their partner commits X, they are tacitly communicating to their partner that retaliation for other contract violations will either be inconsistent or entirely nonexistent. Failing to execute a response to a violated term in a marriage contract signals to the violating partner that there are no consequences to their actions—or that the consequences are not predictable and consistent—thereby rendering the contract useless.

Because enforcement is so crucial, the immediate dissolution of a partnership in response to any violation is neither a prudent nor a realistic approach. Instead, apply one default low-level response to any sort of generic violation and specific, logical, reasonable, and easy-to-actually execute responses to more extreme violations where applicable.

Specific common responses to contract violation include:
- Hurt Feelings and Lost Respect
- Reversal or Correction of Violation
- Specific Generic Cost
- Specific Unique Cost
- Relationship Renegotiation
- Partnership Dissolution

These responses may be enforced in isolation or combined. Some of these responses are, in our opinion, unrealistic to implement in a long-term relationship, but since we have seen other couples apparently use them to some success, we will address them here.

Hurt Feelings and Lost Respect

One of the most elegant responses to contract violation involves nothing more than making it clear to your partner that violating terms of the contract will result in hurt feelings and a lower level of respect for the contract violator. In most healthy relationships, this is more than enough to prevent contract violations. In fact, we feel at least within most relationships, lost respect is far more painful than a few thousand dollars fine.

Among partners who genuinely care for each other and respect each other, this is by far the best default "punishment" to maintain within a marriage contract.

Reversal or Correction of Violation

In some cases, the simplest and easiest way to address a contract violation is to reverse it. This method of addressing contract violations is often used in conjunction with others. If Partner A used joint rent funds on a personal indulgence, have Partner A return those misappropriated funds. If Partner B changed the house temperature to 75 when it was jointly agreed that it should be 68, have Partner B return the house's temperature to 68.

Not all violations can be completely "undone," but even simple correction may do the trick when applicable. If Partner A contractually agreed to quit smoking, then lapsed back into the bad habit, have Partner A quit again. If, in a moment of anger, Partner B called Partner A by a forbidden word in violation of agreed-upon language usage, Partner B must apologize.

Simple reversals and corrections such as these might not feel adequate when used in isolation, as we humans love to see retaliatory punishment and "justice," but sometimes the most practical thing is to merely set right that which is wrong. More serious consequences may be needed for repeat violations, but it serves us well to remember how fallible we are as humans and leave a bit of wiggle room.

Specific Generic Cost

In this case, a specific, discrete, concrete cost is associated with a breach of contract. The archetypal example is a discrete amount of money paid as a penalty toward a joint account, such as an emergency fund. This is most commonly seen in popular media with "the swear jar," into which those who use forbidden words must contribute fees per forbidden word uttered.

When people use these, they typically only use them as a broad punishment for very small contract violations.

This cost should be something that does not delight or benefit a non-violating partner because this might enable a violating partner to feel justified in their actions (e.g., "It's OK that I stay out late drinking in violation of the contract tonight because then I'll have to give him foot massages every night for a week and he loves foot massages!").

Also, keep in mind that partners may see any cost incurred as a fair trade, meaning that it is OK to violate that contract clause as much as one likes, so long as one pays. Generally, we advise against contract clauses that are habitually and casually violated, hence we would advise against contract violation repercussions that facilitate such casual violation.

At the same time, repeat violations to a contract clause may be perfectly acceptable to the violated partner(s) . . . if the price is right. Perhaps Partner A is perfectly happy to have Partner B leave dirty dishes in the sink each night so long as Partner B receives $10.00 each time this happens. Perhaps Partner A really doesn't mind Partner B sleeping around in violation of a monogamy clause so long as they receive a new luxury car for every time Partner B takes a new lover. What matters is that all partners in a relationship carefully think through just how much certain contract clauses matter to them, and determine whether there are certain reparations that could be made to nullify the sting of a particular clause being violated.

Specific Unique Cost

Some contract violations are most appropriately addressed with unique responses.

For example, at one point I (Malcolm) violated the weight clause in our contract by putting on a few too many pounds. As a consequence, I had to give up beer outside of special occasions for nearly a year—a cost that quickly brought me back within an acceptable weight range.

The above cost worked because:
   1) It was reasonable
   2) It was in my best interest
   3) It was self-resolving

Trying to stay with the above three points when designing these aspects of a contract is useful. However, when designing responses, keep in mind that **there is no promise that a cost imposed on a violating partner will not turn the relationship into a net negative for them and cause a dissolution event**. This is especially a problem in the case of contract violations tied to addictions; many people would rather split than endure the cost of their transgression if that cost involves going cold turkey on an addiction.

This type of punishment is best used as a solution for contract terms tied to financial or physical health scenarios in which a violating partner will regret their transgression and want to atone for said failure. In this case, the punishment's core purpose is to help steer that partner's atonement and self-punishment instinct into productive action that ameliorates the problem.

Relationship Renegotiation

In some instances, the best response to a violation involves renegotiation of the relationship contract.

If Partner A gives Partner B very permissive terms in a relationship contract—such as an honors system with regard to how joint funds are spent—and Partner B violates that trust by spending over an agreed-upon threshold on purely personal products/services, an appropriate response (among other consequences) would be to change the contract's rules regarding the use of joint funds to be less permissive.

Keep in mind that any renegotiation that makes a relationship categorically worse for one party can lead to that person leaving the relationship if they feel they have better options elsewhere, even if (and perhaps especially because) that particular party technically deserves retaliatory action.

In other words, sometimes partners realize that both want to stay together even if a certain clause of the relationship is violated, but the current terms of the relationship contract simply are not going to work if one partner cannot trust another to not violate said terms. For example, you want to give your partner the chance to use your credit card responsibly, but if they can't that does not imply that you want the relationship to end—just that the terms dictating the manner in which joint finances are handled need to be changed.

Relationship renegotiation happens organically all the time among those working on default societal contracts and is far more common than dissolution. Typically, these renegotiations happen unilaterally (e.g., one partner cheats, so the other decides they are no longer permitted to meet alone with those of the opposite gender, imposing this as a new rule in the relationship's implied contract) and may ultimately undermine the relationship's structural integrity.

A sustainable renegotiation should incorporate ideas and consent from all involved parties, and, if truly intended to make the relationship attractive on an ongoing basis to all parties, it will likely entail some concessions to the violating party. For example, it may simply not be feasible for one partner to be monogamous; hence, a renegotiation in response to a violation may involve opening up the relationship, which in most cases is a *huge* concession for a violated party to make, but one that may be feasible so long as the violated party is also granted rules that make them comfortable with the new arrangement, such as veto power over certain partner choices, routine STD testing, etc.

Partnership Dissolution

In dire cases, the most appropriate response to the violation of some marriage clauses is ultimately dissolution, though it is possible for dissolution to be entirely absent from marriage contracts. An absence of dissolution clauses in your contract does not mean you will never leave your partner; it merely indicates that you will not be expected to leave your partner over something specific. If a relationship becomes differentially undesirable to any partner when contrasted to other relationships they might secure, that partner will likely leave even if there is no dissolution clause.

If you would like to explore the concept of so-called "dead bedrooms" (long-term relationships without sex), we encourage you to flip to: Sex in a Long-Term Relationship in the appendix on page 464.

COGNITIVE INTEGRATION IN MARRIAGE AND LONG-TERM RELATIONSHIPS

One of the greatest benefits of marriage is that it allows partners to act as a single unit and offload parts of their cognitive load and basic life maintenance to each other. The extent to which partners leverage this feature in their relationships varies widely, with some living almost entirely bifurcated lives (separate homes, friends, bills, problems, etc.) and others nearly melding into a single hive-minded person (working side by side, living together, solving nearly all problems jointly, etc.).

While many choose to minimize cognitive integration with their partners, we would go so far as to argue that cognitive integration represents the core value of marriage in modern Western society, as almost everything else a person gets from a relationship—be that sex, love, or childcare—can be achieved through hiring someone or dating, while cognitive integration is only accessible through a long-term relationship with a person.

To be clear, one can cognitively outsource various elements of one's life to someone who is just on their payroll, and many do exactly that, but doing so is risky. This is a bit like having someone making major strategic decisions at a company who will only work for salary and not equity. An employee who is paid in equity is incentivized to act in the best interest of the company and is less likely to make decisions that are purely selfishly motivated and/or find ways to exploit the company for personal gain. Serious, long-term relationships essentially entail humans making an equity swap with their lives. This is why divorces can be so messy; you, the CEO of your life, must essentially fight for as much of your life's value as you can take back, with a fellow executive who has a major stake in the business.

There are three extremes of cognitive integration. Every relationship exists within these extremes.

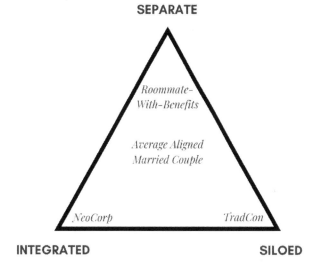

Cognitive Separation

Cognitively separated partners are essentially roommates who have sex, maybe kids or pets, and perhaps (though probably not) some shared income.

Cognitive separation is optimal in cases in which:
1. Partners have no reason to trust each other
2. Each individual prioritizes personal freedom and independence over a relationship
3. At least one partner has a strong ideological belief that prevents them from subverting their sense of self to become part of a unit

Cognitive separation is, ironically, also optimal for relationships in which at least one party's objective function (driving life purpose) revolves around maximizing personal happiness, power, or social status—even though this approach generates the least happiness, power, and success. In cases in which a partner is ideologically motivated to do whatever is ultimately going to give them the most personal happiness, power, or success, the other partner puts themselves in danger by outsourcing some or all of their cognitive load to this self-interested party. (You see this in almost all domains in life—someone striving for personal happiness or fulfillment will always feel less of it and have a harder time achieving it than someone who cares about other things more—see The Pragmatists Guide to Life for more info on this.)

Cognitive separation features two core benefits:
- It is easy to terminate a relationship in which there is no cognitive integration

- It is more difficult for cognitively separated partners to hurt each other

Cognitive separation yields a higher likelihood of relationship termination. This is not just a matter of low exit barriers; nothing about the relationship encourages the partners to grow in parallel, hence within a few decades, partners often become very different people and grow apart. Fortunately, it is easy to bounce back from a cognitively separated relationship, as all parties have been managing their own lives for the most part. This benefit is non-trivial in an age in which relationship separation can be very painful and damaging from a legal, logistical, and statutory perspective.

Cognitive Siloing

If cognitively separate relationships are akin to hunter-gatherer societies, in which each person more or less knows how to survive on their own, cognitively siloed relationships more closely resemble post-industrial societies, in which each person contributes specialized labor and cannot complete every survival-related task themselves.

Consider the idealized 1950s marriage in which the husband processes all family thought and strategies related to work, investing, big ideas, and world affairs, while the wife processes the family's thoughts and strategies related to meals, child-rearing, home keeping, and morality.

Whether leveraging this approach in a TradCon-style relationship or some other fashion, the dynamic remains the same: Certain domains of one partner's life are completely offloaded to another partner. By offloading these large chunks of their lives and minimizing overlap, partners can increase output and skill in the domains in which they specialize and excel, thereby increasing the overall output of the relationship unit.[5]

We do not recommend cognitive siloing among couples in which any partner prioritizes their own happiness or success over the relationship's or family's combined goals, values, and objectives. Whereas a cognitively siloed relationship can certainly form among self-interested parties, such setups typically end in disaster for at least one partner with time. This is because when a person silos a part of their life—whether it be their finances, their income, or their children—and give it completely over to another individual, they give that person enormous power to work against their best interest without them noticing.

The effectiveness of this relationship model is that it offers the efficiency gains created by the domain

---

[5] Reminder: TradCon stands for a "traditional conservative" and is a style of relationship that apes the model common in a few Western countries from the short period between the 1900s to 1970s, during which households were made up of a tiny nuclear family, consisting of a single breadwinner and a single individual who raised children and kept the home. We do not use the full term "traditional conservative" as these relationships are neither traditional nor conservative, but rather a radical and failed social experiment enabled by a period of extreme affluence. This is not to say there are no benefits to the model as it has been reimagined by the 21st century TradCon movement, though it certainly has its flaws.

specialization of each party without the dangers of complete cognitive integration. For example, if only one party is responsible for family finances, home repair, or gardening, they can theoretically focus more time building expertise in that task than if it was split between both parties. However, we must specify this is theoretical, as in the few instances in which this has been studied, the data is not as clear as one might imagine.

Cognitive siloing is commonly used to enable relationships in which one partner focuses on housekeeping and child rearing-related tasks while the other focuses on career-related tasks. The science is unclear whether this style of child-rearing has any benefit to children, and a lot of the data seems to indicate it might be actively harmful to children. For roughly every four studies touting the benefits of being raised in a household with a stay-at-home parent, there are five indicating that children who grow up in households with a stay-at-home parent have higher rates of discipline problems, lower mental health scores, and get lower grades on average (these effects are most pronounced in female children).

While these studies seem to be pretty well controlled for things like income and parent education, we suspect this still might be a correlation issue with helicopter parents, narcissists, and mentally unstable parents being more likely to be a stay at home just because they can't hold a job. It is impossible to control for such factors, so they must bias the data a bit. We, therefore, assume the evidence for and against stay-at-home parenting is more likely to be evenly balanced. No particular approach can be assumed to be superior at this point.

If we take this even balance at face value, it indicates strongly that children are strictly better off when raised in households in which both parents work. This is because the studies that show small benefits to having a stay-at-home parent do not temper these benefits with the benefit of the extra income (children do better in marginally wealthier households). This can be a painful concept to absorb, especially for those who sacrificed careers for what they thought was the best interest of their children. If it makes you feel any better, none of the studies showed a large effect either way, so if you are or were a stay-at-home parent and you didn't have much-earning potential, you likely did not hurt your children *that much* by foregoing a career and at least your children were/are statistically much better off than they would be if they had grown up in a single-parent household. Given that the research on this topic seems to swing both ways at pretty even intervals, we also would not be surprised to see it swing back in the other direction in the near future.

At any rate, the potential pitfalls of child-rearing-oriented cognitive siloing can be avoided by ensuring each member is actively contributing toward the relationship's wealth, influence, and/or power. Divisions, for example, may be made along corporate lines, with partners taking CEO vs. CFO vs. COO positions. Or each partner in a relationship may specialize and rise within a different professional field to protect the relationship from downside risk in recessions.

Both a risk and a benefit of cognitive siloing is that it makes exchanging one partner for another specialist in the same cognitive category fairly easy. For example, it would be easy for a partner to swap out one home-keeping, child-rearing partner for another—or even just hire a nanny and maid.

Those whose specialized value has a time limit are in extremely tenuous positions in such relationships. A child-rearing-specialized female who leveraged physical attractiveness to secure a high-value partner will have little value to her partner and the open market after reaching a certain age. This fact will destabilize her relationship over time. To avoid such dangers, ensure any specialization a partner develops will *maintain* or *increase* its value with time. **A good example of this might involve one partner focusing on building wealth and the other focusing on building influence (through something like politics)—such a relationship would not put either party in a vulnerable position.**

Each partner in a cognitively siloed relationship should regularly audit the value their domain brings to the relationship and take measures to ensure that value does not diminish. Never believe you "lucked out" because your partner handles everything for you. Committing to a partner who handles almost everything for you, from income to chores, puts you in an incredibly vulnerable position. Should that person perish or leave you, you will have next to no value on the open market and be unaccustomed to fending for yourself.

Given the low amount of actual interaction needed for this model to function, it is very easy for cognitively siloed partners to grow apart over time and cease improving themselves. **Because their partners may not fully** understand all the work, stress, and effort that goes into their specialized work and contribution to the relationship, cognitively siloed partners may also come to feel lonely, unappreciated, and unsupported. Cognitively siloed partners must therefore put a uniquely high effort into communicating about their work and achievements, plus supporting the efforts and accomplishments of their partners.

Cognitive Integration

Whereas cognitive siloing usually involves partners taking on different *domains* in their lives (e.g., "I'll work and increase our wealth, you'll build our influence through a political and media career."), cognitive integration entails partners dividing responsibility for different *stages* in the decision-making processes related to some or all domains of their lives (e.g., "I will come up with all proposed solutions, you will vet them, I will make a final call, and then you will execute on our decision."). In other words, cognitively siloed partners divide responsibility by domain, whereas cognitively integrated partners divide responsibility by stage in the decision making and action-taking process.

When people read our books, they often think some chapters are primarily written by Simone and others by Malcolm. This reveals an assumption that we write the books using a cognitively siloed methodology when in reality we write using a cognitively integrated methodology. We talk about what we are going to write together until we have a rough idea of what it will look like, after which Malcolm writes a rough first draft that

Simone turns into something readable, and Malcolm ultimately polishes. This is an example of cognitively integrated writing strategy in that the responsibilities are divided by the stage of the decision-making process rather than the domain.

A cognitively integrated couple may, for example, divide all decisions by complexity (from nuanced detail to big picture decisions), then allow each partner to specialize in one type of decision making. Were Partner A to be tasked with making big picture decisions, they may focus on constantly consuming news media, information, and studies, digesting everything, and ultimately communicating a condensed summary to Partner B. Partner B might then be tasked with using this information to make detail-oriented decisions—information they wouldn't have been able to collect themselves as their noses are buried in the nuances of the detail-oriented decisions affecting their joint lives. Partner B is permitted by the relationship's arrangement to genuinely focus on every problem without removing their nose from the details through the understanding that partner A has their head up and is alert to larger trends that could be impacting their up-close analysis.

If the actions of partners in a relationship were to be illustrated as a tree, and the color of the tree's branches indicated the authority of each member, a cognitively siloed tree's branches would be all one color or another, whereas a cognitively integrated tree would have branches that are vertically striped.

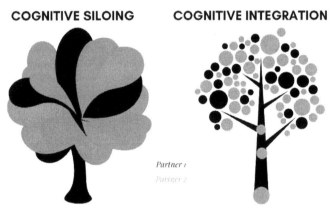

A fully cognitively integrated couple will not have independent thoughts, opinions, or friends (acquired post-relationship start date). Cognitively integrated partners combine their cognitive pathways to the extent that any interaction they have with the world is partially processed by each partner's brains.

For this model to be effective, each partner must be completely comfortable surrendering individuality and allowing someone else to think on their behalf. Independent thoughts and opinions remain but are as a rule are subordinate to the thoughts and opinions of the collective. While most initially recoil from this concept, 64% of the men and 41% of the women we polled agreed that their ideal marriage would be one in which their lives are as integrated with those of their partners as possible.

We theorize that cognitively integrated relationships are poorly represented in public because:
1. They only work for partners with unique objective functions and lifestyles, typically allowing the partners to work together in some capacity.
2. The social absolutism of individual empowerment in the 70s and 80s created a hostile environment for a relationship style that does not value the individual.
3. It looks like enmeshment to relationship psychologists—which means they would counsel against it. While superficially similar to enmeshment, cognitively integrated relationships and enmeshed relationships have about as much in common as poly relationships and relationships in which someone enjoys many sexual partners by cheating on a spouse.

Enmeshment is when the emotional state of the group is imposed on the individual and is most common in cognitively siloed relationships. Enmeshment is characterized by emotional manipulation through guilt, shaming, and a lack of respect for an individual's personal boundaries. Think of the cliché societal image we have of the overly dramatic mother asking her daughter how she could so wantonly wound the mother by not yet being married and pregnant. This is enmeshment.

Enmeshment is <u>mandatory emotional integration</u>

Cognitive integration is <u>voluntary intellectual integration</u>

An easy rule of thumb for distinguishing between the two involves checking how partners regard emotions. Enmeshed partners will place importance on emotions and emotional displays, while cognitively integrated partners will often have the utmost contempt for decisions made under the influence of emotional states and treat emotional displays as the height of character weakness. Cognitively integrated couples rarely attempt to suppress emotional states, but accept that emotions are just an accident of our evolution (or in the case of those religiously inclined, a tool of the devil), something to be experienced, accepted, and calmly communicated, but not permitted to become the driving force behind an action or a decision.

Consider a case in which a woman gets slighted by a coworker.
- **Enmeshed relationship:** The woman guilts her partner for not being as mad about it as she is and spends a half-hour talking about how angry it made her while talking about what a loser the woman who made her angry is and insisting her partner hold the same emotionally charged opinion.
- **Cognitively integrated relationship with a secular objective function:** The woman would note the anger she felt and, understanding that it may cloud her judgment in future dealings with the coworker, sources her partner's perspective to help her maintain objectivity in those situations in a manner that serves the relationship's best interest.

- **Cognitively integrated couple with a religious objective function:** The woman would note the anger and ask her partner to help her focus on how God would want her to respond in such situations so as not to indulge in hatred and anger.

While we are referring heavily to enmeshment, we don't believe enmeshment is a real "thing" or at least not as it is characterized by relationship psychologists. Instead, what we believe psychologists are observing is an emotional manipulation tactic that is bolstered by creating an expectation of emotional alignment. This expectation of emotional alignment is holistically secondary to the emotional manipulation and represents a power-wielding tactic commonly deployed by those in a submissive or subordinate position in a relationship. That is why this tactic is used so frequently by narcissistic-yet-traditional women; they want to *exert* control, but don't want to *take* control through an act of dominance due to their traditional views on gender roles, so they do so instead through emotional manipulation, which requires some expectation of emotional mirroring in their target (though this can go two ways—something common in mother-daughter relationships).

We ourselves (Simone and Malcolm) have a mostly cognitively integrated relationship and aside from undergoing the hassle of setting it up (a process that took about two years), we have experienced no discomfort from the dynamic—aside from accidentally signing off emails with the wrong name from time to time.

This is not to say we don't experience negative interpersonal interactions with each other: Once every couple of months, one of us will fail to live up to the expectations we have set for ourselves as a unit. When this happens, we count on our partner to call attention to the failure so we can take a moment to collectively develop a strategy ensuring we never fail in the same way twice. That said, a partner pointing out an unacceptable failure feels less like an outside attack and more like the voice in your head that chastises you for doing something you knew was stupid.

When someone is in a runaway state of anxiety, fear, or grief, it can overwhelm their cognitive load and prevent them from the mental work required to shake it. When half of someone (their partner) can think clearly, it is much easier to implement a strategy to extricate unwanted emotional states before they fester. In a similar vein, it is very easy to suppress a desire to have "fun" or indulge in self-image-reinforcing activities when a person knows their other half is hard at work.

Of all the couples we know who operate on this model, we cannot think of one that has split up or is not extremely successful in a classical sense—though this is likely not because this model is superior but because a couple must be very well matched and financially secure to even attempt it (everyone we know who operates under this model owns a company with their partner, and we have trouble thinking how it would work if they did not—this also might be why we know more people operating under this model than an average person might, as it is disproportionately represented in married CEOs and married CEOs often know each other).

It is not surprising that cognitively integrated couples tend to be CEOs of the same company, as this was the default style of relationship within the "corporate family" model—in which the partners both raise children together and run a company together from their home—which predates the TradCon model and has dominated the past couple thousand years of Western history. What killed the corporate family model was the rise of the male wage job in an office, which started in the early 1900s and gave birth to the TradCon model. What killed the TradCon was the rise of the female wage job in an office through the 1960s and 1970s. With the rise of the gig economy and work-from-home models of corporate work, we can't help but wonder if we are on the cusp of seeing the rise of a neo-corporate family model (NeoCorp being a term for an iteration of the corporate family model designed for the 21st century).
As a quick aside, it is technically possible to run a NeoCorp or corporate family model in a cognitively siloed fashion as well; it is just less common.

Cognitively integrated relationships require precise circumstances—specifically:
- Closely aligned objective functions that cannot be self-privileging: In other words, both partners have to have the same purpose to their life, and that purpose cannot be to maximize either of their own happiness (or to maximize anything that privileges one individual's cognitive state).
- A hierarchical model of conflict resolution within the marriage contract: Commands must be executed without hesitation. You might think this requires a great deal of trust in a partner, but in reality, all it requires is trust that one has correctly

identified that partner's goal in life, verified that said goal aligns with their own and established that the partner's mental acuity is such that they won't make idiotic decisions.

Though it can squeeze even more productive output from a relationship than the siloed approach, cognitive integration features enormous risks and drawbacks:
- If a person misjudges their partner's motives, unquestionably submitting some of their cognitive processes to the partner could effectively ruin the persons' life.
- Traditional employment is difficult, as truly cognitively integrated couples work collaboratively on everything. Even entrepreneurial lifestyles are difficult, as investors often view romantic involvement of co-founders or co-executives to be too great a risk factor ("What will happen to the company when you get divorced?").
- Productivity plummets when the devices and systems used for cognitive synchronization, such as cloud-based document sharing, CRM systems, and shared calendars, become unavailable.
- The death of one partner can render another significantly less functional than they would be otherwise. Learning how to think totally independently again is a long and difficult process.

THE ECONOMICS OF RELATIONSHIPS

Though not all men and not all women want the same thing, it is still immensely helpful to know what a market, in aggregate, values. If Person A has a piece of gold, he may not give it to Person B—*even if it is of no use to Person A and he does not value gold*—because enough people in society *do* value gold to make Person A careful about how he spends it. The fact that Person A is not *personally* keen on gold does not mean that gold will not have a significant impact on his life. Even those who create the market demand for gold value it due to socialization and not some genetic compulsion to value gold; this fact does not change the value of gold.

We provide this example to make the point that even though not all women and men want the same things, if enough do have similar desires that manifest along gendered lines that will affect the economics of dating where economics is defined as "the study of how society uses its limited resources."

Notes from the Research:
- Women are socialized to want to be desired at a very young age. In one experiment, researchers dressed up the same baby in either a pink or blue gown and let adults interact with it. The adults interacted with the baby they thought was a girl by talking about how pretty it was while when interacting with the boy; they often praised it for its apparent interests (what it was reaching for, etc.). Adult subjects would also take more risks in how

they handled the blue-clad child while treating the pink-clad child as if the pink-clad child were frailer. This suggests that adults' default behavior with children may lead women to become socialized to expect ideal relationships to include protection (physical and emotional) more than men do.
- Statistically speaking, women are more sensitive to partners' status than men, and men are more sensitive to physical appearance (though this likely falls in the "no duh" category).

Economic Trends to Exploit

Understanding different quirks of gender differences in dating and marriage markets can enable you to recognize and exploit trends. We will highlight a few common trends so that you can learn to leverage their currents—and their effects on dating markets—to your advantage.

The Illusion of Hypergamy

Within various "manosphere" communities of the internet, hypergamy is perceived as being an intrinsic female behavior and as a major problem in current dating markets. Though hypergamy is technically defined as the action of marrying someone of a superior class, the going online connotation for hypergamy entails a woman leaving an existing partner the moment a better option arises, the moment they have a chance to trade up.

What is interesting is that this accusation is, surprisingly, factually accurate: When a long- term relationship is terminated, said termination is much more likely to be initiated by the female. More than 70% of divorces are initiated by women. But in this statistic lies the crux of the illusion: Women leave relationships at much higher rates than men both because they are less likely to cheat and more likely to trade up. Why is this?

Historically speaking, women in many societies had severe limitations on their ability to earn income. In such societies, cultural norms developed around men financially supporting their female partners. This cultural artifact still exists as a societal norm even though the earning potential of women has dramatically increased over the past 100 years or so. The cultural artifact can be seen everywhere from men being expected to pay for dates to gift-giving rituals (flowers etc.) and the concept of the stay-at-home wife—even though many will be loath to acknowledge it, recent study showed that only 51% of women even *offer* to pick up the check on a first date.

In nearly every realm, bad actors emerge who either consciously or subconsciously abuse the system to their advantage. In the case of this particular cultural artifact, bad actors manifest as women using men they date to supplement their income and enable them to live a lifestyle above their independent means. When you combine this inevitability with the social stigma that shames men when they financially support a woman who is sleeping with other men, you get a situation in which a portion of the female population expects resources from their relationship partners, but can only easily secure resources from one partner at a time (this is because part of the resource-giving ritual often involves the male publicly exhibiting his relationship with the female, be that on Facebook or at a popular restaurant, and if a male cannot publicly display his relationship with a female, he will be hesitant expend significant resources on her). Should such women feel fairly confident that they can do better than a current partner from a resource perspective, then their most logical move would be to leave the current partner so they can secure resource flow from the more endowed partner.

To put it in other words, "hypergamy" as the manosphere sees it is inevitable in any society in which (1) there is a social expectation that a woman should be able to draw resources from a man and (2) there is a social expectation that a woman can only draw resources from one man at a time (were the second condition not the case, women would just get additional partners, and there would be no reason to trade up). Were this cultural expectation reversed and we lived in a world in which these conditions were applied to men, we feel confident in saying that men would be far more likely to terminate long-term relationships than women—there is nothing "innately female" about being subject to market forces.

Men are not saints in this equation either. In our society, sex is perceived as a core value of a relationship to men—thus when a man feels he can do better than his current partner, he is better off just cheating on this partner with the other woman covertly. This way, he gets sex with other women *and* his current partner: Maximum sex! Society insinuates to men that relationships are for sex and implies to women that relationships are for resources/status. It is much easier for a man to hide that he is getting sex from multiple women than it is for a woman to hide she is securing resources from multiple men. This is why men cheat at much higher rates, with about 20% of men cheating versus around 13% of women.[6]

In other words, the average man (in a society in which men commonly financially support female partners, and monogamy is expected) will be incentivized to cheat with willing sexual partners instead of breaking off a long-term relationship, whereas the average woman (in said society) will be incentivized to end a long-term relationship when a more desirable partner presents themselves—or when she believes she could do better on an open market. This is why men cheat more often than women and why women more frequently end long-term relationships in the pursuit of better mates.

The simplest explanation for this behavioral tendency is that it is solely a product of a tradition around unidirectional resource flow (a society in which men typically give resources to women), not some biological impulse women have to betray men as some groups would argue.

---

[6] With regard to cheating stats: We had trouble pinning down actual numbers, as they differ so much between studies. Some studies showed cheating rates in men being as high as 50%. The one thing that is consistent is that men cheat more often than women in almost every circumstance, except in one study that found married women in their twenties cheating more than men, likely due to their aggregate desirability on the market being astronomically high.

This behavioral tendency yields very interesting externalities. For example, women over 30 or so will notice an alarming dearth of high-quality men in the marriage market, whereas post-30 men will see plenty of eager high-quality 30-something female candidates. This is because high-value *men* with low-value partners stay with those partners, but cheat, while high-value *women* with low-value partners are more likely to leave those low-value partners to look for a better partner. Though this isn't always the case, it happens differentially enough to seriously affect the dating markets as we age.

Here comes the important part: **How can we exploit this dynamic to our personal advantage?**

For one thing, understanding this dynamic grants some predictability around partner cheating and relationship abandonment and enables you to take action to prepare for or possibly prevent these occurrences from happening.

Men are more likely to cheat when they feel that they can do better than their current partner or when the sexual spice from a relationship fades due to the Coolidge effect (see *The Pragmatist's Guide to Sexuality* for more info on this. In summary: Men get more turned on by a new woman more than a woman with whom they have had sex before . . . though this is complicated by some new research showing a similar tendency may affect women even more than men with some caveats).

Statistically speaking, men have very little motivation to leave a partner who is not actively making their lives miserable—so long as they can get away with having sex with other people and believe their partner is faithful to them. Alas, allowing men to sleep around is risky, as there is a chance that a person with whom a man sleeps will attempt to secure non-trivial resources from him. This person may also attempt to hamper resource flow in the man's preexisting relationship or even try to terminate the preexisting relationship entirely in an effort to secure 100% of the potential resource allocation granted from that man (resources need not be monetary; they may also manifest as emotional investment and time).

If letting a guy sleep around introduces exogenous risks, how can you remove almost any risk of a guy leaving you? One strategy we have seen involves taking ownership of additional partner selection. This may sound extreme, but it is not that uncommon for women to select additional partners for their husbands and long-term male partners. This seems to be a strategy uniquely effective in enabling some women to maintain high-value male partners. We are not condoning this strategy per se, just noting it as a potential solution that exists and is uncomfortably successful.

Women in long-term relationships primarily cheat when looking for validation. A woman may crave validation when she no longer feels desired by her current partner or when her partner's validation loses its luster because his value has decreased in some way. On average, women terminate long-term relationships when they feel they can secure a significantly better partner, something that is not the case for the average man. This leads to dynamics that feel very unfair when women leverage their partners' value to increase their own value, then leverage their upgraded value to secure an even better partner (whereas a man would just utilize a similar rise in status to cheat). Fortunately, men can largely prevent cheating by constantly improving their status.

Exploiting Differences in Standards

Another useful "mega trend" among average gender dynamics is that men in short-term dating markets settle for much lower-value partners than women.

Even though some groups deny this fact for ideological reasons, the data makes this trend painfully difficult to avoid. On Tinder, 80% of men compete over the bottom 22% of women, while 78% of women compete for the top 20% of men. If you calculate this out as a Gini coefficient (a measure of inequality across a population that is usually applied to economies and societies), the dating market for men is less equal than 95% of economies in the world. To put it another way, a man of average attractiveness will only be "liked" by 0.87% of women (1 in 115).

The marketplaces created by various dating apps are not all as unequal in nature as the marketplace created by Tinder, but still dismal from a male perspective.

On OkCupid, women rate 80% of men as "worse-looking than medium" and men in this 80% category get their messages replied to 30% of the time or less. On the other hand, men rated only about 50% of women as "worse-looking than medium" and were much more generous to women in this category, replying to them 40% of the time.

Females on the dating app Hinge (another dating app) have a Gini coefficient of 0.324, while males have a still much higher Gini coefficient of 0.542. Were we to compare these Gini coefficients to those of actual countries, the dating economy for women on Hinge would rank as the world's 75th least equal economy, about the same as the economies of the UK or Canada, and the economy for men on Hinge would rank as the 8th least equal economy. Countries ranking this low on economic equality are typically embroiled in active civil war—people are starving on the streets, etc. Countries rarely stay this bad for long, so it dates the book to cite the few in that category now, but for some context, the Gini coefficient experienced by men on Hinge is worse than the economic state of the Congo, Rwanda, or Nigeria (these three only go up to around 0.50 whereas men on Hinge are at 0.542).

Essentially, even in better case scenarios, men still live a daily dating life in which a small minority live like sexual super billionaires and the rest live in abject poverty, while women enjoy a sort of sexual middle-class rank in society. This significantly influences the tactics men end up using when dating online.

It is not uncommon to see women beg to not be sent low-effort messages like "Hey," wishing instead for more thoughtful, personalized messages. This is a reasonable request from a woman's perspective because men reply to 50% of messages women send. Alas, the typical man on an online dating site can't just put more effort into each message. One study demonstrated that lengthening a message from fifty words to two thousand five hundred words increases a man's odds of receiving a reply by less than 10%. This marginal boost in odds does not make the time investment logical if, in a similar time period, he can reach out to nineteen additional women with a "hey" equivalent. If time is a limited resource to a man, it is simply not logical for him to waste it drafting well-thought-out messages in initial online dating outreach.

A woman of average attractiveness scolding a man for sending her low-effort messages online asking for sex is a bit like someone who grew up middle class scolding a homeless refugee who is asking them for change. Refusal to take the mental effort to model what the world is like for others will make their behavior seem quite bizarre. By making an effort to understand the daily struggles of others. You will find it easier to understand them. Through that understanding, you can more efficiently exploit others to achieve your goals.

A fascinating caveat to all this is that gay, male-on-male markets exhibit reply rates that more closely resemble women looking for men (with partners being easy to obtain), whereas female-on-female markets resemble markets in which men are looking for women (with partners being difficult to obtain). This implies that the target gender in any particular market dictates how easy or difficult it will be to obtain a partner.

Again: **How can we exploit this dynamic to our personal advantage?**

Because men rarely hear from women and rarely get responses from women, women can gain a massive leg up in online dating markets by taking the lead, reaching out to desirable men, and sending them thoughtful responses. I, Simone, did this when dating online and found it worked splendidly. I never had trouble securing dates and filling my pipeline with promising leads—heck, this is how I landed Malcolm. I would suggest aiming for emailing at least ten new men a day during any period in which you are sourcing a new partner.

Furthermore, men should learn that online dating is a numbers game. Write a clever (but sufficiently generic) initial message template, contact as many female profiles as possible, and do not waste time on leads that appear to be stringing you along. Furthermore, consider sourcing women outside of online dating apps, leveraging markets in which you might enjoy a higher status. While you might not be in the top 20% when it comes to physical attractiveness and therefore suffer on photo-based dating apps, you *may* be in the top 20% of a social club, academic group, church group, or charitable organization.

Timing Considerations

Instinctual Life Stage Behavioral Impulses

That which is appropriate for you, relationship-wise, may depend heavily on your particular stage in life.

Anyone who has owned a dog or watched a nature documentary about lion cubs is familiar with something called "play behavior," which only lasts for a certain period of time. Just as adult dogs and lions lose their drive toward play behavior and find themselves motivated to do other things, humans experience instinctual changes, feeling the drive to exhibit different behaviors during different life stages.

Shifts in our instinctual behavioral impulses can cause surprise and consternation when an individual repeatedly attempts to derive happiness from an old instinctual impulse. If a person goes long enough without exploring new categories of behavior while older behaviors cease to generate happiness, they may even end up feeling as though nothing gives them happiness anymore (though clinical depression can also cause this feeling).

Changes in behaviors that generate happiness matter a great deal when people make relationship decisions. Someone may assume they never want children because children annoyed them as a teen only to find that later in life, interactions with children cause more happiness than anything else. Plans this person may have made for their lives in adolescence would not anticipate this shift and, if executed, could cause a huge drop in life satisfaction over the long run.

To our knowledge, there is no coherent model that illustrates how our sources of happiness change as we age, so we will have to build one ourselves, gathering data points from personal experience and potentially relevant studies.

In general, we assume that the systems influencing what makes us happy are not that different from the systems that cause us to feel sexually aroused. We have a number of "stimuli" detectors in our brains that generate an emotional reward when they recognize something that fits into a set of pre-defined parameters. These detectors cycle throughout a normal person's life, seem to be inborn and not learned, and have an average way that they function, which varies among individuals.

Just as turn-ons vary between people, stimuli that create happiness vary from one person to the next. For example, while play behavior typically ceases to generate happiness around mid-adolescence, in some individuals, play behavior continues to be a source of great joy well into old age. As with the arousal systems, we have reason to believe that happiness-generating systems were evolutionarily selected by somehow increasing the survival rate of the offspring of those who had them, as they appear inborn and across cultures.

Childhood

Think back to one of your favorite childhood activities that has since lost its appeal. Doing so should give you a clear idea of what it feels like to have an impulse to do something at one stage of your life that subsequently disappears with age.

As discussed, play behavior, which typically manifests as interaction with peers in a physically taxing manner that involves a high degree of touching and boundary testing, is critical during childhood. This play behavior is designed to help children develop social connections and understand the world around them. However, if you as an adult, were to attempt rolling around on the grass, wrestling your best friend, you would likely be able to derive little positive emotion from it—or at least would get bored after only a minute or two.

Childhood is a unique age in that humans appear to be able to derive a high level of emotional output from totally imagined scenarios, leading to most childhood games to incorporate a high degree of imagination. A child can gain almost as much happiness from imagining orbiting earth in a space station as they could actually doing so. Children are even able to gain social stimulation from entirely imaginary friends who amount to nothing more than cognitive models. Perhaps children are afforded this imaginary luxury because it does not distract them from other important tasks that adolescents and adults cannot afford to ignore.

Finally, children derive happiness from pleasing authority figures at this age and look to them for cues about what should make them happy (consider kids pretending to be parents, drive cars, talk on cell phones, etc.). Mimicking authority figures' interests and activities may help children develop knowledge in domains that will be relevant to them in adulthood.

Adolescence

Behaviors that cause happiness in adolescence are problematic in that we often internalize them as core elements of our identities. We begin to believe these inclinations are part of who we are because we feel them strongly at the same time we develop a sense of identity and place in the world, then become confused when we no longer derive happiness from them despite having made life decisions around them (like people becoming video game designers because, as teens, they loved playing video games).

At both this age and in childhood, social acceptance plays a more prominent role in happiness than it does in adulthood. Adults often complain about how small their friend groups become; however, the reality may be that people simply put less time into these sorts of interpersonal relationships as adults because they derive less happiness from them.

In general, studies have shown adolescents are extremely sensitive to social cues and have trouble ignoring them. One study showed that when performing an emotion-themed version of a Stroop test (e.g., saying "sad" when looking at a picture of a happy person), adolescents performed dramatically worse than adults. You will never care as much about what other people think of you as you do at this age.

In contrast to childhood, adolescents do not derive happiness from pleasing authority figures, and complying with authority figures may even cause a fairly strong aversion reaction. We would assume this evolved to help push humans away from their parents once they reach breeding age, both so their parents could give them more siblings and to increase genetic diversity by encouraging movement to other tribes.

Studies have repeatedly shown that at this age in life, novelty creates a stronger positive feeling than it does during other stages. This both creates an urge to explore and seek out novel ideas (learning forbidden knowledge by exploring something relatively obscure, like communism or Wicca, or finding a band no one has heard of). It is often during this stage of life, in which novelty provides excessive positive emotional stimulation, that people decide they want to travel the world—only to find the experience to be somewhat hollow in their more affluent years when they can actually afford to do so.

Some hypothesize that this drive for novelty, combined with the drive for social acceptance, creates the "meta drive" for deviance in adolescents—meaning that youth don't actively have an urge to seek deviant behavior. These feelings may also explain why adolescents often begin to identify as "rebellious" and become confused as to why rebellion feels less fulfilling with age.

Promotion motivation also is statistically much stronger at this stage of life. This means that you get more happiness from pursuing huge, idealistic long-term goals. At this time of your life, you are focused on your hopes for how you can create a better future for yourself and the world, and this drives youths to more idealistic endeavors and ideas.

As for a negative emotion during this stage: People often find children and babies quite annoying as teens. This is likely evolved to prevent them from procreating too early and having to divide their resources at an age during which they are better served by building a stable platform within the tribe to maximize their position within its hierarchy. Position in a tribal hierarchy historically mattered more to one's total number of surprising offspring than getting an early start with kids (this is likely also contributes to people's high sensitivity to social stimuli at this age).

Finally, analysis of twelve million personal blogs for how youths interpret happiness found at this stage exciting things trigger more happiness (this may just be an artifact of novelty leading to more positive emotions at this stage). In general, the anticipation of future goods also caused more happiness in this group with a focus on things like "like finding love, getting ahead at work, or moving to a new town," though, again, this is likely just a combination of novelty-seeking behavior and promotional motivation.

Midlife

Midlife changes in desire are critical as they likely are often the ones that happen after we secure a long-term partner. Often our long-term partners are chosen to optimize our adolescent desires and not those of the longest stage: Midlife.

Research has shown that as adolescents and young adults transition into midlife, they begin to derive more fulfillment and happiness from prevention than from promotion—meaning that goals designed to minimize losses and maintain that which has already been secured become more satisfying and motivating than goals revolving around big wins and changes.

This shift likely ties strongly to the trope of individuals losing their idealism and becoming more conservative as they age. An increased desire to protect what one already has may also explain why humans often move into hobbies focused on "prepperism" or sustainability in midlife, such as gardening and wood working. Marrying someone as an adolescent out of shared, passionate idealism could therefore be a suboptimal life choice

While we haven't seen studies promoting this idea, it seems as though humans may also experience a stronger desire to acquire physical assets and build things at this age. The first half of this is realized through things like land acquisition while the second is realized through fixing up old cars or making Martha Stewart-inspired displays.

In the study that looked at a large number of blogs, they found people at this stage of life got more happiness from things that made people feel "peaceful, relaxed, calm, or relieved," though this may just be another manifestation of prevention motivation.

Long walks and scenery seem to make people happier at this life stage. While the positive stimulus that comes from exploration of totally new things typically decreases at this stage, "surveyance" activities seem to increase (starring at a pretty view, for example). Our assumption is that this behavior might be tied to scouting good camp locations and protecting them by looking for areas close to sources of water like streams or the ocean and where you could see someone coming from a long distance away (a view). But obviously, this is a "just so story" and holds no weight.

Finally, and most importantly for this book, at this age, you begin to develop a strong affinity for both bearing and interacting with children. This often shocks people because most adolescents have an active aversion to children. This desire happens both in males and females and is not tied to adherence to societal gender roles (making it unlikely that this occurs "because society tells us to want children" and more likely that it is a biological urge to procreate and nurture—because your ancestors who had this urge kick in had more surviving offspring than their peers). That said, there is a gender difference in this emotion—it starts younger for women and goes down in severity over time (especially after having some children), while in men it occurs at lower rates but increases over time.

The desire to have a baby is not the only major children-related change that takes place during midlife. While most of the happiness we get from exploring new things decreases with age, the happiness we derive from exploring new things through others increases dramatically with age. So as an adult, while you may not be able to gain as much happiness as you used to from activity X, you can regain that happiness by experiencing activity X *with a child*. The same can be said for resource acquisition: When younger, you gain more happiness through dreams of acquiring great things for yourself, whereas that emotional stimulus seems to shift onto children with age.

Old Age

Sadly, most research we have found on this subject doesn't break out old age from midlife, and we haven't experienced old age ourselves yet, so we cannot easily say how things change.

Note From Personal Musings:
- *Based on anecdotal observations, it appears that people can get "stuck" in a life stage if basic needs during that stage go unfulfilled. For example, if a young man barley ever gets laid during late adolescence, he may build an internal model for himself that receives significant emotional rewards from carnal pursuits long after his brain has stopped naturally rewarding him for putting such time and effort into securing sex. While we most commonly see this with people who were severely deprived of sex in youth, we also see this with those who put off "exploring the world" and spend huge portions of their disposable income traveling as adults.*
To be clear: We don't think people are actually getting "stuck" in a stage of development when this happens, but rather that years of consternation and focus on a specific unmet objective cause strong cognitive dissonance when the objective is attainable during later life stages. Even though such people are no longer inherently driven to these previously unmet-objectives later in life, they convince themselves they are—only to throw immense resources into pursuits that don't ultimately satisfy them.

The Profound Effects of Fertility and Childbirth

No talk of relationship timing would be complete without a discussion of fertility, especially because conventional wisdom does not correlate with present scientific research.

A recent *New York Times* article bemoaned the fact that, while college students overwhelmingly wanted children, they did not understand their time window for having them: "only 38 percent of men and 45 percent of women stated correctly that a woman's fertility declines between 35 and 39 years of age, and only 18 percent of men and 17 percent of women knew that men's fertility declines between 45 and 49." This is funny, as the article bemoaning youth who don't know about how fertility fluctuates with age gets the research wrong. Specifically, a recent shift in research findings suggests the claim that female fertility declines dramatically at 35 is a misnomer perpetuated by bad science that relied on French peasant birth records from the 1700s and thus was not conducted within the context of people who grew up with modern medicine. Does this mean women are forever fertile? Hardly. But it does suggest common perceptions need adjustment.

It appears that what the previous predominant view on fertility got wrong was its perception of a sudden cliff in fertility that appears around a woman's mid-thirties. Instead:
- Female fertility experiences a slow decline
- Male age plays a huge role in fertility, with 40% of fertility problems being male-related
- The age disparity between partners plays a role (a large age gap between partners leads to larger fertility problems—a guy who thinks he can wait until 50 to start having kids and will be fine if his wife is young is rolling dice loaded by the house)
- While rates of birth defects rise dramatically from the ages of 30 to 40, this dramatic rise is from

roughly 0.025% to 1.5% odds—so still low even when they are on the higher end (while keeping in mind that a 1.5% chance of permanently affecting your child's life in a negative way is nothing to scoff at).
- 82% of women aged between 35 and 39 fall pregnant within a year of trying
- If a 35 year-old-woman wants two kids and tries, she will probably get them.

With all that said, none of that really matters for three reasons:
1) If having kids that are biologically yours is super important to you, you should build your life plan, assuming you will become infertile a bit before 40. If the general population experiences moderate drops in fertility with age, *some* members of the population still do experience plummeting fertility. You might be one of those people. It seems unwise to run that risk if you have a choice.
2) Some couples have trouble conceiving, for a wide variety of reasons at *any* age. Fertility treatments tend to be more successful on younger patients, so to make the most of these expensive and uncomfortable procedures, it would be best to undergo them as early as possible, when yields are likely to be higher.
3) Even if your personal fertility remains sky high through your thirties and even your forties, society on average has the perception that fertility plummets around age 35, meaning you will have to combat that stigma on dating and long-term relationship markets. In other words, men who want kids will generally assume a woman in her

thirties is too old to have them and thus will not marry her—her actual fertility is irrelevant to her ability to secure a partner, and only her perceived fertility matters.

Should you want to avoid these risks but also advance your career a bit more before having children, you can always do what we did: Bank a large number of healthy embryos in your twenties or early thirties so that you do not have to worry about doing so later. Though keep in mind, this costs a lot (we spent over a $100K banking 27 healthy embryos).

Finally, keep in mind how having children affects earning potential. Parent status increases the hireability of men. In one study conducted on the subject, dads who indicated they were part of a PTA on their resumes were called back for interviews at a much higher rate. Conversely, women in this experiment were asked back for a second interview at less than half the rate of those who did not mention the PTA. In general, men earn an average of 6% more for every child they have (and live with), whereas women earn 4% less. This suggests that for a married couple earning an equal salary, every child yields an average net bonus of 1% in higher income. There have also been studies showing a productivity increase in the office after having children (in men at least)—a productivity bump that is highest for men with two or more children (with fathers becoming 52% more productive on average after the birth of twins).

This is all very strange to us, as within our companies (which are roughly 90% female), we have noticed that mothers perform exceptionally well. Studies also show mothers are more ambitious than women without children, with mothers being 15% more likely to want to become a top executive.

Essentially, having kids is a strict net benefit to a family's career (unless the woman is earning more than the man in a relationship) and is a huge earnings boost for gay male couples. As a downside, or potentially an upside, having a child will also make partners more critical of their friendships, with 69% of women and 67% of men feeling satisfied with their friendships before having kids and only 54% and 57% feeling the same way afterward.

For those monstrous ghouls who value happiness over money, the jury is still out on the subject of children. Studies looking at how children affect happiness yield a broad range of conclusions. Some suggest children increase happiness and life satisfaction while others argue the opposite. We read no clear consensus. The one thing on which these studies do seem aligned is that parents with very young children are less happy.

Those afraid of dying would be well-served to review the twin studies (studies that contrast identical and fraternal twins separated at birth and raised by different families) exploring how much of a person's consciousness is preserved in their genetic code. Everything from a person's political inclinations to the way they interact with friends is hard-wired into DNA and can be inherited by biological children. Better yet, parents get to choose the person with whom they mix their DNA to create their next iterations. If all that isn't enticing enough, you as a parent can give the next iterations of yourself any type of childhood you want them to have. As for all those biases and crusty old ideas stuck to the walls of your mind like scum on the side of a pot—well, this next iteration of you will get to choose which of them it accepts. Children are not burdened by their parents' memories—only memories parents choose to share. Did we mention that you get to create as many new iterations of yourself as you want? We will never understand this cryonics and life extension contingent of people trying to live forever through freezing themselves and religiously adhering to wacky diets. It just seems like such a waste when most people are born with all the bits they need to live forever and in a way that is about a billion times better than living forever in your current body.

The Wall & How Dating Dynamics Change at Age 30

Nowhere is the sexual dimorphism in human dating more salient than the dynamic change that happens when those playing within the sexual, dating, and relationship markets hit their thirties. Namely: Male market value steadily increases past age 30, whereas female market value drops. Colloquially, this phenomenon is commonly known as "The Wall" and is well attested to in statistical analysis of both dating website behavior and research data.

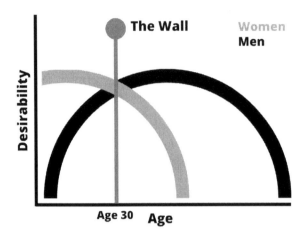

Typically this dynamic is presented within the narrow view of the ticking biological fertility clock, which obscures the larger issue: Women prefer to date men who are their age or slightly older, whereas men prefer to date younger women. Statistically, this means that a 26-year-old woman will have more online pursuers than the average man but, at age 48, men have twice as many online pursuers as the average woman.

To understand how this works, let us look at a hypothetical college campus in the middle of the woods, in which the only available partners are members of the opposite gender and all members follow the rule of women-only dating guys in their grade or older and men only dating girls in their grade or below. A first-year female is a desirable partner to men in their second, third, and fourth years, while a first-year male is only a desirable partner to first-year girls—who simultaneously have a choice of any guy in the school. By the time they are both in their fourth year, the boy is a desirable partner to any girl in the school, whereas the girl is only a desirable partner to other fourth-year boys (who have the choice of any girl).

This may not seem like a big deal, but the effect is enormous. If we define the period between second and third year as equilibrium, then each gender will find it about four times harder to secure a partner in their low year than at equilibrium and about sixteen times harder in their low year than their easier year (they can only target one fourth the population and that quarter of the population has access to four times the potential partners). Imagine if you had to put in sixteen times the amount of effort and time to earn your same salary! We will call this equilibrium "The Wall," and in our adult life, it occurs around the age of 30 for heterosexuals looking for a long-term monogamous relationship.

In the real world, The Wall affects dating dynamics even more severely than the hypothetical college model would predict. Why is this the case? And why does this happen to women around age 30 and not around age 39, the midway point of the average human lifespan? We have different theories on this—maybe you can settle it for us.

Malcolm argues: The answer becomes pretty clear when you look at the data. OkCupid did a study of what age of partner men and women prefer throughout the course of their lives. Men within every age cohort preferred women 20-23 on average, while women preferred men slightly older until they hit 30, then slightly younger from 30 to 40, and at any age past 40, women prefer 40-year-old men. The Wall surfaces at the age of 30 and not 39 because, on average, all age groups of men prefer women between 20-23 and it takes women a few years to realize that it isn't just a string of bad luck for them: It really does become astronomically harder to secure a decent guy after the age of 26 or so. This also means that after the age of 45, the market dynamics of The Wall, and specifically the disadvantage it gives to women, largely disappear as both females and males prefer younger people. Thus "The Wall" should really be thought of more as "The Trough"—but that just doesn't have the same ring to it does it?

Simone argues: The equilibrium point at which woman should really start to feel a crunch is actually around 39, but the age at which women start to really realize that they can't secure the same high quality of partner with the same amount of effort—as well as the age at which women internalize that their fertility is beginning a downward slope—is around age 30-31. Upon realizing this, women begin to panic, especially if they had planned on having kids because they feel they are running out of time. Much like how populations can trigger economic collapses by getting spooked and making a run on banks, women can trigger a Great Dating Depression of viable male partner availability by making a rush on all plausibly good male long-term partners when they get spooked at around the age of 31. (Look up the data on "panic buying" for interesting examples of this phenomenon and how it plays out in different areas, For a recent example of this, consider the toilet paper shortages that broke out during the COVID-19 pandemic.) Alternatively, it could be argued that women are acting rationally. If they see their value dropping on the dating market with no hope recovery, they may start trading against their expected future value instead of their current value.

Another possibility for your consideration: The Wall could just be a result of female libido increasing dramatically in women when they hit age 30. Women between 30 and 40 have more sexual fantasies, more fantasies about men who are not their partner, more casual sex, cheat more often, and more one-night stands than their college-age counterparts. As to why this is the case: The most accepted current theory is that women evolved increasing sex drives to keep their birth rates steady despite declining fertility (the increase in sexual desire maps pretty well to declining fertility). As one would predict from this theory, after menopause female sex drive often decreases precipitously, though surprisingly a woman's sexual satisfaction increases with age despite this lower sexual desire. This complicated picture contrasts with men whose libido peaks in their teen years, then remains fairly constant.

Note from the Research:
- One study that mapped each gender's desirability to the other over time found that after the age of 18, female desirability decreases logarithmically while male desirability increases until the age of 50 with a parabolic increase. Women's logarithmic decline meets men's parabola around the age of 30, at which point the average woman becomes less desirable than the average man. This paper would thus argue it is rational that The Wall starts at 30 and there is no mystery at all.

As a society, we used to warn young girls and boys about this dynamic with concepts like "the old maid," but as that concept was offensive, we swept it under the rug. A lack of proper warning puts many responsible, hard-working women who truly want long-term relationships at a huge disadvantage in the long-term relationship market. The fact that a woman is going to have an easier time securing a higher quality partner when she is younger is daunting—even offensive—because it hurts the feelings of women who did not take advantage of those years or felt they couldn't properly secure a good relationship without sacrificing their budding careers. That said, it is cruel not to warn young girls that they are going to have to put in at least five times the amount of time and effort as a 35-year-old to secure the same quality of partner they could have at 25.

We cannot imagine what it would feel like to pass the wall without understanding the economic forces at play that drives handsome guys with good jobs to cease being so eager to go on public dates. A perfectly reasonable woman experiencing this shift would mistakenly think something is wrong with her, not realizing she is caught up in something much bigger. An entirely level-headed woman would reel in horror at the amazing partners she squandered not knowing how hard such partners would be to come by only half a decade later—or grieve at the realization that she never indulged in the joy of being treasured and pursued by most people she came across when she had the chance.

Worse still, in modern Western society, even the most open-minded of little girls are socialized to look down on people who marry in their twenties. They see such people as less educated and poor because statistically they are. To avoid seeing themselves as uneducated, imprudent, and poor, ambitious young ladies make plans to start looking for a husband at a "respectable age to get married," like 28. Not only do we raise women to *not* be aware of this cliff, but we are enthusiastically hurling them off the edge.

Simultaneously, men deal with a bizarre mirror phenomenon: A Tinder study found that an attractive 34-year-old man has a much easier time attracting women his own age than a 26-year-old man, but that the 34-year-old will attract women in the 26-year-old age bracket at the same rate as the 26-year-old. In other words, not only can the 34-year-old male attract 34-year-old women easier than a 26-year-old man can attract 26-year-old women, but he can also attract 26-year-old women with the same ease of a 26-year-old man. That said, this effect is not felt by most men that strongly, as most men are not in the "attractive man" category.

We find it hilarious that many pick-up artist gurus are generically attractive men that magically develop their systems for easily getting laid by lots of women at around the age of 30. What genius role models these men are. Remind us to share our ingenious system for getting free sand at the beach.

Fortunately, an awareness of "the wall" phenomenon can be leveraged to develop a strategy that maximizes the quality of long-term relationship partners available. If a heterosexual woman is looking for a TradCon or NeoCorp relationship and wants to make optimal use of her changing market value, she is best off utilizing the period before she is 19 for experimentation and casual dating, as by age 20, the training wheels should be off and she should be focused on finding her long-term relationship partner with the expectation of securing one before or around age 27. Given her astronomical value on the market between ages 20-23, she should not waste even a few days of those years off the market unless there is a real possibility of a long-term relationship with the target in question.

This timeline is onerous in that it requires major life decisions to be made during periods many people are still emotionally developing and thus even if it does allow one to better take advantage of their changing value on the market it is not necessarily the best strategy for all women looking for a TradCon or NeoCorp—keep in mind marriages before 18 have a 60% chance of divorce, this contrasts with an average 30% divorce rate for first-time marriages of those 23 and over and a 5% divorce rate of those 35 and over. **Life doesn't always have a "correct" answer. Sometimes life presents us with a few solutions, each with a unique drawback.**

Another factor any heterosexual woman looking for a TradCon or NeoCorp relationship should consider is that if she secures a marriage partner during her prime age range, she will, on average, have a much worse aggregate desirability upon divorcing and will be targeting a very different pool of men. In other words, a woman who secures her first husband in her early twenties will, on average, have a harder time securing a second husband of equivalent quality—this is doubly true if she had kids during her first marriage. This is of course assuming that the divorce happens before the age of 50 (as we have mentioned, the market equalizes again in later life) and assuming she fails to increase her market value in some other way during the interim (by securing a better job, for example, or getting a prestigious college degree), but even with improved market value, securing a high-value second partner will be hard.

While one can always find exceptional deviations from the norm, this a clear trend in aggregate—one of those shitty realities we like to hide from young women. Hiding these realities can ultimately cause immense harm through the poor decisions this ignorance causes, like: "Let's just try out this marriage thing; I can always get divorced and give it another shot if it doesn't work out." While not realizing that the period of her life she is expending on the "trial" will be her most advantaged time on the marriage market. Worse, that the guy in this little experiment loses nothing by expending the ages between 25 and 35 with a "trial wife" because when he hits the market again, he will statically be able to secure someone even better with less effort.

There is a reason why men are more than twice as likely as women to remarry after a divorce. While some would argue the reason is that women realize marriage is a raw deal after going through one, we imagine this is more of a "sour grapes" scenario than a lucid analysis of the benefits of marriage for a woman whose personality is compatible with one.

Should the idea of an older partner not be disagreeable, targeting older groups while at an age range of peak desirability (age 20-23) provides women with access to a spectacular market arbitrage opportunity as few other young ladies are interested in pursuing such a strategy. Nevertheless, those looking for a lifelong marriage and children should disregard the older-men-gold-digger strategy: Statistically speaking, the wider the age gap in a relationship, the shorter the relationship and the higher the probability of genetic abnormalities in offspring it produces.

What can men learn from this?

Men looking for TradCon or NeoCorp relationships are best off casually dating until around age 25, after which the search for a more permanent partner should begin. We suggest age 25 as a starting point instead of 30, seeing as the hunt to find a wife may take around eight years of sustained effort, and while it is not talked about as much as it should be, men experience declines in fertility after age 30. In general, if the man is looking for a TradCon relationship, with a wife who stays at home, he can afford to start on the older end of the spectrum, while if he is looking for a NeoCorp, with a wife who works alongside him, he may even want to start looking as early as around 22, as he will be optimizing for a partner of a roughly equivalent age, not wanting to take the earnings hit of partnering with someone earlier in their career.

This book's gay readers have our hearty congratulations, as they will not have to contend with The Wall. That said, gay relationships do exhibit higher average age disparity. Among heterosexual couples, a male is on average **2.4** years older than a female (this age difference persists across cultures, but it is exaggerated in more "traditional" cultures like in Egypt, where average age difference stretches to over **5** years). So just how much higher is the average age gap in gay relationships? It is over **9** years among male gay couples and around **8** years among lesbian couples.

Marriage

Let's take a moment to dig into some data about the changing landscape of marriage to see if we might help you extract something of strategic utility.

In the US, marriage is and has been in open retreat. From 2000 onward, married 25-34-year-olds comprised 55% of the population while their never-married peers accounted for a paltry 34%. By 2015, this married group had slipped to 40% of the population, overtaken by their never-married peers who had quickly climbed to 53%.

It is currently predicted that 33% of those in the US who are currently in their twenties will never wed. Historically, only 10% of the population never married.

What is happening here? Perhaps men's' lower wages relative to women have dampened their confidence in dating markets; however, the fact that regions in which men *do* maintain disproportionately higher wages than women do not enjoy higher marriage rates suggests this is not the case. Specifically: Regions affected by the fracking boom, which yields increased wages in predominantly male jobs, did not see the increase in marriage rates we would expect if increased wage parity was a marriage killer.

The declining popularity of marriage also doesn't seem to be due to any lack of desire to marry or a fear of committing to a woman. Surveys show neither of these reported desires has significantly decreased (even though groups like MGTOW—heterosexual men who choose to forego relationships with women—are on the rise, the stats make it clear that their sentiment is not leading to a shift at a society-wide level).

We theorize that two concurrent phenomena are causing this phenomenon: (1) A significant drop in the amount of investment required for a high-value man to secure sex (on average studies show, attractive men don't just expend less energy to secure relationships, but also invest less in relationships once they have them) and (2) increasing female independence and control over fertility (women neither need a male partner to support them nor do they even technically need a male partner, or any partner, to have children).

In countries like the US, in which female college graduates by far outweigh male graduates—and yet women want male partners who match or exceed their own education level—there are just not as many viable pairings as there used to be. These dynamics together have "broken the ecosystem." High value men invest less in relationships because they do not need them to secure sex. High value women invest less in relationships as they depend on men less and outperform men more. Mechanisms for fixing this system are honestly quite fun to explore; we will cover some at the end of the *Pragmatist's Guide to Sexuality*. It is also worth keeping in mind that the system may not need "fixing"—maybe this is just a natural transition period between one system and another better system.

Notes from the Research:
- You have an increased risk of divorce if you marry someone with a large age or wealth difference from you.
- 73% of married men said that within 9 months, their partner had become the center of their lives
- College-educated women with independent sources of income have a very low chance of divorce (less than 20%).
- Over the past 50 years, the number of people living together without being married has increased by 900%. In some countries like Norway, this has become the new cultural norm for a long-term relationship de-throwing the "marriage model" This shift may soon solidify in the US as well: As of this writing, only a quarter of Americans disapprove of unmarried couples living together. Nearly half of Americans disapproved of such behavior in the 80s.
- It is normal to live together for long periods before marriage. Two-thirds of married couples live together for more than two years before marriage. Scientists used to think this increased the risk of divorce, but when you control for age of marriage (younger couples cohabitate more) and look at larger data sizes you don't see cohabitation before marriage having a negative effect.
- Expensive weddings and wedding rings increase the probability of divorce. Engagement rings costing $2,000 to $4,000 are associated with a 1.3

times greater probability of divorce when contrasted to rings costing between $500 and $2,000. This does not imply that couples should forego weddings and rings at all. In fact, larger wedding crowds and honeymoons are associated with a lower chance of divorce. Thus the ideal wedding from a statistical standpoint is an inexpensive one attended by a large number of people, followed by a nice, long honeymoon.

Appendix: *Interested in digging into more data on securing a husband? Flip to Securing a Husband on page 401 in the appendix.*

Geography

An individual's ability to find, vet, and secure sexual and marriage partners varies widely among locations. A robust 55% of relationship-seeking singles claim it is difficult to meet people where they live. Dynamics can be shifted favorably by simply changing locations.

For example, New York is a men's market for dating, being a place where men—and significantly older men—secure much higher-value female partners than they would be able to secure in other markets. On the other hand, Seattle is a woman's market, which changes the strategies that are successful. Seattle, for example, is the only market where longer form message outreach significantly improves reply rates for men on dating sites. This market is so bad for men that there are two men for every woman within some segments.

Extreme cases aside, how will geography affect your dating life? Counterintuitively, those living in cities with more singles generally have a lower probability of forming a relationship. This makes relationship formation rates lower in large cities like Los Angeles, New York City, and Miami, but higher in medium-sized cities like Colorado Springs, El Paso, Fort Worth, and Louisville. The surprising dynamic stems from the default cultural expectations different cities present—when seemingly everyone is in a relationship, the average single person will feel more pressure to form one as well.

Which markets are best for each gender?

Males looking for females should go where there are the most single females per single male:
1. Memphis, TN
2. Jacksonville, FL
3. Fort Worth, TX
4. Charlotte, NC
5. Richmond, VA

Women looking for men would be best served by relocating to markets with the most single males per single female:
1. San Francisco, CA
2. San Jose, CA
3. Seattle, WA
4. Salt Lake City, UT
5. San Diego, CA

It is difficult to provide equivalent recommendations for gay men and women. While men outnumbering women in a city might give a woman a market advantage, the

same cannot be said about a preponderance of other gay men in a city. Also—and this pains us to say this—we could not find any charts of cities that break out gay women and gay men, so all we can provide is the top five cities for LGBTQ individuals in general, population-wise:
1. San Francisco, CA
2. Portland, OR
3. Austin, TX
4. New Orleans, LA
5. Seattle, WA

As tempting as it might be to circumvent the limitations of local geography by entering a long-distance relationship, the average duration of a long-distance relationship is only four and a half months. While we would hardly argue that there are no ways to make a long-distance strategy effective, we think it important to highlight that they require more persistence and creativity. We also suspect long-distance relationships should be divided into two categories: Those that were in person, then split up due to life events, and those that were created and initiated among people who are physically separated. We suspect the second category is far more stable.

The Human Mating Season

Humans seem to have something of a mating season, which is weird because no one ever talks about it. This season lasts from Christmas through Valentine's day and reaches its peak on the Sunday after New Year's day (which in the dating industry is called Dating Sunday). This increase in dating activity can be seen very clearly in data from dating apps; however, seasonal fluctuations in dating behavior are not just a dating app phenomenon. There is actually a seasonal increase in sexual interest and desire over the same period. You will see an increase in Google searches for pornography and prostitution over this period. (We would really love to conduct more research to determine whether this is a cross-cultural phenomenon and whether or not it affects genders differently.)

We are not sure what one can take away from this functionally speaking but thought it was too cool to not include here.

Choosing Not to Have a Partner

Among men and women alike, there has been a growing movement of people who have decided that a relationship is simply not worth the emotional effort, risk, or cost.

Among men, the most predominant of these groups is MGTOW: Men Going Their Own Way—a fairly large online community who argue that relationships as traditionally structured are so systematically unfair to men they are not worth engaging with. While not all MGTOWs have sworn off relationships entirely, opting instead to pursue novel models of relationships, the group and movement in general is helping to reduce the stigma of living forever single as a man.

There is no uniquely monolithic anti-relationship subgroup of women; however, factions do pop up occasionally and we expect to see a movement in this direction again in the near future.

Most research indicates that being in a good relationship is better than being single. Most research also indicates that being single is better than being in a bad relationship. Those who have sworn off sexual/romantic relations entirely have justly observed that, for some individuals, the economics of relationships do not act in their favor, and these people in particular are better off staying single.

Some men simply do not want the risk associated with choosing the wrong partner. The cost of a divorce, alimony, and a mutinous partner taking their children is incredibly high for many men (women have a leg up on all those fronts in divorce courts within most Western countries). Combine this hazard with the high cost of dating and the extreme effort required if a man is handicapped by a low market value, and it is hard to fault someone for concluding they will be far better off alone.

Many women feel as though they have been given a similarly raw deal. After all, many studies indicate that women are less happy if they choose to get married (though the data is all over the place here—it seems like marriage ultimately has a neutral effect on women). It is easy for women to look at these studies in isolation, consider friends who got screwed over through marriage, feel somewhat underwhelmed by the realistic options they have in potential partners, contemplate the sacrifices required to enter and invest in a long-term relationship, and ultimately decide that marriage is just not worth the effort.

We do not suggest that foregoing romantic relations is always the optimal choice for women and men disadvantaged in their respective markets. We only want to clarify that it is not an actively stupid or illogical path. Should you find yourself at a disadvantage in marriage markets, you might consider finding other ways to satisfy needs in your life otherwise satisfied by relationships. Consider just how bad a toxic relationship can be to a person's quality of life. Consider how rare intentional, emotionally mature humans really are—two traits we would argue are prerequisites for any truly successful relationship.

Historically, any self-realization that the odds of securing a quality, trustworthy partner are very low would not be enough to stop someone from trying to secure a partner—at least if one wanted sex and/or children. Now, thankfully, we have better options. We can, if we want, get all the benefits of a relationship from other things. Want sex? Pay for a hyper-realistic sex doll, pornographic virtual reality rigs, or prostitutes (pending availability and legality). Want kids? Pay for a surrogate or enter a co-parenting relationship. Want new relationship energy? Casually date. Want company? Make some good friends. Want to feel needed? Build a charity. Want unconditional love? Adopt a dog. The only two things one cannot get without a committed long-term relationship are the social and personal validation of having a high-value partner and the benefits of cognitive integration (though this is only true if you value validation from people who would only see you as "complete" if you have a traditional relationship and many people who do "go their own way" just don't care what these sorts think of them).

The research is nevertheless very clear about single parenting: One-parent homes raise children who have much lower-quality lives in every area, from income level to alcoholism. This effect is more pronounced in single-parent female houses than in single-parent male houses, which are not drastically worse than two-parent houses (though this is likely correlational and not causational, given how hard it is for males to win custody in a divorce). Perhaps this data is driven by failed marriages and unintentional parents. Perhaps as more people choose to go their own way and, as singles, raise children on their own terms and with all the care and intentionality they deserve, these stats will change.

"BAD" RELATIONSHIPS

A book on relationships that neglects to explore bad relationships in depth is akin to a book on explosives that exclusively discusses how delightful it is to blow things up. We are sure it's really, really fun to play with explosives, but explosives and relationships are also super dangerous. A bad relationship can be incredibly hard to leave. A toxic partner can completely ruin a life. Those not capable of identifying and extricating themselves from bad relationships should not be dating, period.

We characterize all "bad" relationships the same way and in a manner that deviates significantly from cultural norms, so buckle up and prepare to be offended.

A "bad" relationship is a relationship in which one of the partners would be better off not participating—from the perspective of their objective function (the thing they are trying to maximize in their lives, be that happiness, wealth, offspring, etc.—see *The Pragmatist's Guide to Life* for more on determining and pursuing objective functions). As we define a relationship as *a collaboration among participants who believe they differentially gain from a partnership,* all "bad" relationships exist due to one of the participants being incorrect in that belief.

"That doesn't sound so offensive" a person may conclude, perhaps not having thought through the real-world consequences of the above statement. By our definition, it is possible for a physically abusive relationship or a marriage plagued with regular marital rape to be "good"—where good is a differential term rather than an absolute term (i.e., the relationship is shitty, but staying in it is still the best option available to them).

Why do we use this metric? We care about actually helping people, and this definition is far more practically useful than any other metric if we are trying to write a guide that offers utility for everyone, regardless of their goals and predilections. Frankly, a large portion of the population would be quite satisfied to be in a relationship with an attractive billionaire who regularly beat them. They might argue that the abuse is better than having to get a minimum wage, nine-to-five job they live in constant fear of losing, leaving them unable to support themselves or their kids. Depending on a person's value system and alternative options, an abusive relationship could still be a net positive for them.

A relationship guide that pretends this portion of the population doesn't exist betrays itself as more concerned with virtue signaling than helping people. **Another person's objective function is not our choice—we are just here to help people get what they want on their terms.**

Thus, to us there is only one way a relationship can be bad: If a person *incorrectly* thinks they differentially benefit from being in a relationship. There is a panoply of ways a person can develop an incorrect belief as to whether or not they benefit from a relationship. By examining these pathways, we can come to a better understanding of when we may be entering into a "bad" relationship or when a relationship we are already in has become negative.

Fear of Change

Fear of change exists as a major component of all long-term relationships and only gets worse with time. Leaving a partner takes work. Leaving a partner requires change. Leaving a partner exposes one to the possibility of failure.

Anyone who hates initiative more than they care about their own happiness and effectiveness (i.e., everyone) will find leaving a partner to be a nightmarish endeavor. To avoid the hassle and uncertainty of change, people will desperately conjure excuses to convince themselves that leaving a current partner is not something they should be doing on any given day. We have personally known people who stayed with a partner who they wanted to leave for years because they were always somehow able to conjure up a new excuse as to why every particular day or week was just not the right time to end things.

If you know you need to leave a relationship and have ever once put off breaking off before, now is always the right time to do it unless breaking up immediately puts your personal safety at risk.

Incorrect Judgment

Many people remain in suboptimal relationships due to incorrect judgments about the differential benefits of their relationships. Someone in an abusive marriage may believe that their children will be worse off growing up in a divorced family than they are growing up in an intact (albeit abusive) family and that assumption may be incorrect. Alternatively, someone might determine that they would be unable to secure another partner of equivalent quality at their age, and they may be totally right.

Incorrect judgments of the value of a relationship exist because it can be genuinely difficult to predict how a vastly different future might play out. It is just as possible to leave a good relationship (one in which a person is differentially benefiting) due to an error in judgment as it is to stay in a bad one. The person who is afraid that no one else will want them may be right. When we trivialize that fear, we make people in bad relationships cling to them with increased enthusiasm because we show them there is a risk that we have not taken sufficient time to evaluate their situation and are happy to wash our hands of their wellbeing as soon as the make the choice we deem "correct."

However, there is one incorrect judgment we can happily dispel right now: The common assumption that "all relationships are secretly alike this behind closed doors." **This is false:** not all couples fight, not all partners end up emotionally unavailable after a few years, not all people will blame their partners for their own failures, not all spouses take their anger home, not all women gain excessive weight after having a baby, not all men cheat, and not all relationships are abusive. This is not to say that every relationship *you* have may consistently yield a certain dynamic; some people have habits that turn all of their relationships toxic. If you experience regular, large spats in every relationship you have had, you are likely the cause of that dynamic, which is good news because it means you can end it.

The Most Important Skill in Dating: Avoiding the Local Optimum Trap

The local optimum trap is the primary culprit leading many to remain in bad relationships. The number one skill in dating is an ability to break up with an ill-matched partner. Whether the goal is sex, securing a husband or wife, or merely improving a long-term relationship, the success of any given "relationship life" is as much dependent on an ability to identify a "bad" partner and leave them as quickly as possible as it is on an ability to secure a "good" partner.

Breaking up with someone is difficult because doing so typically makes your life worse for a period. A relationship is almost always a local optimum. A local optimum is a state that you can only leave by first going down. Being trapped in a local optimum is like standing on a hill and seeing a mountain: To get to the top of the mountain, you must first walk down the hill. A decision to leave a relationship is a decision to make your life worse—at least in the short term. Our society does not prepare us to pull the trigger on decisions like that.

The most common form of bad long-term relationships occurs among couples who, while not great together, are not so bad as to lead to a quick dissolution. These couples stay together because doing so is always easier than breaking up, and through staying together longer, they become more deeply ensconced in their local optimum. The longer a person stays with someone, the higher the cost of leaving them becomes: "But… we just bought a couch/puppy/apartment/house together!" they think to themselves when confronted with dissatisfaction.

The hills these couples stand on never get higher, but the valleys around them continuously grow deeper and deeper and deeper.

After however many years, a worrying proportion of these couples decide to get married— again, not because the participants are a good match for each other, but because the cost associated with leaving continuously rises and things like starting a family are time-sensitive.

The local optimum trap extends beyond long-term relationships into casual dating and even casual sex. If you can recognize someone as a bad pairing on the first date instead of on the third date, you gain the ability to test two other potential partners on nights during which you would have otherwise wasted time and money on the suboptimal partner.

Even when only looking for sex, people will hit this trap. A guy going to a bar to secure a partner for the night may end up spending half the night chatting with someone who has no intention of going home with him, and by not breaking off the conversation, this guy has likely blown his chances of getting laid that night. This man has succumbed to the local optimum trap. In the moment, it may indeed feel pleasant to linger for some time talking to an attractive person at the bar who, while clearly not sexually interested, is still happy to chat. It is also painful to bear the awkward solitude experienced after disengaging from this person and attempting to chat up someone else. That is the essence of the local optimum trap: What a person is doing at a particular moment is more pleasurable than what they will need to endure to get to where they want to be.

How can we avoid this local optimum trap? How can we avoid wasting a night—or our entire lives—on the wrong person? Consider the following three scenarios

Escaping the Local Optimum Trap in Long-Term Relationships

Realizing you are in a differentially bad long-term relationship is extremely difficult. Getting out of a relatively stable yet suboptimal long-term relationship requires a huge amount of willpower, initiative, and work. Asking how to get out of a relationship like this is like asking how to not be addicted to heroin. The best answer is: Do not allow it to happen in the first place. The best interventions to protect yourself from a suboptimal long-term relationship are those designed to weed out poor matches during the dating process, which we described above.

✿ The Pragmatist's Guide to Relationships

What if that ship has sailed? What if you think you are already in a suboptimal relationship?

It is not easy to soberly evaluate the quality of a relationship in which you already find yourself, especially if you have been in that relationship for a long time. If you are determined and driven enough to tackle this endeavor, we recommend you first determine your objective function. Determine which thing(s) you believe have inherent value that you wish to maximize with your life (see our last book, *The Pragmatists Guide to Life* for guidance on determining your objective function without having someone else, a particular group, or your culture push you in any particular direction). Once you have determined your objective function, ask yourself if your partner in your relationship aids or hampers the maximization of that objective function.

In attempting to determine whether your current long-term relationship is worth maintaining or not, avoid leaning heavily on societal tropes of negative and positive relationships (e.g., "We don't fight much, so our relationship is good" or "He cheats on me, so our relationship is bad"). Features that society labels as classically negative or positive in a relationship may not ultimately matter that much to you or your values and objective function.

You may not even like your long-term relationship partner, but ultimately deem your relationship to be "optimal" as defined by this guide. You may, for example, hate your husband, but have an objective function around maximizing the success of your offspring and be aware that leaving this man would put your offspring in a differentially disadvantaged position. That said, anyone who chooses to stay in a relationship that is at least partially harmful in the name of objective function maximization must VERY CAREFULLY validate their conclusions, as in many cases they are poorly substantiated and more a product of habituation than logic. Depending on the standard of evidence you require, this evaluation may involve anything from looking at what happened to your friends' kids after their divorces to reading the latest scientific literature on the subject.

If you are not yet in a long-term relationship, take a sober-minded moment to build a set of heuristics telling your future self when to leave a long-term relationship that has ultimately proven to be suboptimal. Create this relationship ejection protocol now, before you meet any eventual long-term partner, because your future self is going to lose objectivity. Future you may do everything in your power to evade escape from this bad relationship. To protect yourself from this folly, even consider making an informal contract with your friends and family, so that if you ultimately are too weak to execute your relationship ejection protocol despite all the alarms sounding, they can sweep in and save you from a loss of objectivity.

Avoiding The Local Optimum Trap While Dating

Dating can largely be broken into two categories: Casual dating and dating with the intention of securing a long-term relationship. After high school and college, casual dating is extremely dangerous, as it can lead one to fall into an unintentional long-term relationship-of-least-resistance with a lackluster partner.

Chronic casual dating is usually driven by a fear of long-term relationships or an addiction to new relationship energy. Regardless of your motivation to casually date, you should know how to properly drop suboptimal partners before any significant logistical or habitual attachment forms.

Eliminating someone you are dating is quite distinct from eliminating a sexual target because personality becomes an important factor. Each participant in a date must ascertain as quickly as possible whether there is, or is not, a promising relationship to explore. Each of us (Malcolm and Simone) implemented different strategies to this end; both were fairly successful.

Simone utilized a five-question post-date evaluation to determine whether someone was a candidate for a second date. Each question had a score of 1-10. Dates that scored under 30 were obvious rejects. Dates scoring 30-40 might be worthy of a second date for further evaluation. Dates scoring above 40 had immense potential and warranted significant investment. At least personally, Simone's average score of first dates was 16. *Note: We talk about this system and the questions used in detail later in the book.*

Malcolm followed a strategy in which he quickly probed for personal attributes of his dates that would be problematic in a long-term relationship. This ranged from desire to have children (or at least flexibility on that point) to the date's objective function and general worldview.

This enabled Malcolm to quickly drop dates who exhibited behavioral red flags and helped Malcolm signal to dates specifically *why* they were not well matched (e.g., "I want to have a large family and you just clearly stated you are strongly against having kids").

Note that **the most effective dating strategies lead people to break up with you more frequently—not less frequently.** For example, Malcolm used to tell women on the first date he was looking for a wife and only escalated things from there in terms of transparency on future dates. This led many women to dump him fairly quickly. Breaking up with bad potential partners quickly is a thousand times better than staying together with a poorly matched partner. Being dumped by a bad long-term partner is a sign of success not a sign of failure. Whenever people tell us they have recently broken up, we congratulate them and comment on how relieved and pleased they must be. It is a shame our comments are met with such odd looks of resentment and surprise—good, healthy relationships don't break up.

Avoiding The Local Optimum Trap While Looking for Sex

Note: If you read the appendix chapter on looking for sex when you are young, this portion of the book can be skipped. It is the less nuanced "bulldozer" version of the same strategy that has more utility in the types of loud "high stimuli" environments adults use to look for no-strings-attached sex.

If you only want sex, the key piece of information you must secure to avoid the local optimum trap is whether or not a target is receptive to the idea of having sex with you. Your primary mission when looking for sex, therefore, should be to make your intentions clear without outright stating them so that your target may turn you down quickly if interest in sex is not mutual.

Studies have repeatedly demonstrated that among those looking for short-term sexual partners, looks prevail as a judgment factor in men and in women looks and dominance displays are predominant. Statistically speaking, if you are the average person looking only for sex, very little interaction is required to judge your own interest in sex with any given person. The only thing that is tricky is judging the interest of your targets.

This can be done through sexually suggestive topics of conversation (if the target engages with sexually suggestive topics enthusiastically, there is likely interest) and **non-sexually suggestive** physical touches (if non-sexual touches are engaged with enthusiastically, there is likely an interest). If the target appears receptive, you may move to more sexually suggestive touching, after which you may invite them somewhere private. If the target has already shown interest in sexually suggestive touching and consents to relocation to a private place, you may then invite them home and engage in full sexual congress (if a target engages in reciprocal touching when in a private space, the likelihood of sexual interest is very high, and this invite can be made without much fear of rejection).

This strategy will result in your inevitably crossing small boundaries with targets who do not ultimately turn out to be interested in you sexually. These experiences may be awkward for you but know that they are well worth any mild discomfort experienced. Why? This strategy vastly decreases the odds of accidental sexual escalation with a target in a way that made them feel pressured into consent. In an ideal world, any target not interested in having sex with you will say "no" as quickly as possible rather than after significant time and monetary investment or—much worse—*after* you have had sex . . . but we do not live in an ideal world.

Be extremely clear with consent before engaging in sexual contact—especially oral sex and hand-to-genital contact, which can "feel" less severe in the moment than penetrative sex, but if you have misjudged consent will have the same negative impact on your life.

Clear consent matters a great deal when you are only looking for sex. Why? An adult who is primarily looking for sex and skilled at securing it is probably sleeping with around fifty people every year. If this adult sleeps with 50 people a year and misjudges consent in only 5% of cases, they are ultimately raping an average of 2.5 people a year. Whether or not you count a "misjudgment of consent" as rape, society does, and those who engage with a high number of sexual partners are setting themselves up for serious legal and/or reputational damage.

If you ever hear someone championing a sexual strategy designed to get someone to sleep with you that involves pressuring a target past comfortable, conscious, active consent and that person has not yet been accused of rape, you can be fairly certain the strategy is not effective, or they have not been implementing it for an extended period of time. And if they have been accused of rape . . . why are you copying the strategies that took them to that place in their lives?

Also avoid strategies that involve securing no-commitment sex from industry colleagues, fellow members of a friend group, schoolmates, or coworkers. A target's connection to social groups relevant to you adds an additional social cost to rejection—sometimes to you, and sometimes to the target. In cases in which the target feels your social connection increases the cost of their rejecting your sexual advances (i.e., you are a bigwig in an industry important to them, or you are their boss or direct manager), they are far more likely to allow you to push them out of their sexual comfort zone. Again, even if you don't personally ascribe to this definition of rape, dealing with the fallout of accidentally pushing someone past their comfort zone is not worth something as trivially easy to obtain as sex.

Appendix: *If you want to dive stupidly deep into the nuanced topic of the types of partners to avoid, see the appendix section A Guide to Avoiding Crazy on page 479. While it has some good info, it turns into a boring, pedantic ramble at times.*

Avoiding The Local Optimum Trap While Single

A large portion of the population is better off single than they are dating a random person. In addition to making the slog of dating even more tiresome, this reality can create the illusion that even if you were able to obtain an ideal relationship, being in that relationship would be worse than being single (a uniquely tempting illusion, seeing as it's true for a minority of the population). This illusion is often used as an easy excuse to not bother with pursuing an optimal long-term relationship at all.

Both recreational dating and single life is fun for most, while dating in search of an ideal long-term partner is stressful and exhausting. Don't let the hard work required to find an optimal partner occlude the fact that life with this person will be better than life alone.

Predicting When *Your Partner* Will Determine Your Relationship to Be "Bad"

One surprisingly common relationship strategy involves keeping a partnership just above a "breakup point" while harvesting all the benefits that one can from said union. To implement this strategy effectively, a person has to become skilled at judging when a partner will hit their breakup point and always stay just above that point.

Two common strategies are leveraged to prevent a person from hitting a breakup point. The first is to improve the relationship's value to this person while increasing the cost of breaking up. We call these "stable strategies." The second is to increase the cost of breaking up dramatically while decreasing the value of the relationship, we call these "unstable strategies."

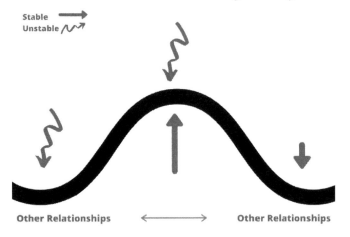

Stable Versus Unstable Dating Strategies

Stable strategies are typically better for both parties, as a partner will be willing to do more to maintain a relationship that gives them more, however unstable methods are common enough to warrant exploration—if only to arm readers against a partner attempting to apply it to a relationship.

There is a wide array of both stable and unstable strategies for increasing breakup costs.

Examples of stable strategies:
- Increasing the number of shared friendships
- Developing rapport and close ties with a partner's family
- Getting married
- Buying a house (or otherwise consensually intermingling finances)
- Helping their partner enter a career field in which a breakup would hurt the partner strategically (like politics or a job at their family's company)
- Buying a pet together
- Consensually having kids together

All of these strategies significantly increase the cost of ending a relationship.

Unless you are certain you want a long-term relationship with someone, do not engage in any of these stable strategies. Be wary if it appears that you are being lured into one of these traps if you do not wish to enter a long-term relationship. These are not things to take lightly. However, if a long-term relationship is your goal, these stable relationship escalation mechanisms are generally great signs.

✱ The Pragmatist's Guide to Relationships

We label the above strategies as "stable" because their deployment does not necessarily decrease the value of the relationship. An unstable strategy is one in which a person decreases the value of their relationship but increases the cost of a breakup more than they reduce the value of their relationship.

Examples of unstable strategies:
- Threatening to harm oneself if the partner leaves
- Threatening to harm a partner if they leave
- Getting pregnant without a partner's consent
- Attempting to convince a partner that no one will want them if they leave (i.e., lower the partner's perception of their own aggregate desirability)
- Threatening to post nude photos of a partner if they leave
- Commingling or otherwise integrating finances without a partner's full consent (such as by taking out a loan in their name).

Unstable relationship maintenance strategies can be effective in extreme moderation but are not recommended. No matter how high someone makes the cost of a breakup, once a confident person realizes they would be much better off single than in a relationship with said person, they *will* leave. Destabilizing a relationship with the above strategies turns every day into a battle to keep one's partner from realizing the relationship is worth leaving by incessantly escalating behavior. A person only has to lose this battle once to lose their partner forever. Still, as stupid as unstable strategies are, they can be moderately effective in the short term—thus why they are so common in emotionally abusive relationships.

Furthermore, there is a special kind of crazy person who tries to use unstable strategies on people with whom they are *not* presently in an active relationship. Such individuals may try to convince someone they have a lower aggregate desirability in order to trick these targets into valuing a relationship with them. The classic example here is a person insulting someone after they are turned down (e.g., "if you won't date me, you must be slut… Now do you want to date me?"). However, more aggressive examples of this strategy, like faking a pregnancy after a casual one-night stand, are hardly unheard of.

We genuinely do not understand how people think these strategies will lead to a desirable outcome for their pursuer. Thinking that someone would see a person attempt one of these strategies and delude themselves into believing they would be better off in a relationship with that person goes beyond stupid to the point at which we question if all humans are fully sentient. If someone attempts one of these strategies on you, we strongly recommend cutting off all contact immediately. People who think like this, no matter how hot they are, will never add anything of value to your life on the aggregate.

Enjoying this subject? We welcome you to take a deeper dive in the appendix:
- To learn how to more effectively predict and respond to cheating behavior, visit: Why People

Cheat Rather Than Leave a Relationship on page 455.
- Younger readers less familiar with social norms around lying in relationships may enjoy: Lying in Relationships on page 522.
- For more information on how to minimize the chance that you hurt someone in a relationship see: Hurting People in Relationships in the on page 507.

OUR INEFFICIENT BIOLOGY

Let's look at how our bodies affect us when dating. The human body is hardly appealing, oozing disgusting, smelly fluids not just from every orifice, but every pore. Despite this our brains trick us into thinking they are desirable. Just as our brains betray us into somehow finding these gassy, greasy, fleshy bodies arousing, they betray us into all sorts of other unconscious behaviors and predilections.

The Funny Ways We React to Testosterone

Testosterone is one of these fun chemicals that just completely screws with your brain and can make it do all sorts of weird things. It is often thought of as a masculinizing hormone; however, it is critical not just in female and male sexual development but also in male and female cognition. Even more fascinating: Average testosterone levels in humans started crashing a few decades ago across western society (it has gone down 30% since the '80s) and scientists do not know why—but more on that later.

There is a myriad of cool research findings related to testosterone. For example, a man's level of testosterone seems more related to where they grew up (childhood conditions) than their ethnicity or present location. One study found that Bangladeshi men living in the UK who grew up in the UK had a similar level of testosterone to other UK men, while those who grew up in Bangladesh had much lower levels.

We are fascinated by how testosterone affects looks. Higher levels of testosterone can lead to all sorts of negative aesthetic effects ranging from acne to increased probability of balding at an early age. Among women, an unnaturally high amount of testosterone causes male features to begin to develop, such as extra body hair.

The positive aesthetic effects of testosterone generally seem to outweigh their negative counterparts when testosterone is high but not to extreme levels. Moderately high levels of testosterone are associated with an increased probability of higher and more defined cheekbones (if one is exposed to high levels of testosterone during early development), muscle definition, and increased masculine features in both males and females.

The muscle definition increase caused by testosterone is quite pronounced. An individual with more testosterone in their system will develop more muscle mass and denser muscles at the same level of exercise. As muscles burn more calories than fat, those with greater muscle mass will have an easier time maintaining a lower weight overall. This is why people take testosterone in the form of steroids when they want to gain muscle quickly and easily. Unfortunately, this exogenous testosterone is recognized by the body, causing it to stop producing its own testosterone and shrinking the size of the testicles.

If testosterone makes both guys and girls into chiseled (if hairy) Adonises with gorgeous cheekbones and rippling muscles, why do we not naturally produce tons of the stuff? Alas, testosterone is also poisonous and is the primary reason why men have shorter lifespans than women (well maybe, this has long been an accepted idea in biology, but recent evidence suggests that if height and risk-taking behavior are controlled for it could be wrong). Moreover, men with more testosterone may die at even *earlier* ages than men with lower testosterone levels (we write "may" because, again, some new studies contradict this finding). Some hypothesize that testosterone in men is something like peacock feathers on a male peacock: It signals to women that a man's genes are so splendid that he can excel *despite* being exposed to a chemical that is constantly killing him.

Furthermore, women are not *always* attracted to high testosterone. Instead, women differentially prefer high testosterone men when they are most fertile. We discuss this in a lot more detail in *The Pragmatist's Guide to Sexuality*.

From an intelligence perspective, the effects of higher testosterone are fascinating. Testosterone appears to act a bit like a chemical that overclocks your brain's processing and can either lead to better performance or burnout. For example, when young boys were tested for intelligence, those at both the highest levels and lowest levels of intelligence had much more testosterone than average boys.

Testosterone also affects general cognition. When individuals are dosed with testosterone, they are more likely to prefer luxury brands of cars, watches, pens, or clothing. This preference appears tied to higher testosterone individuals being more motivated to elevate their social rank. This may be tied to the association between higher testosterone levels and higher levels of ambition, aggression, and threat processing.

We wonder: Could the above fact, combined with the crash in testosterone that has happened since the 80s, be a major contributor to the trend of millennials appearing more frugal than early generations—with even wealthy millennials spending much less than previous generations at equivalent levels of wealth?

What you likely care about is how testosterone affects a partner's mating behavior. An increase in testosterone will lead to an increase in sex drive in both men and women. Higher testosterone also leads to an increase in fetishistic interests (though at ultra-high levels, testosterone can have the opposite effect). While some studies indicate testosterone only increases masturbation behavior in females and does not increase sex drive in either sex, the finding runs contrary to conventional wisdom and most other studies, so we regard them with skepticism.

Given the effect of testosterone on sex drive, one could—purely for idle fun—theoretically estimate the sex drive of a person just by looking at their physical features and behavior. For example, women who have very defined cheekbones, as well as women with a keen interest in traditionally "masculine" pursuits such as contact sports, may have higher sex drives, as both characteristics indicate the presence of more testosterone in their systems.

The effects of testosterone on mating behavior extend beyond mere increases in sex drive. Men with higher testosterone show higher rates of mate-guarding behavior (attempts to prevent their partners from sleeping with other men). This is somewhat ironic, as a polyamorous lifestyle increases testosterone levels but also would make strong mate guarding impulses more problematic. Testosterone-driven mate-guarding behavior is not what you might consider to be the sweet kind of mate-guarding behavior (e.g., buying flowers and otherwise just trying to be *better* than other options) but rather the cost inflicting kind (e.g., threatening other men to stay away). This mate-guarding behavior is probably linked to the increase in activation you see in threat processing regions of the brain associated with testosterone, which also may be responsible for the "roid rage" phenomenon (a rise in uncontrollable, violent outbursts) among those who supplement with a lot of testosterone for bodybuilding purposes.

Fluctuations in the amount of testosterone your body produces can be triggered by all sorts of experiences. For example, testosterone levels increase in men after repeated wins and decrease after losses. In other words, testosterone gives men greater psychological momentum: When they're on a winning streak, the rise in testosterone encourages them to take riskier risks. These findings are reinforced by studies conducted on birds, fish, and mice, which have shown that either being in competition with other males or winning competitions against other males increases testosterone. *(As nerdy as an aside this is, we cannot help but note human males are basically playing life under "Warhammer" Orc rules, the more they win, the* more muscly they get and the more they want to fight.) What's more, men in higher positions of power often have more testosterone, and striking power poses in men can increase the output of testosterone.

Threats to a man's masculinity may also trigger spikes in testosterone production—or at least spikes in testosterone-esque behavior. Male study participants who were told that they had a lot of "feminine knowledge" after taking a quiz would choose to be shocked by a higher voltage in a subsequent exercise in which participants received a harmless electric shock than participants whose masculinity was not threatened by this statement. Is that not hilarious? People are so funny.

Fascinatingly, testosterone (as well as cortisol, a hormone associated with stress) decreases significantly in men who are in long-term relationships. It seems this decrease is tied to a feeling of love for a partner. Essentially, when a man's brain decides it is safely pair-bonded and doesn't need to keep hunting new sexual partners, it lowers testosterone production—like a government deciding to decrease military spending in a time of extended peace. This lowering of cortisol and testosterone likely takes place both to lower the negative effects of testosterone on the body when it is no longer of utility to reproduction, and to lower a man's sex drive and risk-taking behavior to allow for more dedicated focus on resource gathering.

Nevertheless, the effects of long-term pair-bonded relationships in testosterone can be easily reversed. While testosterone decreases while in a marriage, it increases after a divorce.

This relationship-triggered reduction in testosterone has all sorts of ancillary effects, ranging from behavior changes (men with lower testosterone are less aggressive, less dominant, and less sexually motivated) to physical changes (such as lower muscle mass and thus more fat accumulation at the same level of diet and exercise). If a man with whom you are in a relationship starts getting a bit softer, but his exercise and diet have not changed and his sex drive decreases along with decreasing aggression levels, these changes are a sign that he may love you. These hormonal changes obviously create problems if you were specifically attracted to a man for his higher testosterone levels (which is understandable, given that high testosterone men are more attractive in a masculine sense).

What if character traits associated with high testosterone are what you like *most* about men? How do you still find a man attractive after he falls in love with you and decreases production? Worry not; there is an easy solution: Individuals in the polyamorous community (both males and females) have the highest testosterone levels of any population. As long as you keep your man's hunger for new females (or males) satiated with a constant stream of partners, his love for you should not have any effects on his testosterone production. Simple and easy.

Both smoking and obesity affect testosterone levels. Obesity-induced drops in testosterone are quite ironic: Because fat produces estrogen, which downregulates testosterone production, it becomes harder to lose weight when there is weight worth losing.

What we find uniquely titillating on a societal level is that when men see themselves as disempowered or "hierarchically lower" in their society, they down-regulate their testosterone production. For this reason, researchers have found lower testosterone levels among unemployed individuals. This finding sadly does not explain the crashing testosterone rates across Western society: While one may hypothesize that these changes are tied to rising obesity rates or economic recessions, such factors were controlled for in the studies that investigated them. No—it appears that men in general feel less empowered now than they did a few decades ago, even when they have the same jobs and better overall standards of living.

While some claim to be horrified by this grand hormonal shift society, we do not see any reason for concern (well at least not as much as concern for something like sperm count degradation which is also happening). Continued monitoring of the situation should be sufficient for now. Perhaps an overall reduction in testosterone is exactly what society needs given the "free radical problem," in which unattached men cause higher rates of social problems—as well as terrorism (this is a topic we dive into in much more detail in The Pragmatist's Guide to Sexuality).

All in all, the effects of testosterone are fascinating. While we would love to say the same of estrogen and progesterone, their effects on sex drive, attraction, and body structure are pretty boring in comparison.

Note from the Research:
- Women administered testosterone will call opponents' possible bluffs more in a card game based around bluffing but bluff themselves less in a way that hurts their ability to win the game. This is likely due to an increased aversion to losing status—something that can happen either due to someone successfully calling out them in a lie or someone lying to them and getting away with it.

Monitoring Personal Hormonal States

A relationship psychologist who helped us construct this book had a really interesting idea for women we thought was relevant here: Specifically, she claimed that women who tracked their ovulation cycle with a focus on how it affected their impulses were more faithful to their partners and had longer relationships. She claimed that cycle tracking made it easier for women to identify whether a fluctuation in hormones was driving them to do something that they would not do under other circumstances.

Specifically, women might consider monitoring how their stage in their menstrual cycle influences the likelihood of:
- Engaging in passive-aggressive stunts
- Starting arguments
- Being unfaithful
- Wanting to break up the relationship
- Lashing in some other way

For example, a woman may find that she needs to be sensitive about verbally lashing out at her partner during her luteal phase. Understanding that her impulse to act negatively toward her partner is likely hormonally driven can help this woman disassociate from the impulse ("That's the hormones talking, not me") and let the desire pass by without acting on it.

Kissing and Touch

Kissing sparks the nerve endings on your lips, causing a surge of dopamine and oxytocin: The chemicals that cause people to feel as though they have an emotional connection. Kissing is, therefore, an effective strategy if you seek to make individuals feel bonded to you. Perfecting and implementing kissing early in a relationship can be of great utility when it comes to locking down targets. Unfortunately, the dopamine and oxytocin surge triggered by kissing is a two-way street and can compromise your own ability to think objectively.

Kissing is a very recent cultural development—at least as a tool for facilitating romantic pair-bonding. Kissing is only seen in 46% of cultures and differentially appears in cultures with distinct social classes (e.g., it is very rare in hunter-gatherer communities). In hunter-gatherer and other societies devoid of romantic kissing, kissing behavior appears only between a parent and their children (likely as a pair-bonding tool as well). One exception to this hunter-gatherer rule is seen among tribes that live in the circum-arctic region (Inuit people, for example), but this just appears to be a way for people covered head to toe in thick furs to have human contact.

We love looking through history to see how past cultures experimented with kissing as a tool for facilitating pair-bonds. Probably the most awesome appropriation of kissing can be found in the practice of kissing a lord's hand in feudal Europe as a sign of devotion. What makes this so awesome? Hand kissing is like romantic kissing without the downside of two-way pair-bond creation. With hand-kissing, only a monodirectional pair-bond is cultivated: From servant to master. Suffice to say a working knowledge of neuroscience, cross-cultural anthropology, and medieval European cultures can yield some tactics to help one efficiently enthrall others.

General touch has similar pair-bonding effects. Honestly, lips only seem to cause a uniquely strong effect due to the high density of neurons they harbor. We imagine something like naked cuddling would have about the same effect in aggregate. In fact, a number of studies have shown that activities that cause this kind of activation, such as cuddling, backrubs, hugging, and kissing all are positively correlated with relationship satisfaction. There are gender differences, though: males report significantly stronger arousal while being the active partner doing the touching, whereas females report a stronger sensation when being the ones touched.

Notes from the Research:
- A study of 140 couples found that affectionate touch leads to couples becoming calmer and more constructive during a heated conflict. This is not at all surprising given that affectionate touch triggers both the release of endorphins and oxytocin.
- A recent (2019) study in Scientific Reports found a positive correlation between countries' Gini coefficients and the prevalence of kissing. In other words, countries with higher inequality exhibit more kissing.

Blue Balls

Blue balls is a term for a discoloration of the testes and pain associated with a long period of arousal not punctuated by release. There is a common misconception that "blue balls" are not real. In reality, when a male is aroused, the arteries dilate in his genitals, and his veins constrict, causing them to fill with blood. As a result, not just the man's penis, but also his balls are, on average, double in size when he is aroused.

Human blood appears blue when looked at through the skin because red light has a longer wavelength than blue light, causing it to be absorbed deeper into the skin, whereas blue light gets reflected before it is absorbed by deeper veins. This ultimately has the effect of making your blood appear blue and thus a man's testes appear blue when they are engorged with blood for a long period of time (actually, the same thing happens to the female vulva and clitoris, leading to "blue vulva"). The pain this condition causes can be easily removed with an orgasm or decreased arousal and an ice pack.

Mate Guarding Behavior

Behavior falls under the designation of "mate-guarding" when its objective involves increasing the probability of maintaining sexually exclusive access to a partner. In humans, mate-guarding manifests as anything from putting your arm around someone in public (to demonstrate to others they are "taken") to sleeping in the same bed as your partner or adorning your partner in attention-grabbing possessions like jewelry (people who use this tactic are statistically more likely to be jealous partners).

Better knowledge of mate-guarding behavior will help you identify, contextualize, and suppress the mate-guarding impulse in your brain. Why suppress mate-guarding behavior? As we will discuss below, it can often yield very counterproductive results.

The most common mate-guarding behavior in human females manifests in the ostracization of other desirable females. Females increase this behavior when they are ovulating and will increase it further if a potential rival is also ovulating. Some studies have also found that women dress more provocatively when ovulating and are less likely to introduce their partners to other provocatively dressed females.

In other words, the most common type of mate guarding behavior in women is to either denigrate other women or prevent their partners from spending time with other women.

In general, the level of mate-guarding behavior a female will exhibit can be judged by how attractive she believes she is relative to her partner (more on that shortly), her level of Machiavellianism (more Machiavellian personalities engage in more mate-guarding), how liberally minded she is towards sex, and the level of intimacy in her current relationship (with more intimacy being tied to less mate-guarding).

While it is easy to separate genetically ingrained and socialized mate-guarding behavior in women because we can look at how their behavior subconsciously changes when they are more fertile, we cannot use this same pattern with men, whose fertility does not regularly fluctuate.

Men who see themselves as less attractive when contrasted with their partners engage in more mate-guarding behavior, such as public displays of affection and attempts to prevent their partners from interacting with other males. Simultaneously, females who view themselves as more attractive than their mates are more likely to resist these forms of mate-guarding behavior. Women with less attractive male partners have also been found to resist mate-guarding behavior more vigorously if they view their partner as less wealthy than their peers, be more likely to flirt with other men, and experience more frequent thoughts about breaking up.

Female resistance to mate-guarding behavior increases further when a woman is fertile. The more fertile a woman is, the less she will like having her current pair-bonded partner demonstrate to others that she is off the market, and the more she will fantasize about sex with individuals who are not her pair-bonded partner. When a female is fertile, she is even more likely to be drawn to events like parties at which she might meet non-pair-bonded partners. Resistance to a male partner's mate-guarding behavior is also more pronounced in women who engage in abundant mate-guarding behaviors themselves. Finally, males who have higher digit span ratios (low testosterone males) will also receive much more female resistance to mate-guarding behavior.

This interplay of male mate-guarding action being met with female resistance and subterfuge suggests that mate-guarding subtly signals to females that the male to whom they are bonded believes that he "needs" to guard them. As a result, male mate-guarding behavior may lower a female's estimation of her male partner's value.

Studies have shown the more mate-guarding behavior a male partner exhibits (e.g., the more possessive and controlling he becomes), the more likely a female is to want to sleep with other partners, and ironically the more likely she is to successfully sleep with others. Alas, few studies look at female mate-guarding behavior—wish we could say if this was a two-way street, but we don't know.

Mate guarding is not only a warning sign to a partner that they can likely secure someone better. Possessive behavior can also be a sign of shady behavior and dishonesty on the part of the mate-guarding partner. For example, people who utilize coalitional mate retention tactics (mate retention with the help of social allies, such as friends) are more likely to be dishonest (higher in extraversion, lower in conscientiousness).

Does theory on attachment styles interest you? Visit the chapter Attachment Styles on page 531 in the appendix. In short, the concept of attachment styles, which has become popular among relationship psychologists, strikes us as suboptimal for various reasons we will happily delineate in the appendix, but not bore readers with presently.

The Cognitive Effects of Birth Control Pills

Recent research has shown a significant, if small, effect on cognition by the standard hormone-based birth control pill. Specifically, women on the pill have a harder time recognizing emotions on other people's faces. We don't really think there are any takeaways from this—we just find it interesting.

The Genetics of Love

Another really cool study, this time out of Binghamton University, shows a correlation between the Oxytocin Receptor gene (OXTR) and martial strength. It appears that our perception of love—how much love we feel for our partner and how quickly we feel it—is impacted by our genes.

While neat, this genetic basis kind of sucks when you think about it. Some people may just not feel as much love as others as genetic factors make it more difficult for them to maintain relationships. We also suspect this same pattern carries over to romance displays, with some individuals just being born with a much larger impulse to make them.

The G Spot

While some early studies claim to have found the mythical G spot, a more thorough investigation has shown it likely does not exist as a real anatomical feature. Instead, the G spot appears to just be the location where the internal part of the clitoris, the urethra, and vagina all intersect, leading to more stimulation.

Length of Sex

In a Canadian study, women reported that intercourse usually lasted seven minutes and foreplay 11 minutes, while men estimated intercourse typically lasted for 8 minutes and foreplay 13, meaning that heterosexual adults typically think sex lasts between 18-21 minutes. Contrasts this with women's ideal: 14 minutes of foreplay and 19 minutes of sex and men's ideal: 18 minutes of foreplay and 18 minutes of sex (for those doing, the math the ideal sex session is 33-36 minutes, while the average actual session is 18-21).

Fancy all this random biology stuff? Explore it in detail in *The Pragmatist's Guide to Sexuality*.

Avoid Partners Who Want to Be Happy

Our strong warning against partners who live lives dedicated to their own happiness has a biological—as well as ideological—basis (which we already covered).

A couple studies out of KU Leuven and the University of Melbourne School of Psychological Sciences found that individuals who place more importance on personal happiness exhibit increased rates of depression and anxiety. They also show that surrounding oneself with individuals who push for happiness or motivational imagery meant to encourage happiness (imagine a "hang in there" cat poster) increases one's perception of failure and makes it harder to move on. Admittedly the studies are a bit more nuanced than we are giving them credit for—specifically, they only show feeling pressured to not be depressed increased depressive symptoms and found that the presence of motivational posters in a scenario in which an individual fails makes it harder to move on from the failure—the rest is an extraction from those findings and other research.

To put it another way, caring about being happy will make it harder to personally be happy and put a damper on the happiness of friends, colleagues, and families. If one chooses a partner who lives a life designed to optimize their own happiness, their biology will conspire to rob them of the one thing they strive for and—plus rob anyone they allow to live in their vicinity of that thing. Happiness-obsessed people are like a black hole of positive emotional experiences.

We imagine this is why religious individuals consistently rate themselves as happier than non-religious individuals. Religious individuals are far less likely to live lives dedicated to maximizing their own emotional states.

This is not to say that one cannot find a partner who is both an atheist and dedicated to something other than positive emotional states. About a third of the bestselling first book in this series, *The Pragmatist's Guide to Life,* is dedicated to helping people think through what may have value to them and to what they should dedicate their lives (be their inclinations secular or religious) and the vast majority of the secular options explored are not focused on personal happiness or the happiness of others.

The Effects of Chastity on Pair-Bonding

There is abundant research exploring how sexual partner count, quantity of sex, and quality of sex affect cognition. While we explore this at length in *The Pragmatist's Guide to Sexuality*, there is one specific finding uniquely relevant to relationships: That in women at least, higher sexual partner count alters the manner in which sex accelerates pair-bonding.

Having sex with an individual speeds up pair-bond formation (love) in women. We use the term pair-bond instead of the word love here, as the word "love" carries a lot of societal baggage that distracts from the larger point.

Sleeping with multiple partners appears to have a permanent effect on the neurochemistry of the female brain. When a female sleeps with a large number of people, the dose of oxytocin her body releases when she sleeps with a new partner decreases. In other words, the pair-bond a female automatically begins to feel for a partner as a result of sexual intimacy declines with each new partner.

This effect can be observed in broader statistics and not just in lower oxytocin levels. The more people a female sleeps with before marriage, the shorter and less happy her marriage is statistically likely to be (these effects exist for men as well, but at a much lower rate). Specifically, one study showed that women who had slept with 16 or more partners before marrying had a staggeringly high 80% divorce rate.

Note from the Research:
- Premarital partner count decreases enjoyment of sex in marriage by 4% per partner for women and 5.3% per partner in men.

There are some bad actors in this research space, trying to massage data to fit an agenda. Should their studies be taken at face value, it would appear that this effect begins after just two sexual partners, but studies showing that do not remove individuals who have been in previous marriages from the dataset. Once amended to be more intellectually honest, the data suggests this effect does not actually kick in until after a woman has had eight or nine sexual partners.

We would be remiss not to mention that some of the studies show that while women who marry as virgins have longer marriages, those who report having only had only two previous sexual partners have shorter marriages than those who report three to nine former sexual partners (so once a women has slept with one person, sleeping with a few more before marrying actually increases the length of her marriage). Most of these studies control for religiosity: Religious people's tendency to sleep with fewer partners and be happier in marriages would not explain this trend alone.

Not many studies have been conducted on the effect of high partner count on males' ability to form strong pair-bonds, so it is difficult to draw any super confident conclusions for men. That said, from the data we have seen, any effect on men is less extreme than that experienced by women. This may be because sex does not facilitate pair-bonding in chaste males as strongly as it does in females. In other words, promiscuity brings a female closer to a male state in this respect, which is why we would not see the effect as strongly in men. All that said, while this specific effect is not shared in the male brain, more promiscuous men absolutely experience neurological changes tied to brain function (specifically, more promiscuous men produce more testosterone on average).

The studies exploring how sexual partner count affects pair-bonding of which we are aware of were conducted within Western cultures, so this may not be an inborn difference in males and females, but rather a product of some sort of acculturation. Cultural pressures can have a pretty big impact on neurochemistry.

This data may come across as both unpleasant and disturbing, but we don't get to choose what is true based on what we wish were true. Enough studies suggest this effect is real for us to feel compelled to report it in the name of intellectual honesty. Fortunately—and we need to stress this as hard as we possibly can—the data does not support that women lose the capacity to feel love if they indulge in sexual experimentation. The data only suggests that sex loses its ability to facilitate/force pair-bonding faster the more a female engages in it, and this, in aggregate, leads to less love in married relationships and thus less happiness. We come to this conclusion based on the lowered oxytocin generated by more sexually experienced women during sex, which would explain the other correlating factors identified, such as shorter marriages and lower reported happiness in marriage.

Despite this, we still think that sleeping with multiple partners is an optimal long-term relationship strategy for women. The increased difficulty in securing a long-term relationship with a man or woman without sleeping with them—in mainstream society at least—is raised to the extent that it is likely not worth the tradeoff of insisting on waiting until marriage for sex.

Keep in mind the competition. Given that a third of women who engage in online dating have sex on the first date, a woman is at a huge disadvantage in her efforts to secure a good partner if she insists on being chaste until marriage outside of religious sub-communities. This is not to say that you should sleep with someone on the first date, just that if your competition is offering sex on first dates, not sleeping with someone until marriage becomes a less enticing pitch to many candidates. It is also far too risky a strategy to hope that one's first serious long-term relationship candidate will be the best one to bond with for life. We could even argue that loosening the strong surges of love resulting from sex will make women more clear-headed in making decisions about who they marry.

It is ultimately a cruel trick that the body would attach someone to those with whom they have intercourse rather than those who are genuinely favorable long-term partner candidates. The strong pair-bond resulting from sex with early sexual partners can be toxic should a woman use the "spark" she felt in her earlier relationships as an indicator of a good long-term relationship match and avoid settling down with an otherwise good match, not realizing that she isn't feeling that spark due to a change in the way her brain processes these interactions and not a product of any decline in partner quality.

We have a fascinating theory around this dynamic: That the decrease in oxytocin production resulting from higher sexual partner counts indicates a switch between polymorphic states in humans, with each state optimized for different tribal social structures.

Essentially, humans may be biologically optimized for both monogamous and non-monogamous tribes, using environmental cues (like partner count) to determine which sort of tribe theirs happens to be. Based on these cues, the brain shifts the manner in which it processes interactions to optimize for one's likely tribal structure.

It would make a lot of sense that a person in a monogamous tribe would benefit from quickly falling in love with a sexual partner, whereas a person in a non-monogamous tribe would be harmed by this behavioral tendency.

We find this potential polymorphic shift to be fascinating, as many people are having sex in a manner that would trigger this system to say: "Aha! I am in a non-monogamous tribe. Better not get overly attached to anyone in particular." and yet many of those same people intellectually expect to settle down into a long-term, monogamous relationship and be happy with it. This dynamic—plus a wealth of other factors—may be contributing to a rise in open non-monogamy in developed Western countries (especially large cities).

NON-MONOGAMY

Many relationship contracts allow one or all partners to enter into additional romantic and/or sexual relationships. Relationships with such permissions participate in the non-monogamy market.

To a certain extent, non-monogamy is becoming normalized within mainstream society. Already, 15% of married couples allow for extramarital sex—though wording like "extramarital sex" implies that the reason people open their relationships is motivated by a desire for "just sex" with others, which is rarely true.

In fact, of that 15% of couples who permit extramarital sex in their relationships, only 24% of men and 22% of women have engaged in extramarital sex during the prior year. Moreover, STD rates among non-monogamous couples have been shown to be no higher than those in the monogamous population. Allowing extramarital sex within a relationship contract does not mean that people are actually constantly having it. The shocking reality is that rates of extramarital sex in non-monogamous relationships are only slightly higher than those in monogamous relationships without these terms, in which partners merely cheat (22% of men and 15% of women).

If non-monogamy doesn't lead to abundant extramarital sex, why do partners opt for it? Aside from the various contractual benefits of non-monogamy that we cover elsewhere in this book, polls show that non-monogamy is often motivated by a desire to spend time with people who have different hobbies and personalities in an intimate context.

Note from The Research:
- In our own study, we found only 66% of females and 69% of males had never been in a non-monogamous relationship. 16% of females and 18% of males were currently in a non-monogamous relationship, and an additional 6% of both males and females preferred non-monogamous relationships but were not currently in one.

Among millennials, favoritism of non-monogamy is even more extreme, with only 51% reporting that their ideal relationship would be monogamous and 20%-25% having tried a non-monogamous relationship in the past. For context, this is roughly equal to the proportion of people who have owned a pet.

That said, studies measuring rates of non-monogamy may be understating the popularity of non-monogamous relationships. Many in the non-monogamous community do not have a primary partner (one they value above others). This means they may not be captured in relationship survey data because, by not having a primary partner, common social conventions may not classify them as having any relationship at all.

This does not mean that a huge portion of the population is regularly having threesomes. Statistically speaking, the most common relationship structure in the polyamorous community is a "V" (in which one partner engages with two partners who are not romantically/sexually engaging with each other) and not, as is commonly assumed, a triad (in which a relationship has three participants and all members engage with each other).

Those unfamiliar with the non-monogamous community may read the above statements and think, "Nice! Relationships and sex without rules are being normalized—I want to try that." Listen, people: Don't open the airlock of a spacecraft looking for oxygen. The world of non-monogamy—including communities who claim to practice "relationship anarchy"—is plagued by more draconian rules than a Victorian dinner party. These rules spread like a disease through polycules (a spiderweb of intertwined relationships), allowing new and increasingly complex rulesets to quickly metastasize.

These rulesets play a crucial role in effectively managing the emotional states of multiple partners, but often are created assuming a liberal worldview among participants and can sometimes be exclusionary to individuals with a more conservative mind set.

While these rulesets make it very difficult for those with more extreme conservative inclinations to effectively participate within the poly community (particularly those inclinations tied to sex adjacent concepts like gender roles, consent, LGBTQ issues, etc.), these very rulesets appear to play a key role in the success of this community when contrasted against past attempts at normalizing non-monogamy in Western Culture. Specifically, these rulesets encourage people to develop effective methods for managing emotional and sexual interactions, which spread faster than our culture would normally allow—at the cost of picking up random political artifacts along the way.

Some hackles may be raised at the realization that we are discussing all forms of non-monogamy as though they can be roughly grouped within the poly community. Many identifying as polyamorous would point out that their approach to relationships is uniquely distinct from the approach taken by other non-monogamous people, such as swingers, and would furthermore highlight the significant differences between open and poly relationships.

We group all non-monogamous communities together because it is difficult to socialize as any sort of non-monogamous individual in an English-speaking metroplex for more than a few years without becoming entangled in polyculture (assuming one is under 40). Polyamory is just too prevalent these days to avoid. Those who realistically plan to have a sustained open relationship will be engaging with the larger polyverse.

Why is Non-Monogamy Not the Norm?

Statistically speaking, individuals in polyamorous relationships report higher relationship satisfaction rates than their monogamous counterparts (non-monogamous relationships also do not appear to have negative effects on children who grow up with their parents in them—but the research is pretty weak at the moment). That said, non-monogamy carries some huge drawbacks.

Jealousy looms high on this list and is hardly unjustified as within the world of non-monogamy; people often *do* lose their partners to paramours. Sharing a partner with other people requires a pretty high level of security with oneself and one's partner in the best of situations, and just like any relationship, you can't pretend like taking risks will always work out in the best interest of everyone involved.

As mentioned earlier, not all people appear to exhibit the same levels of jealousy when faced with the same stimuli (in the same way, two people will have different arousal reactions to the same image). It is likely that a portion of the population is too jealous in nature to experiment with non-monogamy.

That is not to say that people in polyamorous relationships don't experience fear and jealousy. A fear of being replaced is normal. The fact that many monogamous people secretly experience some discomfort when they can't engage in a relationship with an additional partner is not an indictment of monogamy. The fact that many poly people have some fear of their partner leaving them—and that this fear causes jealousy—is not an attack on poly lifestyles.

Time constraints are far more of a problem for non-monogamy, in our view, than the emotional pain experienced as a product of jealousy. Maintaining relationships with multiple partners simply takes far too much time. The maintenance of multiple sexual and/or romantic relationships is even worse than having friends as a time sink because romantic and sexual connections with others compromise your ability to think objectively and thus pragmatically deploy your time as a resource.

Consider how much of your time and effort casual dating consumes. Now, consider how much of your time and effort a long-term relationship takes up. Now, think about how much free time you would have if you did both at the same time. Also, keep in mind that managing two partners requires managing *three* and not just two relationships: You must manage each partner's relationship to you as well as each partner's relationship with each other (depending on the type of polyamory you are practicing). This VASTLY increases the emotional effort and time that must be spent to maintain these relationships in a stable context.

This time sink issue can be mitigated by joining pre-existing polycules featuring other partners who take it upon themselves to expend the lion's share of the temporal and emotional effort required to manage and maintain the complicated relationship so you don't have to. That said, attempting to save time by shirking relationship maintenance duties and acting as a free rider is hardly an ideal solution and will put you in a vulnerable position.

Though you might be tempted to attempt just dipping your toes in non-monogamous markets in an effort to save time, you cannot really half-ass participation in non-monogamous communities and gain their full benefits. While it is true that poly individuals show more relationship satisfaction than strictly monogamous individuals, poly individuals are not the only non-monogamous folks out there. People who identify as swingers show no improved relationship satisfaction, and people in open relationships show lower relationship satisfaction rates than strictly monogamous individuals. Just technically having an open relationship is not, apparently, a viable solution. **While poly relationships are statistically better than their monogamous counterparts (if you judge "better" by relationship satisfaction), open relationships score the lowest on satisfaction of any relationship type.**

Another drawback: Participating in non-monogamous communities, which sometimes by proxy leads to association with other kink-friendly communities, can have some negative social effects among those who *also* mix, either professionally or personally, in conservative communities. Association with a non-monogamous lifestyle or kink communities could easily kill a promotion or ruin odds of getting elected. For many with "larger" goals in life, this is reason enough to stick with monogamy and a less thrilling intimate life. One recent study that took its participants from Croatia, Italy, and Portugal found that consensually non-monogamous individuals were seen as less loving, less compassionate, and more remorseful than both heterosexual and monogamous same-sex couples.

Non-monogamy does not benefit each gender equally—or at least not in the same ways. While it is true that studies have shown that for men, sexual fulfillment in one relationship will spill over to other relationships they have (e.g., being sexually satisfied with a secondary partner increases sexual satisfaction with a primary partner), studies have also shown that the opposite effect is observed in women (the more sexually fulfilled women are by a secondary, the less they are by their primary partner). It is unwise to ignore research when it is inconvenient, and yet we have seen the first study quoted profusely in poly communities who conveniently leave out the second finding—*despite it being found through the same methods and by the same team*. It would be more prudent to accept the reality that, on the aggregate, there are certain ways a poly relationship can lower the quality of a primary relationship (assuming one is in a relationship that has a primary or a "hierarchy of importance" among partners; this is hardly a universal arrangement).

Roadblocks hampering the growth of polyamory are a shame, as polyamory, when executed efficiently, really could lead to massive cost of living reductions and time efficiency gains. Alas, the sourcing and vetting costs for both men and women are just too high to be worth overcoming the associated social stigmas in most geographic regions.

Note from the Research:
- Are people born non-monogamous? This is a question we explore in *The Pragmatist's Guide to Sexuality*. Our current answer: Probably not. Instead, we suspect polyamory is a form of behavioral polymorphism brought on by environmental conditions—at least in females. As previously mentioned: When a female chooses to have sex with more than a handful of partners, her brain downregulates oxytocin production during sex and upregulates testosterone production in general, increasing sexual appetite and lowering the pair-bonding hormones released during sex (we do not know of any changes in male neurophysiology tied to a promiscuous lifestyle, so it is difficult for us to theorize what causes a mono

or poly preference in males). Our brains may have evolved this mechanism to use the number of sexual partners we have to decide what type of culture we live in and switch from a monogamy-optimized state to a poly-optimized state based on experience. We are unsure if there is a mechanism for turning this switch back. Anecdotally, the answer would be "yes" in that we know people who have gone in that direction.

Thinking about Joining the Poly Community?

Are you thinking about building your relationship within the polyamorous community? We strongly encourage you to be intentional about how you go about doing it.

Ensure you understand the nature of your local polyculture. The sad reality is that even if you are inclined to non-monogamy, the culture in your local area may not be conducive to your goals or needs. The non-monogamy community is not a monolith. Even if some geographic iterations of it might suit you, others may not (the community in San Francisco may work great with what you are looking for while the one in Hangzhou may not).

Membership in a non-monogamous relationship in no way reduces the need for a relationship contract, though it does sometimes delay the creation of one. Just as people frequently forget to ask questions like, "Do you want kids?" and "How will raising kids work, logistically?" in the early stages of a monogamous relationship, many in poly relationships also have blind spots and neglect to broach potentially-deal-breaking subjects until it is too late. A choice to enter poly relationships does not mean life will penalize you any less for waiting to ask important-but-difficult questions until a relationship gets serious.

If you are in the poly community, we strongly encourage you to create a list of relationship goals you want to achieve in the next two decades and that you review these goals with your partners—along with the logistics that surround them. Even if poly works for you now, the long-term dynamics you desire may not be compatible with that sought by other community members in your area.

New Relationship Energy

New relationship energy is that feeling you get early in a relationship with someone you think you might really like. It can easily be as intense and salient as an emotion like love, and it is one of the driving motivators for a portion of the poly community.[7]

New relationship energy is highly addictive. Research at Stanford has shown that new relationship energy has the same effect on a person's brain as pain killers, like highly addictive codeine, and activates very similar pathways. It also appears a portion of the population likely is highly

---

[7] We suspect a key factor in new relationship energy involves not yet having a complete picture of the person inducing it or how they think about you. These two mysteries dissolve in longer-term relationships. This would explain why new relationship energy seems to last longer in long-distance relationships and cyber relationships.

susceptible to new relationship energy addictions (in the same way someone can have a susceptibility to becoming an alcoholic).

Your comfort with the addictive nature of new relationship energy comes down to a question of whether or not you would be against a drug with no negative physiological effects, but that caused people to lose years of their life to an obsession with it.

People need to be aware of the risks before getting involved with a community peppered with enabling pockets that hand new relationship energy out like candy. Some sub-groups of the non-monogamous community seem hesitant to tell members they have a problem because the complicity of these new members is necessary in order for the existing community to access the drug through relationships with new entrants. That said, many groups in the poly community do have cultural norms in place to get individuals developing new relationship energy addictions the help they need.

If you have an addictive personality or suspect you may be susceptible to a new relationship energy addiction, we recommend caution and thorough vetting before entering a poly community sub-group that sees new relationship energy, the behavioral equivalent of codeine, as an unequivocal good. This is only necessary if you believe that addictive behavioral patterns without negative physiological effects are something worth avoiding.

What Monogamous People Should Learn from Poly Culture

Because polyculture must develop solutions to problems that are not as common in a monogamous society, and because the spread of cultural ideas is much more virulent within poly communities due to the web-like nature of polycules, there are many interesting takeaways that a monogamous person can gain through interactions with polyculture.

Consider how polyamorous people cognitively reframe the stories they tell themselves about their experiences in order to produce more productive emotional reactions. This is most commonly seen in the way some poly people address their feelings of jealousy. Jealousy need not be contextualized as a holistically negative emotion.

When feeling jealous about someone who has taken a husband/wife/boyfriend/girlfriend/whatever to a restaurant/event/movie, etc., search for the root of that jealousy. Does the jealousy…
- Stem from relationship insecurity? Then work to improve the relationship.
- Stem from fears the other person is better? Use the jealousy as fuel for self-improvement.
- Stem from fear of missing out because the activity sounds fun? Use the jealousy as motivation to get out and do things more proactively with your partner.

In monogamous societies, we normalize complacency and stagnation in relationships. Is it really so bad to have an active motivation to improve our relationships, improve ourselves, and do all the things we really want to do with our partners while we have the chance?

Those active in poly communities often quote the widely read polyamory writer Franklin Veaux, stating: "Just because I'm hurt doesn't mean that anyone's done something wrong." This particular lesson is critical when dealing with the more complex and mercurial interactions of polycules. This nugget of wisdom is also relevant in monogamous relationships, especially in a day and age in which we seem to have come to believe that never feeling hurt is a basic human right.

The statement: "Just because I'm hurt doesn't mean that anyone's done something wrong" can be just as critical in a monogamous relationship as it is within a poly relationship—especially when it comes to creating an environment that encourages open communication. It can hurt if a partner says "yes" when asked whether they find a co-worker attractive, but blaming or somehow punishing the partner for that hurt (given the fact that humans cannot control who they find attractive) discourages future open communication.

Poly culture has, out of necessity, developed more nuanced terminology dictating how relationship contracts work that clearly differentiates between boundaries and rules. If a clause in a relationship contract you propose relates to **your own body and property**, it is a **boundary**. If a clause relates to **your partner's body or property**, it is a **rule**. Let's go over some examples to get a better grasp of this distinction:
    Rule: "Partner A cannot smoke"

> Boundary: "If Partner A's breath smells like cigarette smoke, they do not have permission to kiss Partner B."

Boundaries are encouraged in polyamorous communities, while rules are not considered to be acceptable. Often people new to poly relationships miss this cultural norm and establish rules that they claim to be boundaries.

For example, Taylor may claim to have presented a boundary that requires Terry to not fall in love with a third partner (asserting that additional liaisons can only be about sex); however, this is actually a rule. To be fair, emotions are out of one's control, and thus this commonly made demand is nonsensical at face value.

Finally, polyamorous relationships can help to augment appreciation of any one partner. Sharing a partner with someone else facilitates discussion of all the wonderful, colorful things about that shared partner that can shed positive aspects of this partner in a new and deeper light. Wouldn't it feel great to gush about a partner to someone whose eyes sparkle in return rather than glazing over? Through an appreciation of this, monogamous couples may benefit from interacting with people who admire their partners and attempt to see their partners through the admirers' eyes.

Compersion

While the poly community has developed a number of novel concepts from which any relationship can benefit, it has produced its fair share of duds as well. The most toxic of these involves a focus on extracting positive emotions through compersion. Compersion—the happiness you feel from seeing your partner happy—seems innocent enough. Essentially it is the joy your mirror neurons create at the thought of joy in another person—especially a person you care about. The poly community uses this concept to flip around feelings of jealousy tied to a partner being happy with someone else. While it serves that function well enough, its normalization has had incredibly negative systems-level effects, causing people who are unhappy or struggling in other ways to be lowered in value within the non-monogamous community even more than they otherwise might be.

The corrupting influences of glorifying compersion indulgence leads to "rich get richer" scenarios in which the happiest, most pleasure-inducing, and expressing individuals get all the attention. This triggers a snowball effect for the emotionally impoverished, in which their emotional poverty makes them less useful to the rest of the community, further worsening their poor emotional states.

One of the core values monogamous relationships claim to offer is to have someone who will be there for you in good times and bad. Whether or not monogamous relationships live up to their fulfillment of this promise is debatable. Anecdotally, we have observed that poly communities that tout the concept of compersion with uncommon virulence are uniquely unable to serve this function, quarantining the community's Debbie Downers more during trying times (such as a depressive episode). Members who do not have a primary partner seem to be uniquely vulnerable to functional banishment when these members fall on emotional hard times.

We are not saying depressed people are immediately nudged out of polyamorous communities, but they do appear to find themselves discarded by some poly communities more quickly than they would have been from monogamous relationships (though the lack of initiative and general malaise that plagues many forms of depression may contribute to this, as poly community participation requires an immense amount of energy and personal initiative).

This only happens in *some* poly communities. Others have developed cultural norms that protect members who go through periods of depression. It is only natural for someone to spend more time around partners who make them feel good as opposed to those who make them feel bad, when given a choice—even if it is only a subconscious decision. The only way to counter this is with active social norms within the community dedicated to never leaving members behind. When you join a polycule, look for evidence as to how they have treated partners during hard times in the past for evidence of how they will treat you.

We may be highlighting our bias here. As you know by now, we believe pleasant and unpleasant emotions to be equally negative artifacts of human evolution. We do not believe people should enter and maintain relationships merely to maximize a certain emotional set to the exclusion of others. Thus, we are somewhat poisoned against the idea that the good feelings you get from a partner are differentially valuable and loath to condone compersion, as it is often contextualized an extension of that mindset. The fact that a partner being sad will make you sad is a good thing, whether or not you are non-monogamous, as it motivates you to improve their mood—and with it, their efficiency. It is difficult to resist the urge to shift attention to a partner who is more fun to be around *when doing so is an option*, hence community social norms and policing are needed to temper this temptation.

The Myth of Our Poly or Monogamous Past

A tedious bunch of pseudo-academics are under the impression that if they can argue humans used to be a certain way and are biologically compelled to be that way, then there is a moral mandate to go back to acting that way. Every few years, one of these moralizing hooligans will release a book in which they commit vulgar and obscene acts with data sets to argue that humans are either naturally poly or naturally monogamous.

Any honest look at cross-cultural anthropology and the data at hand makes it fairly obvious that, while early human tribes leveraged a variety of different relationship styles and social structures, the most common structure was violent, patriarchal, and polygynous[8] (involving one

---

[8] About a quarter of *The Pragmatist's Guide to Sexuality* is dedicated to using historic data, comparative physiology, genetic data, and kinks (otherwise unexplainable desires like getting aroused by seeing someone transform or being immobilized that cannot be

man with many wives and *not* polyamory *or* monogamy). This historical norm does not give us permission to act that way within our own context.

There is also evidence suggesting that our ancestors commonly practiced systematic infanticide, and humans today still experience impulses tied to that practice. We review this evidence and its implications in excruciating detail in *The Pragmatist's Guide to Sexuality*—and yet we are hardly about to call for a good old-fashioned baby stomp every time a single mother remarries.

Why are most major countries monogamous today? The data yields a very simple answer: Monogamous societies have lower rates of almost every major social ailment when contrasted with polygynous ones, including lower rates of rape, murder, assault, robbery, fraud, spousal abuse, and prostitution. This is presumably due to the high number of single men in polygynous societies—we call this "the free radical problem"—but the data doesn't 100% match up.[9]

Monogamous cultures simply outcompeted their polygynous counterparts once human social groups reached certain population levels, even though monogamy wasn't necessarily our "natural" state. The

---

accounted for by socialization, but which vestigially appear in large chunks of the population cross culturally and thus were likely selected for in our ancestors) to attempt to ferret out a clear picture of early human social structures, mating displays, and marriage types.

[9] Again, this discussed in detail in *The Pragmatist's Guide to Sexuality*, but we also heartily recommend referring to a 2009 study titled: *The puzzle of monogamous marriage*.

mere fact that monogamous cultures appear to produce more stable societies does not set a moral mandate for monogamy, nor does it mean that monogamy is more efficient than polyamory. While the occasional description of a tribe or blip in a history book mentions social practices sharing traits of what our culture calls polyamory or "ethical non-monogamy," such groups don't provide large enough data sets to tell us how polyamorous-like models affect the rates of various social ailments. To put it simply, we lack data on how polyamory would play out at a societal level because no modern culture has practiced it at a societal level.

Even were we to hold proof that monogamy yields a more efficient society than polyamory, such knowledge would hardly grant us carte blanche to mandate it. A society in which non-contributing elderly are euthanized could also be argued to be "more efficient," but that doesn't mean we should introduce such policies.

To take another example: Suppose we could show that humans evolved to be prejudiced against outsiders. Suppose we could show that human societies that were xenophobic had fewer social ailments and spread faster. Would any of that mean we should embrace xenophobia within our current culture? Of course not. This whole argument about what is the "natural human state" is just silly.

Neither polyamory nor monogamy is "natural" and we don't have the data to say which is more efficient on a societal level . . . but even if one were "natural" and even if we did have the data to show one was more efficient, such data would not represent a moral mandate to adhere to it. Were we to build our society to be as "natural" as possible, the result would be horrifying. Were we to build our society to be as "efficient" as possible, the result would be horrifying.

The perfect society is not hidden beneath the ocean, practiced by a remote tribe in a dense jungle, or detailed in a leather-bound, dust-coasted tome—it lies bare before us, clearly visible from the Mount Nebo of our minds' eyes. Those looking to build the perfect society and discover the "correct way" to be a human must look to the future and not the past. The perfect society is something we will have to build ourselves.

HOW TO TRAIN YOUR PARTNER

People say partners should not expect to change the people they marry. While we agree that some traits cannot be changed and that it's bonkers to marry a poor match out of love and with the hope they can be fixed later, we also believe that training a partner to permanently transform themselves in a positive way is neither impossible nor difficult.

The notion that a partner—or any person—cannot be trained is absurd. We all see individuals transformed by those with whom they choose to associate. This is how people change when they "fall in with a bad crowd." By interacting in specific ways (either intentionally or unintentionally), people can exert immense control over their peers' personalities, outlooks, behaviors, values, and habits.

Like it or not, we will be transformed by those with whom we spend the most time. As most people spend the most time with their long-term partners, these partners are going to have a powerful impact on who we become.

Suppose Finley thoughtlessly brings cookies to Yael after every fight because Finley knows Yael likes cookies. While this mindless behavior appears sweet on the surface, it will subconsciously train Yael to initiate more fights, having been subtly "trained" by Finley that fights lead to cookies. This subconscious training is common, whether the inadvertent reward for bad behavior manifests as flowers, make-up sex, or even private time after a fight for someone who is otherwise granted very little solitude. While thinking through the long-term consequences of behaviors like this may appear cold and unromantic, it is patently worth sacrificing this societal cliché of romance if it is in the best interest of a relationship. Failure to think through the manner in which interactions with a partner subtly train them does not change the reality that interactions train people.

We would go so far as to say that the most critical skill ensuring a happy and productive long-term relationship—after an ability to recognize and end bad pairings—involves conscious, intentional partner training. A laissez-faire attitude toward training a partner is like a laissez-faire attitude toward training a pet dog. Not housebreaking a dog and letting it pepper a home with steaming turds is neither an act of kindness towards the dog nor an expression of love.

Marry Someone Who Will Work to Make You Better

While you may or may not spend the rest of your life with the person you marry, you will have no choice but to spend the rest of your life as the person into whom your partner transforms you. There is no greater tool for self-improvement than a long-term partner with a vision for your potential that aligns with your own.

A partner that is in all other ways perfect is probably still worth leaving if the vision they have for you significantly differs from your own vision of your ideal self—or even worse—if this partner loves you for who you are. There is nothing more terrifying in a relationship than the words, "I love you just the way you are—flaws and all." Find someone who loves you for your potential while accepting your flaws.

Regard "self-love" movements with caution. Why would we ever want to learn to love ourselves as we are? If we must sit around all day celebrating ourselves, we should at least learn to love ourselves for the improvements we have made and are making instead of just who we happen to be.

It is not difficult to find someone with the same vision of your potential and who also conveniently agrees with *your* vision for *their* potential. The traits we don't like in ourselves are almost always the same traits a partner would happily fight to address, such as laziness, negativity, lack of emotional control, cruelty, or lack of self-control. As long as a partner wants to improve themselves, finding alignment in visions for each other is really not that hard, even when moderately unusual goals are in play.

Once committed partners have agreed on an aligned vision for each other, the training may commence. Simply remember to always react positively or at least neutrally when a partner attempts to train you. While your partner will often be asking you to do challenging things (that make you want to snap at them), the last thing you want to do is train your partner *not* to train you. If you react negatively to your partner's attempts to improve you, you are punishing them for behavior that *should* be rewarded and ultimately discouraging them from continuing important work.

Partner Training Tips

Training people is remarkably easy: Withhold positive stimuli when they do something undesired and bestow positive emotional stimuli when they do something desirable.

> Bad Thing => No Praise or Attention + Disappointment
> Good Thing => Praise and Attention + Pride

To create rewards and punishments when training someone, simply express pride or disappointment. That is it—though it helps to use more colorful and varying verbiage. If a person loves or respects someone, simple words from that person can raise their spirits to the moon or dash their emotional states to the dirt (and a relationship devoid of respect has already failed; terminate it and try again).

Positive emotional stimuli are not relegated to compliments and the like. Any attention given to a target can be a source of positive emotional stimuli. When a partner shares something they are proud of, taking the time to explore it and engage with them will train them to put effort into that work in the future, whereas ignoring them trains them to invest less time in the activity. This is often more of an issue with accidental negative training, such as consoling someone (thereby giving them attention) when they cry, which makes emotional composure more difficult for those who crave attention in the future.

Those who resort to anger or gifts for punishments and rewards will have to continually increase the magnitude of their anger and gifts to elicit the same response. The shouting tantrums will have to escalate in order to land the same impact. The gifts will have to get more expensive in order to yield the same delight. We have all seen relationships destroyed by individuals who attempt to use anger or gifts to guide their partners' behavior.

Getting sad and angry for a day or even an hour in response to something a partner did is not training and not effective because a good partner will not reward such demonstrated lack of emotional control with a pleasant response, lest they encourage more of it. In other words, regular loss of emotional composure merely trains a partner to ignore these outbursts. An intentionally implemented negative stimuli should never take more than one minute to express—any negative emotional display that lasts longer is simply a failure at emotional control.

A simple and calmly delivered verbal affirmation or condemnation is the only reliable method of punishment or reward in the long term. This is also a better method because demonstrating emotional control increases respect, and increased respect makes words carry more weight over time.

Attempts to train partners to change in a way that only yields one-sided benefit lowers the effectiveness of all other training (at least if such attempts to do so leverage negative stimuli). Criticizing a partner for something that is self-serving—something that patently does not align with their goals for themselves—signals to the partner that they should ignore you. This takes the bite out of any expression of disappointment in them in the future, which in turn renders all training more difficult. When trying to train people in a self-serving direction, stick only to positive stimuli and reward pathways.

Partners must be extremely explicit about (1) the behavior they are trying to change, and (2) what the partner being trained could and should have done instead. Punishing a partner without making it clear why they earned said disappointment will teach them to expect punishment without reason and reduces the emotional impact of any disappointment or lack of affection granted in the future. Chances are that well over 50% of the time, partners have no idea what they did to elicit the statement: "You *know* what you did." Such socially stunted statements only breed disrespect and distrust.

When To Begin Training

Training begins with the very first interaction. We have never seen someone successfully start training a partner from any point in a relationship other than day one, so we do not know whether it is possible. Switching a relationship devoid of intentional training to a relationship with intentional training may require a communal flux period in which all partners are removed from their normal routine and settings and able to explore new habits (see our first book, *The Pragmatist's Guide to Life*, for more info on this).

Not only should training, in general, begin as soon as a relationship starts, but training out a negative behavior pattern should occur the very first time that pattern is observed. This can often be difficult, as we are less secure in our relationships early on and thus scared to set boundaries but is nevertheless critical.

For example, at one point early in their relationship, Simone was tight on time and hung up on Malcolm in the middle of an unpleasant conversation. Malcolm made it clear that this behavior was not acceptable from anyone who wanted a relationship with him and talked through other ways Simone could have handled the situation with him, such as explaining why she had to rush off and setting a time to finish the conversation later in the day before hanging up—while also explaining why a behavior like that was bad for the relationship (because it allows one partner to unilaterally shut down unpleasant conversations and disagreements, lowering the couple's ability to overcome meaningful challenges and problems). Annihilating negative interaction types early in a relationship spares partners from developing poor behavior patterns. Furthermore, the oxytocin released in the early phases of love makes it easier to rewrite even deeply ingrained behavior patterns.

Dealing With An Ex's Training

Expect to find—and need to correct in new partners—negative behavior patterns trained into people by former partners, friends, and family.

A problem endemic in modern human casual dating and sex markets is that many males will do whatever young women want in order to date and/or have sex with them because young women are in such high demand.[10] A guy in high school who has an attractive girlfriend willing to have sex with him regularly is not going to risk losing an immensely valuable source of personal validation in order to punish her for suboptimal behavior patterns.

This toxic dynamic does not necessarily represent something intrinsic to the male or female condition. It just happens to be that the sex market in western societies' high schools grants women gatekeeping powers, as society rewards young men for being promiscuous while shaming promiscuous young women. This dynamic hurts both men and women by developing suboptimal behavior patterns in which men pamper women who lose emotional control instead of punishing emotionally manipulative behavior and removing it from their female peers' behavioral vocabulary. If a hot female sophomore wants something and starts crying or complaining, a boyfriend who does not want to lose access to sex with her will find a way to give her what she wants or attempt to comfort her, thus subconsciously training this girl that whining is a good way to get a partner to do what she wants.

---

[10] Malcolm voted to remove this discussion, referring to it as sexist, reductionist, and probably wrong, but was overruled by me (Simone). Fully correct or not, the dynamic presented holds a kernel of truth that may help people to consider some elements of dating in a new light.

Conversely, women of this age, being sexual gatekeepers and living in a society that constantly slut shames them often accidentally and subconsciously train their boyfriends to see sex as both a reward and a woman's core value in a relationship. Men with past partners who allowed this relationship dynamic to occur can become blind to things women bring to the table other than their sexuality. In adulthood, most of this training gets corrected in public, but scars of its effects linger.

The damaging effects do not end there. Because of this same dynamic, men who do not succeed in the sexual / dating market as teenagers often come to associate their number of sexual partners with their sense of self-worth as adults. This might lead men to contextualize women as tools for personal validation because that is the role women played in their early adolescence.

Fortunately, this outcome is largely avoidable should a man consciously decide that it is not wise to sleep around in youth or successfully sleep around while young and realize what a trivial and hollow accomplishment it is. An association between sex and validation only seems to take hold in guys who both wanted to sleep around while young—while they were still figuring out their identities—and failed to do so. It is neat that we are granted such a clear view into a guy's past through the way he engages with others: If a guy brags about sleeping with a lot of women, we can almost guarantee he struggled to find someone who would sleep with him in his youth and begun to define is self-worth around the thing he valued due to its apparent inaccessibility to him.

At a societal level, something as innocuous as an unequal sex market for teenagers leads women to be perceived as tools for personal validation that lack emotional control and are inherently emotionally manipulative while men become perceived as sex-crazed cretins. This, in turn, creates a reinforcing cycle, fueled by societal expectations of masculine and feminine behavior. Interestingly, some of these behavior patterns we now see as intrinsically "masculine," such as an insatiable libido, were seen as feminine before people dated around in high school (literature from the Victorian period frames women as the hypersexual gender). This further adds evidence to the theory that a lot of gendered behavior is trained by partners due to the economics of the sex and dating market.

It may be that much of the behavior we call "masculine" and "feminine" is not actually gendered behavior, but the manifestation of training patterns created by an unequal sex market people often enter when young. Moreover, this behavior can be easily trained out of a person in their adult relationships.

We must be extremely unforgiving when addressing behavior patterns—both in ourselves and others—that were taught by past partners. If a person believes that yelling, moping, withholding sex, whining, crying, giving the silent treatment, extended periods of negative emotion (more than half an hour), claiming offense, or losing composure will lead to them to get what they want, a previous partner (or friend, or family member) likely trained these behaviors into this person by giving in to their demands.

None of these behaviors are acceptable. The only way to end these behavior patterns is to not respond to them emotionally. Sit the partner down and ask: "Is this who you really want to be?" Should they respond: "Yes" or argue that they cannot improve themselves, end the interaction and give them time to compose themselves, then ask them again. If this partner still stubbornly refuses to attempt to improve their emotional control or acts as if doing so is an impossible goal, promptly end the relationship. Such behavior will only get worse and will likely balloon after marriage. If a partner wants to improve, develop a plan for improvement, and provide them with simple approaches to take the moment they lose composure in order to help them amend their behavior.

Accidental Training

Accidental training is discussed in greater detail in this book's chapter on abuse. Abuse and accidental training are often integrally linked.

The most common form of accidental training involves not fully appreciating when someone is making a bid for attention through a negative behavior pattern and accidentally granting them that attention in response to said behavior pattern. Granting *any* attention, whether it be neutral, positive, or negative, is a reward that trains people to continue negative behavior.

Suppose a partner makes a hurtful emotional jab. Demonstrating to this partner that their comment succeeded in causing damage yields an emotional reward for the partner and encourages them to use such attacks in the future. Both parties in this exchange are partially to blame; one behaved poorly and the other rewarded the behavior. Suppose Sidney punches a hole in the wall and Skyler makes a great effort to calm Sidney down: This attention may also be reward—enough to lead Sidney to exhibit future violent outbreaks in the future by making such outbursts harder for Sidney to inhibit.

The key to handling a potentially explosive emotional indulgence on the part of a partner is to never *ever* indulge their emotional outbursts with consolation, validation, engagement, or attention. Disengage from the situation entirely—or better yet—engage an emotional partner in a way designed to snuff out the emotion instead of indulging it.

If a partner is steaming with anger, pull up two chairs, express disappointment in their loss of composure, and make it clear they can do better, but nevertheless invite them to sit down if they feel capable and—in a neutral emotional tone—talk through what made them upset, what they plan to do about it, and how those actions will benefit their objectives in life. You might also consider having your partner discuss and work through the problem in the third person (talking about themselves as though they were a removed, neutral third party); this third-person approach has been shown in several studies to help people address heated, personal subjects in a more logical, level-headed fashion.

After addressing the emotionally-triggering issue in a logical fashion, discuss a separate topic with your partner for half an hour or more before returning to the delicate subject (if it must be revisited at all). This enables you to demonstrate to partners that you care and are emotionally engaged, but in a way that trains them to not indulge in an emotion for an extended period of time.

Maintaining a Positive Relationship

Maintaining positive emotions in any relationship is often regarded in dating books as some kind of secret that requires hard work. We suppose positive relationships *are* hard work, just as not being a turd of a human is hard work. *C'est la vie.*

Humans relate to their lives through stories. When we are asked to determine whether we like our lives, we first construct a story about what we have experienced in life, then ask ourselves if we are the type of people who would like living that story. When asked if we like our relationships, we do the same thing: Tell ourselves a story about our relationships and, based on how we have chosen to see ourselves, decide whether that person is happy in this narrative we constructed.

To ensure a partner thinks positively about a relationship is to ensure the narrative they are telling themselves about that relationship fits their ideal narrative. Obviously, this isn't always possible because we do not always know the nuances of these stories—there may be some backstory or subplots of which we have not yet been

informed that powerfully color the narrative. Fortunately, **there are several common elements in the stories people like to tell themselves that can be reliably hijacked:**
1. Belief that one got the better end of the deal
2. Belief that one is in an exciting, special relationship
3. Belief that one is a good person
4. Belief that one is desired by a desirable partner
5. Belief that the relationship moves one closer to one's goals

Signaling That The Partner Got the Better End of the Deal

People want to believe that they are with a partner who is of higher value than themselves. Putting too much effort trying to demonstrate high market value to a partner stinks of insecurity. Conversely, failure to even attempt to appear desirable signals to a partner that they may have chosen a lackluster partner.

The key is to interact with partners in a way that highlights one's best qualities without specifically drawing attention to those qualities. Find opportunities and utilize environments that remind partners what makes you valuable. Bring partners to events that reveal they are in a relationship with someone that others admire and value.

Just don't cite romantic interest from others in an attempt to demonstrate high personal value to a partner (e.g., "That checkout clerk was hitting on me like crazy"). Such behavior is often a sign of low social intelligence. Low social intelligence may be a desirable partner trait to those who like to be able to easily manipulate their partners, but we generally do not celebrate it.

Making the Relationship Feel Exciting and Special

People want to believe that their partner likes being in a relationship with them and likes them as a person. Working this into a partner's internal narrative about the relationship can be a little tricky, as showing too much affection early in a relationship can lead someone to believe that they are with a partner that is lower value than them.

The key to circumventing this problem while still building a strong positive relationship involves **complimenting shared moments rather than complimenting that partner directly**.

Instead of: "Your hair looks beautiful."
Say: "The way the sun is shining off your hair right now is beautiful."

Instead of: "You are a great bowler."
Say: "That moment you got an all-time high score in the bowling alley and everyone applauded was unforgettable."

Instead of: "That was the best sex I ever had."
Say: "I really liked the way you did X; it blew my mind."

Not only does this form of compliment have a very low risk of making a partner think less of the person delivering it, but it makes them think *more* of shared moments, which facilities the creation of a narrative in which the moments associated with the relationship are just slightly more magical and better than other moments (which conveniently happens to be another thing almost everyone wants from a relationship).

Once a relationship becomes well established, it becomes safe to add direct compliments to the mix. Focus on statements designed to make a partner better about themselves. All partners benefit from partners who enjoy positive internal narratives. A higher level of self-respect will lead to more happiness in a partner's life and greater success in their career. There is, however, one exception: Relationships built around the Dominance Lure are compromised when dominant partners become overly affectionate.

Making Partners Feel Like Good People

People want to believe they are good. Partners are more likely to enjoy and want to stay in relationships that make them feel as though they are good people. To create this perception, reinforce narratives that highlight how the relationship has helped to make you a better person. For example, reinforce narratives in which they helped you accomplish something you would not have been able to do on your own, like quit smoking or cut ties with an abusive friend. Through these kinds of stories, the relationship comes to play an important role in the partner's personal narrative of being a good person.

While it is tempting to show a partner how good they are as a person by demonstrating how much you rely on them in daily life, it is unwise to come across as weak and in need of a partner to be strong. While this may be a story that some people want to tell about their relationship, more often than not it is a negative story. Deep down, we all want to believe that our partners can act as a safety net if somehow our lives hurtle out of control, and having a dependent partner breaks that fantasy.

Making Partners Feel Desired (by a Desirable Person)

People want to believe they are sexually desirable, and yet according to some polls, one in seven adults is living in a sexless marriage. As 57% of people living in a sexless marriage report that, aside from sex, they feel they have the ideal partner, improving a partner's narrative around a relationship's sex life can nudge a relationship fairly close to perfection.

As we discuss further in the appendix, the biggest problem in a relationship with a dead bedroom—a sexless relationship—is not the lack of momentary sexual pleasure that comes from a lack of sex, but rather the story it causes people to create. Narratives involving someone not being sexually desirable can be quite psychologically damaging to many, especially for those whose sexuality comprises an important part of their self-identities. Expressing sexual interest in and satisfaction with a partner while focusing on all the magnificent things they do will do much to improve the story they tell about the relationship.

In long-term relationships, compliment a partner's physical appearance at least a few times a day and express wonder at how attractive they are. In short-term relationships, these compliments can be less frequent and more roundabout in their delivery. In both short and long-term relationships, compliments shown through actions or facial expressions are far more valuable than compliments shown through words (i.e., a hungry glance up and down a partner is worth far more than the words: "You look sexy").

The need for sexual validation often becomes greater in long-term relationships as more time passes since partners last received sexual validation from a third party. Without frequent validation and reinforcement, a partner may come to believe that the relationship is being held together by forces totally independent of sexual attraction (e.g., "maybe he is just with me for the kids"). This is not an issue if sexual desirability is not a core part of a partner's core identity, but it is a huge problem if sexual validation *is* a core part of their self-image.

We realize some who buy into the prevailing social narrative are tempted to believe that most sexless relationships are the product of female partners withholding sex. While we couldn't find hard data on this, a cursory look at the communities dedicated to helping people in sexless relationships suggests this isn't true. Statistically speaking, female attractiveness declines with age faster than male attractiveness, males are subject to the Coolidge effect causing frequent interaction with the same partner to yield lower erotic output (though researchers have recently observed a similar affect in females), and studies repeatedly show that male testosterone and sex drive both decrease when they are in love and in long-term relationships. Many more dead bedrooms than one might imagine are comprised of men who are no longer motivated to sleep with their wives.

Reassuring Partners That The Relationship Helps Them Achieve Their Goals

People want to believe their current relationship is moving them toward their long-term goals. To ensure that a partner can tell themselves a story in which this is happening, establish long-term goals with them. Sit them down and have them paint an ideal life. Make joint plans detailing how this ideal life will be achieved and kick off conversations reflecting on all the progress that has been made—thanks to close collaboration and support—since the relationship started.

Focus on important elements of the partner's narrative around which they have insecurities. A partner may want to believe that they are independent, but secretly they are not sure they can make it on their own. These features make up landmines in a relationship that are easy to unintentionally trigger, even through well-meaning behavior. If, for example, a partner is insecure about their independence, the relationship might incur serious damage through a gesture—if however kind—offering support should that partner ever fail, as this signals to them that their worst fears about their lack of self-reliance may be true.

Two great examples of this from Malcolm's life:
1) A woman who broke up with Malcolm because he complimented her intelligence more than her looks. While she was secure in her intelligence, she

had insecurity about her appearance, and this led her to create a narrative in which Malcolm only appreciated her for her intelligence. This, in turn, made her feel ugly and ultimately contributed to the relationship's demise.
2) A woman told him that she felt negative emotions when he called her beautiful. She felt very secure in that she was classically beautiful in an elegant way, but what she really wanted was to be seen as "hot" and "sexy."

The takeaway from these two examples is: Don't ever assume all women want to tell themselves X story, and all men want to tell themselves Y story. Take time to get to know each partner's insecurities to avoid stepping on landmines resulting from treating them as "Generic Female A" and "Generic Male B."

INTERNAL COMMUNICATION

It is unarguable that communication makes up a core pillar of any healthy relationship. Just how central that pillar is may sometimes be exaggerated. We posit that poor communication is often blamed for other types of relationship breakdowns.

Communication problems in a relationship can typically be solved with one simple rule: Put 100% of the onus for bad communication on the communicator and not on the person who was supposed to be listening. The listener cannot know what important information is not being shared and therefore cannot ask for it, and a communicator can always ask for information to be repeated back to them in the listener's own words if there is any doubt in the effective transfer of information.

Many schools of thought about relationships choose to say both partners are at fault when communication breaks down and blame communication for situations in which poor communication is merely a byproduct of a bigger problem.

For example, A partner caught cheating may attempt to deflect responsibility for their infraction by claiming that their cheated-upon partner was not properly meeting their needs. The cheated-upon partner responds by saying they did not know they were not meeting their partner's needs, at which point these older schools of thought blame this relationship breakdown on poor communication.

A sober analysis of this chain of events nevertheless makes it clear that a lack of communication is not to blame for this breakdown. Even if there were better communication, cheating would still have occurred. **Using poor communication as a scapegoat is just a tool for sharing blame in a failed relationship.** In this hypothetical case, the actual cause for the breakdown may have been something like a lack of respect for the cheated upon partner, meaning that having sex with them no longer granted the cheater the validation they craved, hence they sought out an external source of validation to still feel virile or sexy.

There are two reasons we fall back on blaming communication:
- The first is that communication is presumably fixable rather than just an innate breakdown in how partners perceive each other. It is hardly productive for a relationship therapist to tell a couple one needs to learn to see the other in a different light for a relationship to survive.
- The second is that communication, being an act that requires multiple individuals, is always both partners' fault. This distribution of blame makes poor communication easier to accept as a "reason" for relationship problems, especially when the real cause of breakdown involves the personal failure of only one party in the relationship, or something that our society treats as trivial, such as someone's desire to maintain a certain personal narrative.

It helps to share the blame for relationship failure because the type of person who is unilaterally responsible for a relationships failure is more likely to change their behavior and engage in discussion about that behavior if it is pointed out to them in a way that doesn't make them seem like the "bad guy".

We also see many situations in which a lack of communication exists because honest communication would damage the relationship. This is less of a communication issue and more of a core failure in the relationship, in which unpleasant truths are met with punishment. A man may find another woman to be sexy, have a strong compulsion to sleep with her and know that this other woman would reciprocate his advances, but may not communicate this to his wife because this reality would cause the wife to become livid. This is relationship failure caused not by a communication problem, but rather by a poorly designed relationship contract: One that prohibits attraction to other people (not a choice) instead of just infidelity (a choice).

Any relationship contract, implied or negotiated, that forbids an emotion is destined to lead to poor communication. In monogamous relationships, this often falls into the category of forbidding a partner from finding anything else sexually arousing but is not limited to monogamous relationships. In unhealthy polyamorous relationships, these toxic clauses can manifest in contracts that forbid either the emotion of jealousy or the act of falling in love with another person.

Be it expressed within a non-monogamous or monogamous relationship, love is an emotion like any other. It is not something over which we have control, and it is not a magical compass pointing you toward happiness or moral righteousness. It is totally possible to develop love for someone outside a primary relationship or to no longer feel love for a primary partner *even when everything else in a relationship is going perfectly*. Being able to communicate feelings to a partner is critical. Feeling love for someone outside of a relationship or not feeling love for a primary partner is not a sign that the relationship has "failed" and *must* be dissolved. Quite frequently, it is best to *not* act on these feelings, which are often fleeting and poorly correlated with the logical best interests of all those involved.

This is not to say that relationship contract clauses banning emotional indulgence should not exist in a relationship contract. We would go so far as to say that *all* relationship contracts should forbid emotional indulgence. By emotional indulgence, we mean not just feeling an emotion and calmly communicating that you feel it, but also "acting out" an emotion through something like crying, pacing, or raised voices.

We are not arguing that communication is never a problem. It often is.

Genuine breakdowns in communication commonly stem from an assumption among partners that they have the same desires and thought patterns. Love romantic, candlelit dinners? It is easy to assume a partner *must* be aware of this proclivity, but failure to communicate it clearly waives any right to expect such awareness. People are not mind readers.

Communication also fails when a partner assumes they only need to communicate important things once. Sometimes partners are too distracted to fully digest the gravity of a comment, request, or complaint. For example, Frankie may tell Aziz that something Aziz does is bothering her. Aziz may then alter his behavior a bit and, after not hearing about the issue again, assume it to be resolved. Meanwhile, Frankie may still feel the issue has not been resolved and secretly build resentment. It is easy to believe a situation has been resolved if you hear a complaint, alter your behavior, and don't hear the complaint again. In this situation, the majority of the fault in a healthy relationship would lie with Frankie.

Effective Transference of Information

Never assume a partner has properly internalized a concern, need, or comment unless they can eloquently describe that thing back in their own words while showing full attention and making eye contact.

Consider using a standardized format for communicating important information.

A good template for this format is to:
1) Express what this partner needs to know
2) Express how important this point is
3) Ask this partner to repeat what you have communicated in their own words

This process can be made even better when it is conducted through writing, such as email or a shared document. This will create a record of your communication, which removes the onus from the communicator. If a partner claims to have never been told about something, everyone can turn to an unambiguous record to determine what really happened.

This can sound onerous, but given that we use emails and a shared Google doc for just such purposes ourselves, we can vouch for the inconvenience being minimal. People communicate far fewer important things than one might think and many of those things are repeats of topics hashed through before ("When you do X, I feel Y," "I am acting with this long-term plan in mind," "Here's my checklist for a properly cleaned kitchen," etc.).

How do we, Simone and Malcolm, avoid miscommunications? We send all important communications to each other via email, as we use our inboxes for task management and can therefore turn important requests and comments into to-do items. We email important requests and comments to each other several times a day. Most of these emails are related to company operations (in addition to writing these books together, operate a number of small-to-medium-size companies and lecture at colleges and universities), but they may also involve household tasks, shopping needs, weekend planning requests, and comments on issues that worry, fascinate, intrigue, inspire, or bother us. These "official" communications are, as a rule, kicked off with a subject reading: Task: [Request Goes Here]. Whenever an email subject line starts with "Task," the other partner is expected to read the message carefully and regard it as a priority.

Common requests look like:
- Task: Follow up with Julian Holgrove regarding contract signature
- Task: Pick up double A batteries when grocery shopping today
- Task: Ask Clara Handel why she did not hit her numbers this month
- Task: Review and counter approve clean kitchen check list

We have agreed that each partner is obligated to review these requests. If unable to complete them, the partner receiving a request must respond promptly with whatever clarifying questions or additional information might be relevant.

One of the most cardinal of "sins" within our relationship involves one of us allowing ourselves to get annoyed at the other for an uncompleted task that was not sent in this format. We should expect verbal requests and comments to be forgotten if we cannot immediately act on them. Even now I, Malcolm, will sometimes ask Simone why some project has not been done to be countered with the reply: "Did you send it in a task request?" (I forget more than Simone does.)

When we have a more complex discussion, like what the standards are for a clean kitchen or how will we educate our kids, one of us will write a summary of the discussion's key points in a Google doc, then send it to the other for counter review in a task item to ensure we both took away the same core points and are aligned on next steps that should be taken.

Several have told us they are with a partner who would never agree to have their demands written down. This is a giant red flag of an abusive relationship dynamic. There are only two reasons a person would refuse to have a record of communication:
1. They don't value the relationship enough for it to be worth the few minutes it takes to write something down a few times a month.
2. They believe that a written record will disproportionately be used against them, insinuating they subconsciously realize they utilize systematic gaslighting to their advantage.

Gaslighting is a type of very serious abuse in which a person misrepresents previous events or conversations in an attempt to convince their partner that they occurred in a fashion that runs counter to reality.

Just because a partner makes a request does not mean that request must be honored.

For example: One partner may tell the other that they really hate it when the other person puts the toilet paper on the roll flipped under and not over. The other may acknowledge they hear and internalize said position, but then explain why they still hang toilet paper the way they do. The manner in which this disagreement in toilet-paper-hanging-philosophy should ultimately be resolved would depend on the terms of the relationship contract. This is not a breakdown in communication.

Genuine disagreement in preferences or goals is possible, even with perfect communication. Should you reach a point with a partner at which you have communicated a genuine difference in preferences, either implement the conflict resolution clause in your relationship contract or, in more critical situations, amend the contract.

A breakdown of communication—and a serious violation of almost any relationship contract—would involve the person who had decided to not change the way they are handling toilet paper to ignore their partner's request while failing to explain that they are choosing to ignore the request and provide some reasons *why* they are ignoring the request.

On a final note: Communication must occur alongside both self-knowledge *and* emotional regulation. **We strongly advise against entering a relationship that lacks any expectation of emotional regulation—the expectation that both partners will actively attempt to regulate their emotional states.** Not having this expectation gradually erodes even relationships in which everyone is acting with the best of intentions.

As an example of how well-intentioned interaction can become detrimental when there is no expectation of emotional control: A couple has an emotionally heated discussion. After one "says their piece," they ask the other if they have anything to add. The other replies that they are feeling defensive and as such want to shelve the conversation until they calm down. About half an hour later, the individual who shelved the conversation then asks their partner why they are giving them the "silent treatment" and their partner explains they were just trying to respect the boundaries set when it was requested the conversation be shelved.

The toxicity in the above relationship occurred not just because the partners became emotionally heated, but because they went so far as to shelve the conversation in an effort to coddle one of the partners' failures to control their emotional state—an action that both exacerbated their disagreement and trained the individual being coddled to not control their emotions. Failure to normalize an expectation of emotional control can lead even those with good intentions, emotional intelligence, and self-knowledge to fail in their attempts to communicate.

Learning to control your emotional state is easy, assuming you are post-puberty (so your frontal cortex is fully myelinated) and are not drunk. The "muscles" required to do this—the prefrontal cortex's inhibitory pathways—get stronger with practice, and thus emotional control becomes easier with time. Relish opportunities to practice self-control, knowing they will make you stronger.

Ignored Communication

There is almost no behavior more toxic to a relationship than ignoring attempts to communicate.

It should never happen that your partner attempts to communicate with you, and you either shut them down (by closing a door on them) or ignore them. If you do not

have time to talk with a partner who is trying to communicate with you:
1) Clearly explain you don't have time right now
2) Schedule time to talk about the issue

Ignoring communication with a partner hurts them. It emotionally punishes them for attempting to communicate with you about an issue that probably isn't much easier for them to bring up. Ignoring communication stifles future communication. This is doubly bad when conversations are avoided merely because they may be uncomfortable. This avoidance trains partners to never share anything that might cause discomfort and will likely kill the relationship over the long run.

This point is complicated by instances in which one partner does not realize the other is trying to communicate something. Personally, we began to notice that our relationship was stronger when we lived and worked in spaces in which we could hear each other from any room. Even though we knew the other person was probably just too far away to hear when we asked for something and there was no response, it still caused a small impulse of resentment—even though we knew said resentment was entirely illogical. We circumvent this problem by creating a policy whereby we only attempted to communicate with each other in larger areas when we were already making eye contact.

Bids for Attention

A partner may also make a bid for attention, which they intend to act as a subtle form of communication, but which is not recognized as such by the partner. A partner poking you then running into their room, a partner inconspicuously listening to a show loudly near you, or a partner saying to themselves, "Boy, I sure would like to go on a walk," may all be requests for engagement—though emotionally stunted ones.

This form of communication becomes problematic when one partner expects the other to see their bid for engagement as clear, obvious, communication. In a long-term relationship, we recommend training your partner to never attempt this subtle communication by going out of your way to clarify and call out these subtle cues while never rewarding them. But, rewarding your partner when they plainly tell you they desire your attention. Learning to tell your partner you want attention may be embarrassing, but doing so prevents miscommunication in the long run.

Self-Narratives and Communication

People have an internal narrative about who they are, which they attempt to reinforce through the process of validation discussed earlier in the book. One of the key tools we as humans use to reinforce these narratives is attempting to get others to see us through the lens of our own ideal narratives.

This means two important things in the context of relationships:
1) People have often found that certain stories, anecdotes, or lines of conversation are good (or at least they believe they are good) at convincing

others to see them the way they want to see themselves. They often "start" with these lines of conversation when they first meet new people. Prepare to hear your partner's same image reinforcing stories a thousand times if you regularly meet new people in the presence of each other. Expect that these stories eat at your sanity. Your partner's desperate need for validation, the same need most people have, will lower your respect for them.
2) Just as we try to reinforce what we think about ourselves through the way others see us, we try to reinforce the story we want to believe about our relationship by imposing it on the view of others. This becomes a problem when the way each partner sees their relationship is not aligned, and their stories conflict in a social environment. For example, both might be trying to tell a story in which *they* are the ones who "wear the pants in the relationship."

Fortunately, like virtually every potential pitfall in a relationship, these problems can be overcome by intentionality.

List the lines of conversation, stories, and anecdotes that each partner tells often. Discuss why you tell them. Decide if they are achieving their purpose. Finally, throw out the stories that do not achieve their goal while perfecting those which have value while also crafting and practicing new, joint stories you can tell together.

Malcolm and I do this regularly with a focus on crafting stories with a strong, engaging narrative structure.

Specifically, we like them to have a rising "plotline" and increasing steaks followed by a "conflict point," which is then resolved with an unexpected behavior that paints a certain story about us.

For example: In our first date story, Simone builds up the impact of the moment by stressing how inexperienced she was. She creates an expectation of "romance" by describing the fancy restaurant, and subverts the expectation with Malcolm sitting across from her explaining that he was looking for a wife and expected to find her through the pre-vetted pool of Stanford MBA students.

This moment of subversion is both entertaining to the listener and elicits, what are for them, unusual conversation pathways that challenge aspects of what they believe should be normalized behavior patterns while reinforcing the intentionality of our relationship in the eyes of others. It also paints a picture of us as a couple that is willing to break social conventions in the service of expediency. Finally, it finds a way to both drop Simone's chastity and Malcolm's education in a way that is germane to the rising action—these are things that are used by people living on autopilot to judge others and thus, as cringy as they are, still are of utility to signal.

REKINDLING RELATIONSHIPS

How do you keep a relationship "fresh"?

Relationships change over time. Trying to keep a relationship exactly like it was at the beginning is a bit like trying to un-bake cookie dough. Cookie dough tastes great and cookies taste great, but they are not the same thing and you can't reverse the baking process. The emotions you will be able to harvest from a nascent relationship are not the same emotions yielded by mature relationships.

For example: New relationship energy is one of the emotions hardest to recreate in mature relationships. If new relationship energy is critical to your enjoyment of life, we strongly recommend you explore poly relationships instead of resigning yourself to dissatisfaction in a monogamous relationship, unable to extract emotions that a single partner is structurally unable to provide.

While it is true some dynamics and emotions can only be efficiently harvested from nascent relationships, these emotional sets are only preferred by a minority of people. Most prefer the emotional bouquet proffered by thriving, mature relationships. We emphasize the term "thriving," as to be fully enjoyed, a relationship must be better than just "healthy." If your relationship is losing its luster without any explicit conflict or identifiable and extractable necrosis, how can you improve it?

It's easy for a relationship to lose its luster when you feel you've already learned and explored everything about a partner. When you can perfectly predict how a person will respond to any new piece of information and how the flow of any conversation will go, the conversations can begin to feel pointless. There are two solutions to this conundrum.

The first is to ensure that both you and your partner are constantly evolving as people: That you are picking up new information, changing who you are, and adjusting your understanding of the world in response to new information. Malcolm never bores me because he changes his perspective based on new information he collects, meaning if I have the same conversation with him this year that I had with him two years ago, it will likely go in a totally different direction.

Should you find yourself forming a relationship with someone who refuses to update their worldview when presented with conflicting but sound information, or who becomes angry when data does not support their "team's" perspective, enter into that relationship anticipating that said individual is likely going to bore you to tears one day no matter how fiery and passionate they are about the views they hold.

The second is to delve into an aspect of your partner that you are structurally unable to explore in your day-to-day relationship. Luckily, the human brain will process information very differently depending on the medium through which it engages with that information. The iteration of us with which you interact by reading our books would feel nothing like the iteration that manifests through in-person conversations or through instant messaging. This is because you are literally interacting with different parts of a person's brain depending on your method of communication with them. If you make a concerted effort to get to know these other aspects of your partner, you will have the chance to fall in love all over again.

You may even find yourself missing one of your partners' manifestations if you don't use that method of communication much due to the structure of your daily schedule. For example, after having to communicate with each other in letters and journal entries while I was in the UK getting my graduate degree and Malcolm was living in Seoul, we came to appreciate the written-form iteration of each other so much we occasionally plan trysts with those parts of ourselves by scheduling a week apart, during which we can only communicate in writing. We recommend this to anyone who is interested in seeing their partner in a new light.

One of our favorite case studies on this front involves a couple that met and fell in love through online gaming, but eventually physically moved in together and married. They preferred the virtual, written, aspect of each other so much that while they tried at first to live a "normal" married life, they eventually settled into a cadence in which they cohabitated and slept together, but communicated and dated virtually and in writing. This couple presents not a failed relationship, but rather two people mature enough to recognize how to access the parts of each other they loved most and creative enough to operate outside the narrow bounds of vanilla, "ideal" relationships as defined by mainstream media.

Changing the medium of communication isn't the only way to explore a new aspect of your partner. The internal models we cultivate of ourselves—the self-identities that guide our automatic actions—will change in response to our environments. The person someone presents around family is often radically different from the persona they display at work. Engaging with your partner in new environments permits you to meet new iterations of them, whether that means playing an MMORPG with them (an online game like World of Warcraft) or joining them when they go drinking with a friend group with which you don't typically interact.

Don't go overboard with this approach: It may lead to problems if your partner has trouble being who they are in these other social settings when you are around—it could be that a key element of them being someone slightly different involves your absence. Fortunately, there are still two easy paths forward should this be the case.

Try spending a week assuming the identities of characters with different names, backstories, and pre-established dynamics with each other. This can feel silly as hell, but depending on how you approach life, it can also be a pretty fun adventure. Acting out different personas also presents a means by which you can try out radically different relationship dynamics, switching up dominance roles or deciding to be theatrically romantic to an extent that would be comical if tried in a different context.

Should you be too much of a coward for roleplay (don't blame creativity: Studies show people can become more creative when encouraged to make an effort), you might also consider taking on a new activity with a partner—bonus points for activities that are exciting.[11] This far-more-vanilla (but nevertheless enjoyable) tactic enables you to generate novel schema in your lives in which each of you has the opportunity to be someone slightly different and see each other in a fresh light.

[11] For more info on this see *Couples' shared participation in novel and arousing activities and experienced relationship quality* in the Journal of Personality and Social Psychology

ABUSE AS A CONCEPT

The relationship industry uses the concept of abuse to label certain behavioral sets as categorically unacceptable. Abuse is the line that, when crossed, means a relationship has gone from acceptable to unacceptable. We understand the intent with this categorization. The reigning concept of abuse allows for emphasis to be placed on just how unhealthy certain behaviors are and through this emphasis it creates cognitive dissonance in both the abuser and the abused: "I am not abusive, so I won't do X" or "I would not allow myself to be in an abusive relationship, so when my partner does X, that means it is time to leave."

Actions seen as classic abuse include:
- A partner hitting you
- A partner gaslighting you (trying to convince you your memory of events is inaccurate)
- A partner secretly tracking you
- A partner breaking into your email account
- A partner ignoring consent

Without these clear lines, it can be hard to break through the cognitive momentum that holds together a slowly deteriorating relationship. Without this strong distinction, it can be nigh impossible to recognize that a partner whose bad behavior has been slowly escalating has finally reached a breaking point. People say, correctly or incorrectly, that while you can't throw a frog into a pot of boiling water without it hopping out, you can still boil a frog by putting it in a room-temperature pan that you slowly bring to a boil. Along these lines, the concept of abuse with which most of us live acts like a thermometer with a red line on it: We might be sitting in pots with dangerously rising temperatures, but at least we have the red line on the thermometer letting us know when to jump out.

But here's the rub: The temperature at one degree below the red line is negligibly different from the temperature one degree above the red line. It is best to get out of water when the temperature is rising, not after it reaches a boiling point. In this respect, this model of abuse fails, allowing relationships to easily continue to exist in states of hostility just below the red line on the thermometer.

The Pragmatist model of relationships requires neither an external concept of morality nor the concept of abuse to create relationship termination forcing functions. Someone following the Pragmatist model who is genuinely mistreated and put in harm's way by a relationship is more likely to terminate a relationship well before it fits mainstream society's definition of classic abuse.

To a Pragmatist, the concept of abuse is pointless. It applies standards, which may or may not apply to your own personal values and best interests, of what is and is not acceptable in your relationships. A dynamic of near-absolute dominance that mainstream sentiments would categorize as abuse could be a preferred situation for some. Consider 24/7 Total Power Exchange relationships and Taken in Hand relationships, both of which feature long-term consensual non-consent agreements (i.e., one partner prefers a relationship in which they do not have to give consent to the other within certain predetermined boundaries)—some actively seek out such relationship dynamics. At the same time, dynamics that mainstream sentiments deem to be harmless or even laudable, such as monogamy or sharing a bank account, could feel abusive to some.

Some even categorize anything that is "extremely unequal economically" as abusive. Within this definition, having one partner make the majority of a family's financial decisions (investments, taxes, etc.) is considered abusive—and yet this dynamic exists within almost any sane construction of a relationship as an effort-saving measure.

Traditional models of abuse might even classify a relationship in which one partner takes the lead in major strategic decisions (such as where the partners live) as abusive. We would argue the opposite: That most relationships in which this doesn't happen are hugely suboptimal, representing a lack of self-knowledge and humility among their participants. After all, among any two individuals, one will be better at strategic, long-term decision making related to certain domains. Insisting on making these decisions equal is either a sign that the individual worse at this type of decision making is unable to admit their inferiority on the subject or that they do not trust their partner to take them into account and source their feedback when making strategic decisions.

By freeing yourself from using traditional conceptions of abuse as a forcing function, you can become better equipped to predict classically abusive behavior, lower the probability of it, and increase the quality of your relationships as a whole.

Proto-Abuse vs. Abuse

When you conceptualize abuse as a red line, it becomes harder to recognize behaviors that lead up to this abuse, which, if recognized early enough, could be halted, thereby lowering the probability that classically abusive situations will arise in the first place. In other words, abuse exists on a spectrum of behaviors, and optimal relationships feature low overall levels of these behaviors. To highlight behavior that can easily turn into "classic" abuse (causing physical harm, gaslighting, crossing personal boundaries related to privacy, becoming unproductively controlling, etc.), we will discuss "proto-abuse" (or as Malcolm prefers to call it: "general dickishness").

Proto-abusive behavior is generally classified by society as normal and acceptable within relationships. For example, while a person locking themselves in their room during an argument or snapping at a partner and raising their voice after a long day of work may not meet any classical definition of abuse, it would fall squarely within the category of proto-abusive behavior that can evolve into classic abuse through a number of channels. Proto-abusive behavior lowers the quality of a relationship *even when* it does not evolve into classic abuse.

Why is it important to recognize proto-abusive behavior, even at its lowest levels of output? Early recognition of proto-abuse can help you spot bad relationships earlier.

Failure to recognize low-level proto-abusive behavior may ultimately cause it to be reinforced.

When recognized and dealt with promptly and intentionally, proto-abusive behavior can be eliminated from a relationship—similar to how dermatologists remove pre-cancerous cells from your skin (and like a dermatologist removing pre-cancerous cells, this is not fool-proof—you can always miss things about a person, but a regular checkup never hurts). If you recognize a partner talking to you with a raised, emotional voice, calmly sit your partner down and discuss it the first time it happens, negatively reinforcing the behavior and working to ensure that not only does it not escalate while decreasing the likelihood that your partner emotionally raises their voice at you again.

We are not arguing that abuse is not as bad as people make it out to be or that abuse can be systematically prevented in all instances. We merely argue that certain behaviors are correlated with relationships that become classically abusive. Learning to recognize and deal with those behaviors may help to prevent a situation from escalating to abuse as traditionally defined. Classic abuse aside, proto-abusive behaviors are toxic and ought to be addressed when possible.

More in the Appendix
You will notice we try to avoid the topic of more severe classic abuse, such as domestic violence. Severe, classic abuse is neither pleasant to read about nor something for which we have a clear and simple solution. Sure, we can provide advice on how to handle a partner who sometimes raises their voice and storms out of a room,

but we are not qualified to give generalized advice to someone whose partner threatens to kill your kids should you leave them and means it.

Our exploration of abuse is more focused on how we address the topic as a society and how abuse affects relationship strategy. Moreover, abuse is not something with which we have extensive personal experience, so any thoughts we have on the subject must come from the data, interviews, and personal theory. Keep this in mind when reviewing our advice. If you would like to read more on this topic, go to page 513 in the appendix, to the section titled Abuse.

Notes from the Research:
- Double-blind, placebo-controlled TMS (trans magnetic stimulation, which allows researchers to temporarily shut off parts of the brain) research at the University of Pennsylvania has shown that stimulating a person's prefrontal cortex increases their likelihood to define an instance of sexual or physical assault as morally reprehensible. While this doesn't exactly have real-world implications, it does highlight that even our own view of moral right and wrong is evanescent and often outside of our logical control.
- The cognitive impact of abuse is not just tied to its severity and frequency. When judging the gravity of an abuse case, society typically looks at the worst individual incidents of the abuse and the frequency of such incidents. While not a terrible methodology, the approach yields a poor understanding of the actual psychological impact of abuse. One of the most critical details when

determining how impactful an abusive or proto-abusive behavior will be is how predictable and regular it is. Proto-abusive behavior that occurs randomly, leaving its target constantly on edge, can lead to a deeper psychological scar than more classic abusive behavior that occurs only under very specific, regular, and predictable conditions. For information on this, see research on the effects of unpredictable chronic stress versus predictable chronic stress as well as the tangentially related concept of "learned helplessness" (again, the research on this topic is way more nuanced and in conflict than we make it out to be).
- One interesting study even showed that introducing predictable stress in mice during their adolescence caused neurological changes, increasing mTOR signaling activity in the prefrontal c1ortex, which lowered their anxiety and stress in adulthood.

Accidental Training of Proto-Abusive Behavior

It is possible for victims of proto-abusive behavior to have accidentally trained or emotionally reinforced this behavior without realizing what they were doing.
If you neglect to pay attention to the manner in which you react to a

> DANGER! DANGER! We just stepped on a PC landmine. Despite the fact that the person most motivated to end proto-abusive behavior is the victim of that proto-abuse, any admission that a victim could have lowered the probability of their predicament may be misconstrued as an argument that victims are responsible for their own abuse. This is akin to suggesting that kids who were told to look both ways before crossing the street are responsible if they are run over by a texting driver, or that women who were told to carefully monitor their drinks at bars are responsible if they are drugged and raped. Let's be reasonable: This is a patently ridiculous argument, and every lucid human knows it. Alas, we still confidently predict that some keyboard warrior more obsessed with virtue signaling than actually helping people in bad relationships will write an angry review of this book based on this argument. We could easily remove this section and not have to deal with such nonsense, but we have chosen to leave it in because we think there is a real chance it may help someone.

partner, it is remarkably easy to accidentally train them to exhibit low-level proto-abusive behavior.

This is done in three ways:
1. **Proto-abusive behavior is rewarded**: This involves giving someone exhibiting proto-abusive behavior

what they want (e.g., Giving positive attention to a partner after they pick a fight with you out of the blue to "calm them down"). This subconsciously trains them to continue leveraging that behavior and may even encourage them to ramp it up.
2. **Proto-abusive behavior is not punished:** This is why proto-abusive and abusive behavior is so common in high-power-distance relationships (in which one partner has much more power than the other). Those in subordinate positions are less equipped to stamp out bad behaviors when they worsen.
3. **Proto-abusive behavior is believed to be necessary:** If a partner is unable to communicate boundaries, needs, and feelings through normal conversation, they may feel their only choice is to resort to proto-abusive (and eventually) abusive behavior. If one partner tells another, repeatedly, to stop blowing communal rent money on designer clothes, and those calmly delivered requests are repeatedly ignored, this partner may come to believe/feel that abusive behaviors such as emotional manipulation, yelling, and even physical violence are the only communication pathways that actually work.

This third point is why proto-abusive behavior often correlates with unreasonable expectations from a relationship, as the partner with unreasonable expectations will adopt it out of desperation after their calmly communicated unreasonable expectations are not met. A partner may, for example, *expect* their relationship to provide them with ample spending money, and if they feel that money is not being provided, despite their repeated, calmly communicated requests, they might feel driven to circumvent their partner and… well, ultimately resort to proto-abusive/classically abusive behavior, such as expressing their resentment by escalating to verbal abuse, limiting intimacy, and so on.

The very second you first spot expectations like this, unless extremely dire circumstances are forcing you to stay in that relationship, **end it**. It is functionally impossible to change a partner's unreasonable expectations. A relationship based on a mismatch of expectations cannot be repaired. The relationship will almost certainly end up being reciprocally abusive. Keep in mind expectations can be unreasonable and poorly matched in many ways: With money, lifestyle, health, appearance, behavior, fidelity, sexual activity, and so much more.

Some common examples:
- "There will always be money for anything I want"
- "I will never be expected to have to budget my spending"
- "You will never find anyone or anything else attractive"
- "You will always want sex exactly as often as you do now"

In addition, mismatched expectations create relationships in which proto-abusive behavior emerges among what would otherwise be totally reasonable, emotionally stable people through a similar mechanism. Consider a relationship in which one partner is a Southern Baptist that believes if their children will be eternally punished if they do not adhere to a specific type of Christianity, while their partner is a Muslim who has contrasting beliefs with equally severe consequences for their children. From the perspective of each partner, reaching a compromise that puts their children's souls at risk is worse than acting abusive towards their partner, hence proto-abusive behavior will emerge from this disagreement and spread throughout the relationship. Just because a relationship has proto-abusive elements doesn't mean there is a clear bad guy.

Outside of the aforementioned types of incidents, how can the likelihood of proto-abusive behavior be lowered?

The key to halting the growth of proto-abusive behavior is to identify and apply negative reinforcement against this behavior at its lowest levels of output—even when the worrisome behavior is not directed at you. Suppose your partner steps on a Lego in an area where your child was clearly building something and had received permission to do so, then yells at your child in an angry tone for "leaving it on the floor." This is called displaced aggression. Essentially, they are transforming their pain into a form of aggression with a specific outlet of blame in order to lower their experience of pain and shock. Displaced aggression exists across many mammals. Even rats lower their stress levels by attacking and hurting other rats—and that displaced aggression *really does* help them feel better (though, of course, now two rats are stressed and not just one).

At any rate, if you partner lashes out in displaced anger at your child (or classmate, colleague, family member, friend, pet, neighbor, stranger, etc.) and you reinforce the behavior by doing the same or taking no immediate action, but separately comforting the lashed-out-at party later, you are subconsciously signaling to your partner that this behavioral response is acceptable, thereby increasing the probability of displaced aggression behavior in the future. If, however, you make it clear in the moment that this displaced aggression—which we would categorize as proto-abusive behavior—is *not* acceptable, you will lower the probability that this behavior will continue and escalate.

The displaced aggression scenario outlined above is probably the most important thing in a relationship to watch for in terms of proto-abuse—not only because displaced aggression really does help you feel better, but also because society normalizes this behavior. Society tells us that "I had a bad day at work" is an acceptable excuse for snapping at a partner, and that "sorry, I was in a really bad place at the time" is an acceptable excuse for belittling a partner in front of their friends. By making it clear from the start that no form of proto-abusive behavior—not matter widely accepted it may be—is ever acceptable in your relationship, it is easy to prevent such behavior from escalating above its lowest conceivable levels of output.

Other low level proto-abusive behavior patterns that, if not stopped at their lowest levels of output, often evolve into classic abuse are:
- **Unilateral conversation control:** Hanging up the phone in the middle of a call, locking the door to a room, storming off for hours/days, subjecting a partner to the silent treatment, etc.

- **Emotionally escalated communication:** Raising one's voice at a partner, slamming a door, punching a wall, throwing objects, etc.
- **Loudly broadcast self-pity:** Crying, whining, complaining about things one cannot change, etc.
- **Threatening to hurt oneself to influence a partner's behavior:** "If you leave with your friends, I will sit at home doing nothing all day" can quickly escalate to: "If you leave with your friends, I will kill myself" if it is reinforced.
- **Showing no remorse for lying after being shown evidence of a lie:** Lying is a hard one, as it is common in a relationship for someone to genuinely misremember something. You know you have a real problem when you present clear evidence that a partner is lying, and they still refuse to admit it.

Just as we categorize some widely accepted behaviors as proto-abusive, we see other behaviors, which many flag as signs of early abuse, as entirely fine (if sometimes a bit unpleasant)—so long as those behavior patterns are primarily enacted in order to improve all partners' quality of life and ability to achieve goals.

Specifically:
- **Controlling finances:** Financial control is often a tool used in abusive relationships, but one partner being responsible for financial decisions might also simply be a smart division of labor. Simone, for example, manages all of our bank accounts and the flow of our income, whereas Malcolm makes all of our investment decisions. We find this

arrangement to be quite optimal, even though each of us is surrendering control with regard to certain financial domains.

- **Denying impulsive behavior:** Somebody denying a destructive impulse in their partner is not abusive—even if their partner finds this denial unpleasant in the moment. For example, someone pouring out all your alcohol after you show up to work drunk or restricting your finances if you appear to be about to go on a spending spree at the mall or blow through part of your kids' college fund at a casino is not abuse.
- **Discouraging destructive interpersonal relationships:** Humans suck at ending toxic relationships. A partner who encourages you to end friendships that are clearly holding you back, encourages you to stay away from a genuinely abusive parent, or who does not consent to you sharing a hotel room with a coworker who has a reputation for being sexually aggressive is not *necessarily* exhibiting proto-abusive behavior. This one holds a special place for Simone, as one of the first things Malcolm did when we started dating was argue her friends were holding her back, and she needed to make more ambitious ones. Should Simone have followed the social convention that a partner telling her to not hang out with friends was being abusive, she would not have had all the success she has enjoyed as a result of Malcolm's mentorship. Thus while telling you who you should be friends with *can* be a sign of an abusive relationship strategy, it is not *necessarily* abusive. Scrutinize the reason behind the request. Is it motivated by jealousy of your

friends or a concern for how your relationship with them could affect your relationship with your partner? Then it is likely abuse or proto-abuse. However, if the advice stems from a desire to improve your lot in life, then it is likely not abuse or proto-abuse. Someone telling you not to hang out with meth heads is probably not being abusive.

Note from the Research:
- An eight-year study conducted by Germany's University of Alberta, looking at 554 people after a breakup, showed that eventually the new relationships they formed featured the same dynamics present in relationships they had left—this happened after the glow of the honeymoon phase had faded. Specifically, participants' relationship satisfaction levels stayed the same, their sexual satisfaction levels stayed the same, and their ability to open up to a partner remained unchanged. Read into this what you will; to us, this finding suggests that the research participants' relationships stayed the same because most people stay the same. Most people don't take personal responsibility for most of life's failures and, as a result, fail to make the changes necessary to avoid creating the same relationship dynamics over and over again.

Love Does Not Equal Caring

When talking about the subject of proto-abuse, one point cannot be emphasized enough: Loving someone and caring about them are not the same thing.

Given the extent to which our society glamorizes the emotion of love, it is very common for someone to assume a partner's love for them somehow makes up for abusive behavior. Whether or not an abusive partner loves the person they abuse is almost as irrelevant as the abuser's ability to find a picture of the abused person arousing. People would be seen as crazy for saying: "It is OK that he hits me because he becomes aroused when he imagines me," and yet many have no problem saying: "It is OK that he hits me because he feels the emotion of love when he imagines me." Both situations are just emotional reward mechanisms tied to our mental image of a person—and yet they are treated wildly differently.

It is incredibly common for one person to hurt another in an effort to protect or maximize their ability to extract the emotion of love from interactions with the victim. Abusive partners commonly pressure their beloved victims to make bad career decisions or threaten violence if their victims suggest leaving the relationship. These people do this because love feels great, and they ultimately do not care about those from whom they are using interaction to extract this emotion.

It is far more important to find someone who cares about you than someone who loves you.

Here are some easy ways to determine that someone does not care about you:
- They say: "If you loved me, you would X."
- They say: "I only did Y because I love you so much"—where Y is something that hurt you.

- They pressure you to make a decision they know is not in your long-term best interest in order to spend time with you (e.g., They make you late to work because they wanted to kiss you longer).

The most dangerous human you will ever meet is someone who loves you and does not care about you. If you run into someone like this: Run—run as fast as you can. Such people will not change because, fundamentally, you do not matter to them. All that matters to those who love but do not care about you is how you make them feel.

We often see people make no true Scotsman arguments on this topic. They say things like: "By definition, love only leads to positive actions."

We ask any who hold this position to bear in mind that the person most likely to commit a war crime is the type of person who "knows" that:
1) Good guys only do good things
2) They are a good guy

Consider how dangerous these two beliefs are when held together:
1) Love only leads to good acts
2) "I love my partner" / "My partner loves me"

Defining love as always positive makes it harder for people to leave abusive relationships when they love their partner—something that happens very frequently. Just because someone is abusive and bad for a victim does not mean the victim will not love them. No emotion is only capable of motivating evil action or good actions.

Emotions are merely signals: Things we evolved because they helped our ancestors have more offspring. Emotions are not barometers that indicate the morality of actions they inspire.

ATTRACTIVENESS STRATEGIES AND RESEARCH

"OK—enough with the boring relationship advice," you may be thinking. "How can I become SMOKIN' HOT??? Uh . . . You know—from a *pragmatic* perspective."

Society gives us these pretty solid guidelines maximizing aggregate attractiveness:
- Be fit
- Be young
- Be confident
- Maintain low/middling weight
- Practice good hygiene
- Get rich

Simple, right?

A look at some of the strongest research findings makes the topic seem fairly uncomplicated. Initial romantic interest, among both men and women, is almost entirely based on looks.

However, pick up artists (mostly male groups who try to figure out how to maximize their success on the sex market) would argue that there is more to attractiveness—that there are ways to "game the system." Are they right? Digging into the research on this subject was a lot of fun because at first, the results did not make a lick of sense.

The Puzzle

We started by exploring one of the strategies most suggested by male pick-up artist communities: Adopting "dark triad" personality traits (narcissism, Machiavellianism, and psychopathy).

Research backs this up: **Women appear to find men exhibiting dark triad personality traits to be more attractive**, and men leveraging these traits get more sex on average (the research also shows women exhibiting dark triad traits get more sex).

Cut and dry, right? Why did we find the studies so confusing at first?

Well, well, well . . .

Multiple studies looking at generosity and kindness have also shown that **men who are more generous get more sex**. In one study, participants of equivalent income levels were given $100 and an opportunity to donate a portion of it to someone else. Those who donated the most also had the most sex. But it doesn't end there: Studies that looked only at *reported* kindness levels also found that **kind men get more partners**.

To confuse things further, studies have found that women find facial features associated with men who naturally express dark triad traits extremely unattractive (a disdain that does not even drop when females are drunk), which seems to imply that an individual only *pretending* to exhibit these traits will have much more success than someone who was born exhibiting them.

So what? Pretending to be a dick will get a guy more sex, but if he is *naturally* a dick, he will get less sex? Being narcissistic sociopath gets a guy more sex, but so does being generous and being kind?

The results for female attractiveness are just as surprising. While we found all the standard stuff we expected to find, such as women being seen as more attractive when wearing red or laughing at a date's jokes, some stuff was just . . . bonkers. For example, the female group that seems to have the biggest single advantage is (drumroll!!!): Older women targeting younger men.

"But wait," you think, "I thought young women were the hottest?"

Upon exploring its fantastically large dataset, OkCupid found that a 40-year-old woman has better luck hitting on a 25-year-old man than she does hitting on a 55-year-old man. What's more, a 30-year-old man is more likely to respond to a message from a 50-year-old woman than he is to respond to a message from a woman in any other age group.

We know this looks like it contradicts what we have said earlier in the book, and this doesn't change our earlier advice—just hold your horses and we will explain. We are not the types to withhold information just because it doesn't fit our narrative.

The Solution

We were able to find dozens of well-conducted studies just like those above that seemed to contradict each other—*and* societal expectations. After a while, we realized that we were looking at the results from the wrong angle.

Ultimately, these studies are saying the same thing: **Both males and females find control groups extremely unattractive.** We do not think we have seen a single study in which the control group was found to be more attractive. These findings line up with our own experiences, societal tropes, and even other dating strategies that are user-reported to be effective.

It is a common trope that "nice guys" and "nice girls" always lose. This platitude may be true—just not in the way people like to interpret it (usually in an effort to protect their egos). We know from the data that both generous and kind men get more sex, so it is definitely not that *niceness* is an inherent turnoff. When someone is described as nice, it can mean many things, but perhaps most often "nice" means "generally inoffensive and unremarkable." "Nice" is the positive thing we say about someone when we have nothing else to say about them, and no personality trait is less attractive than being unremarkable and unmemorable. This is true for both women and men.

Perhaps in this context, "nice" is just a euphemism for "basic." The concept of "basic" comes from the slang terms "basic bitch" and "basic bro," which are perhaps best described through YouTube videos on the subject. To us, "basic" can be taken as an adjective to describe someone who is "vanilla" or a "control group human." If "basic" describes you, you may *through sheer mediocrity* be in a lower league than you otherwise would be had you developed a more distinct personality.

This explains why 40-year-old women have such high success rates with 20-year-old men. The type of 40-year-old old woman who uses dating websites to hit on 20-year-old men is very unlikely to be describable as "basic." The fact that average people are major turn-offs also explains why the dark triad strategy has become so popular among some males. Most guys start attempting to get laid by trying to be as generic and inoffensive as possible, which ultimately negatively affects their attractiveness. Trying to be a narcissistic tool also happens to make one stand out, as it is rare for young men to exhibit dark triad traits openly in a social context (plus play-acting as though they have dark triad traits also likely helps men separate themselves from their contexts, thereby increasing their confidence and decreasing fear of rejection).

You do not have to be an irritating tool to secure partners. You only need to be extremely unusual within your market, and you should preferably embody a clear trope (or traits with trope potential). In other words, you would be well-served to embody an archetype that exists within people's minds from movies or literature but that does not commonly exist within society. Exhibiting tropes does *not* involve peacocking. Peacocking is a tactic developed by the pick-up artist community that involves dressing and acting as ostentatiously as possible. While peacocking *can* work through the trope pathway (as being ostentatious and socially unaware fits many unusual tropes), there are many less douchey ways to attract partners using tropes.

Anecdotally, Malcolm had a relatively low success rate with women until he switched to being as nerdy as possible in an environment in which unashamed male nerds were rare. After making that change, his success rate shot through the roof, and interestingly, his extreme nerd act boosted his odds with preppy girls just as much as it improved his odds with nerdy girls.

Any persona you can adopt that is "safe" from criticism, and common within your local dating market is going to completely devastate your ability to secure a partner. Defining, creating, and becoming a genuinely unique personality is one of the easiest ways to dramatically raise your aggregate desirability.

Less Practical (But Immensely Fun) Tidbits on Attractiveness

There is fascinating and nuanced research describing everything from color preference differences by gender to the impact of facial symmetry on mate selection, matching partners' movements, body language, and ovulatory cycle preferences. We are not going to cover this research. Why? As interesting as they are, these studies present red herrings from a relationship strategy standpoint.

Knowledge of these studies will not move the needle enough to make a difference in your life and may even distract you from focusing on more useful, practical tactics. You will learn infinitely more about dating strategy by seducing just five partners than you could learn from reading an entire book on arousal patterns—though if you simply cannot resist, check out this tomes sister book, *The Pragmatist's Guide to Sexuality*.

Having read this far, you will not be surprised that we cannot resist going through *some* studies and unique concepts that have practical implications. Below are some of our favorite informational tidbits, ranging from things that society gets wrong, to choices that are more nuanced than we pretend, and beauty tips that have been lost to history.

Prepare to feast yourself on a delicious array of findings related to attractiveness and:
- Eye Dilation
- The Tradeoff Between Attractiveness and Competence
- Wealthy Male Preferences
- The Difficult Male Market
- Ethnicity
- Stoicism
- Intelligence Differentials
- Smells
- The Closing Time Effect
- Heavy Breathing Sounds
- Personality Traits Tied to Looks
- The Pratfall Effect
- The Kawaii Effect
- Protean Signals
- Friends and Groups
- Metaphoric Language Use
- Waist-to-Hip and Chest-To-Waist Ratios

Eye Dilation

We probably piqued your interest with "beauty tips lost to history," so let us start there. This one bugs the hell out of us. Modern research has shown that when you look at someone you find attractive, your eyes dilate, and when you see someone's eyes dilate while they are looking at you, you will find them more attractive. In ancient Rome, women used an Atropa Belladonna (literally translated, beautiful woman, because of its use but now more commonly known as deadly nightshade) extract to dilate their pupils in order to appear more attractive (and more intelligent too, as dilated pupils also conveniently increase judgments of intelligence). It is shocking to us that such an effective beauty trend would have died out just because it was derived from a mildly deadly plant (heck, we inject our faces with botulinum toxin in the name of beauty... what is so crazy about deadly nightshade?). Given her ophthalmic background, Simone would nevertheless like to point out that while there are safer methods to get the same effect these days—artificially dilating your eyes exposes them to sun damage. (So to be clear we are joking here, if any idiot kills themselves or goes blind by putting a plant in their eyes which literally has the word "deadly" in its name that's not on us. People stopped using this plant because it can literally and actually kill you, don't be an idiot.)

The Tradeoff Between Attractiveness and Competence

When we say that the choices we make around attractiveness are more nuanced than society lets on, this is especially true in women. While determining which style she should adopt in an effort to enjoy better professional success, Simone reviewed a number of studies looking at how people perceive women. Much to her dismay, she found that increased attractiveness, approachability, and likeability appears to correlate inversely with perceptions of intelligence and competence. For example, glasses and short hair are seen as less attractive, plus they make people seem less approachable, but they also correlate with higher perceptions of intelligence competence, whereas long hair has the opposite effect: Long hair makes people appear more attractive and approachable but also less competent and intelligent.

Wealthy Male Preferences

Gold diggers, we have a hot tip for you: What wealthy men find attractive is typically the inverse of the "bimbo social archetype" (large breasts, long nails, heavy makeup, revealing clothing, jewelry, long hair, heavy makeup, etc.). Studies have shown that the wealthier a man is, the more he finds small breasts attractive, while the poorer a man is, the more likely he is to find large breasts attractive. More specifically in our own survey data, poor men have a strong preference for large breasts, middle-class men have a small preference for large breasts, and wealthy men have a strong preference for small breasts. It appears to be that we have a system in our brains, influenced by our perceived security, that looks for wives with larger fat stores if times are lean. Why do we say that? Men *also* prefer larger breasts when they are hungry, and other studies show men prefer fatter women when they are stressed. All of this is in the aggregate of course—many individual wealthy men prefer large breasts.

Wealthy men also appear to have a strong preference for androgynous characteristics. While the financially insecure may be optimizing for the survivability of their partners (through fat stores), the financially secure may be optimizing for the number of kids they can still get out of their partners (youth), which is often signaled by androgyny. There may be more at play, however: A man who feels insecure about his position in the world may have a much stronger preference for a woman showing heavily gendered traits who would reinforce his position as the masculine breadwinner. A man craving masculine validation would find the "bimbo social archetype" very attractive indeed, whereas a man who feels more secure about his place in the world is more likely to look for traits in a female partner that are more commonly associated with strength, intelligence, and practicality.

Now that we think about it, every major *male fashion trend* that started among less financially secure communities that we can think of emphasizes masculinity (consider blue jeans, hip hop style, and gang-inspired styles), whereas most fashion trends that started among wealthier groups (aside from those that merely copied martial styles) emphasize more feminine/androgynous traits in men (think of the dandies of the Regency era or emo styles for something more modern).

Moreover, society features heavily ingrained tropes emphasizing that poorer men (e.g., construction workers) are more masculine while wealthier men (e.g., heirs) are more effeminate. Perhaps these patterns, along with the trends described above, are two pieces of a puzzle that we have not yet put together—the answer is on the tips of our tongues. It cannot be as simple as wealthy men just feeling more secure in their sexuality; there must be something bigger going on here. We would say it might be a downregulation of testosterone among men once their bodies decide they do not "need it" to secure mates, making the ideal of the social archetype of the ideal wealthy man less masculine, but we know that unemployment causes a lowering of testosterone, as does feeling like your position in society is lower, so the inverse is happening. What could it be???

The Difficult Male Market

While women may feel as though they are subjected to unreasonable standards of beauty, men are actually much more likely to be rated as unattractive. A whopping 80% of men are rated as having below-average attractiveness by women (contrast this with men who only see 50% of women as below-average attractiveness), this really sucks seeing as women will score men's personalities as consummate with their looks (back when OkCupid had separate scoring metrics for looks and personality, it found that people almost always had the same score for each). Companies like DateHookup found similar results. This troublesome connection between perceived personality and attractiveness is caused by something called the halo effect, which affects perceptions of both men and women, but affects men more negatively, as women on average rate much higher on attractiveness than men do. Fortunately, studies make it clear all is not lost: Men can improve their attractiveness by maintaining good hygiene and building muscle.

Ethnicity

There's no dancing around the fact that ethnicity/race significantly influences partner choice. We debated including this section because talking about racism is always a potential minefield but decided that ignoring it and pretending it has no effect dating is infinitely worse. (Note: While we took our data from a few sources for this section, most of it comes from an analysis of around a million OkCupid users in the USA from way back in 2009. So the data primarily is looking at who messages who on dating apps and how likely they were to write back when messaged.)

If you are a man, being anything other than white, Pacific Islander, or Native American significantly negatively affects how likely women are to respond to your online advances. In OkCupid's dataset, women were far more racially motivated in their dating practices than men.

If you are a female, men will reply to your advances at about equal rates regardless of your ethnicity—unless you are a Black female, in which case they are less likely to by a fairly large margin. Even Black males were less likely to respond to a message from a Black female than a female of any other ethnicity—similarly, Black females were less likely to respond to Black males than they were to any other ethnicity (again, this is all according to these old OkCupid results so there may have been some selection bias in the data set).[12] What makes this even more striking is that despite replying to them at lower rates, Black women found Black men more attractive than other ethnicities (according to an OkCupid rating of attractiveness from a similar time).

Some other interesting things to note:
- An OkCupid study that looked at attractiveness ratings by ethnicity over time from 2009-2014 found that while people claimed to be less racially motivated in their choice of partner in 2014 than in 2009, as time went on their preferences did not show their behavior had changed. Apparently, people know that being racial motivated in dating is worse now. but haven't decided to change their behavior.
- Except in the case of Asian men and Asian women who both seem to see each other as much more attractive as time went on.
- Men get way lower reply rates when contrasted with women. In fact, the most-replied-to male ethnicity, white men, got a lower response rate to their advances (29.2%) than the least-replied-to female ethnicity, Black women (34.3%).

---

[12] We took a deeper dive because we found this data so shocking and wanted to make sure we were not misreading it: On average Black women responded to 34.1% of messages sent to them—but only to 28% of messages from Black men. In contrast, Black men responded to 46.9% of messages sent to them while responding to only 37% of messages from Black females. Black women responded to Black men more than any other ethnicity did, while Indian, Middle Eastern, and Native American men responded to Black females as much or more than Black men did.

Let's be clear—there is no such thing as an "inherently hot" ethnicity. Instead, these preferences are a product of socialization and societal racism. How can we say that so confidently? Were certain ethnicities inherently more attractive, we would not expect only one ethnicity to prefer mates of other ethnicities. Even if only one ethnicity preferred mates of other ethnicities, it would just be way too much of a coincidence if this group also happened to face the most prejudice within our society. As to why Black Americans message other Black Americans back at lower rates: Large scale systematic racism in America and the effects it can have on internalized racism aligns with other famous studies, such as Dr. Kenneth Clark's "doll experiment," in which Black toddlers were found to preferentially chose white dolls to play with back in the 1940s. It is just sad to see this bias so alive and well within today's dating markets. We suppose it is not a surprise to most Americans that prejudice is prevalent enough in our country to significantly influence dating preferences.

All that said, if socialization is the mechanism of action, we would be keen to know why women appear to be socialized differently than men in this instance. Why are women showing a racist predilection against all non-whites, Pacific Islanders, and Native Americans, whereas men only show a strong racist predilection against Blacks? These preferences may be driven by the manner in which our culture associates the concept of masculinity or femininity with certain ethnicities. Alternatively these preferences could be tied to a trend we noticed in the studies we conducted for *The Pragmatist's Guide to Sexuality*. Female participants in our research reported consuming less erotic art featuring disadvantaged groups—specifically material featuring overweight individuals of the opposite gender (f2%, m21%), older individuals (f34%, m48%), or poor people of the opposite gender (f18%, m23%). Your first thought may be that women merely consume less diverse sexual material, but when romance novels and erotic fanfiction is included in the data set, such is not the case. We can only speculate on why this pattern exists (and is, confusingly, not observed in the consumption of interracial porn (f35%, m36%)).

Stoicism

Stoicism has become a popular philosophy among online groups tangential to the pick-up artist world, such as the Red Pill community. We find this ironic, as while research does show stoicism helps in securing long-term female partners, it also suggests that stoicism doesn't help in obtaining sex.

Specifically, one study that had men signal stoicism by working despite being in poor health found that women find stoic partners more attractive, but only as potential long-term partners. Stoicism in this study did not appear to affect short-term attractiveness ratings.

Intelligence Differentials

Studies show that men prefer women who are less intelligent than they are. Some researchers have hypothesized that this is due to an assumption that such women would be more financially dependent on their partners (i.e., will be unemployed) and thus will have more time to raise a family and run a household.

We think it is much more likely that the team didn't properly control for the wealth of its participants and that if it were to only look at wealthy men, interest in a relatively less intelligent female partner would be far weaker. According to the data we collected as research for *The Pragmatist's Guide to Sexuality*, wealthy men do indeed prefer intelligent women. Preference for lower female intelligence could also reflect societal constructs that devalue relationships in which the female partner is "better" than the male partner.

Smells

While there are all sorts of interesting studies exploring smell and attraction, one of the most famous findings is that females prefer the smell of shirts worn by men with symmetrical faces (another trait tied to attractiveness) and the more fertile the women were at the time of the study, the more they preferred those shirts. This is one of those effects that is backed up by a cluster of research and healthy replication.

The Closing Time Effect

The Closing Time Effect refers to the phenomenon in which individuals begin to perceive the opposite gender as being more attractive as it gets later into the night. Further studies on this dynamic have nailed it down a bit more: The Closing Time Effect only works on *pictures* of the opposite gender. The effect does not appear among people in relationships, nor is it caused by alcohol. The effect is stronger in males and appears to make pictures of attractive people more attractive while making pictures of ugly people even less attractive. This effect means that if you are hot, your odds may improve later in the night, but if you are unattractive, your odds may *decrease* later in the night.

Heavy Breathing Sounds

If you put headphones on someone's head that are playing heavy breathing sounds, they will (on average) rate individuals they are looking at to be more attractive. We are frankly not sure how to use heavy breathing sounds to boost perceived attractiveness outside of chatting someone up while they happen to be listening to audio with heavy breathing sounds, but what this finding *might* suggest is that relaxed, more focused states increase perceived attractiveness. It could be that heavy breathing sounds compelled research participants to focus on their own breaths and begin relaxing. (Now I am giggling imagining someone reading this book and walking up their crush breathing heavily while asking them out.)

Personality Traits Tied to Looks

Studies have shown certain personality traits to be associated with facial "looks" (a study participant can guess certain elements of a person's personality at a rate above chance just by looking at pictures of their face). People find faces to be more attractive if they also find the personality set a stranger would associate with those faces to be more attractive. For example, if you are attracted to nerdy personalities, you will also be more attracted to those with nerdy-looking faces.

This might seem obvious, but it has pretty severe implications for people attempting to maximize their own attractiveness. Specifically, those born with facial features associated with a specific trope will be somewhat locked into "playing that trope," assuming they want to maximize how hot others find them in aggregate (as opposed to appealing to a specific individual). We wonder if this could also be applied to makeup tutorials. People might be able to better target specific individuals by emphasizing facial features associated with personalities they like.

The Pratfall Effect

We love this one: The Pratfall Effect describes how people find high-value partners who make mistakes to be more attractive. If you are super clumsy but not otherwise high value and attractive, put back that bottle of champagne—this effect only works for people who are perceived to be otherwise attractive and competent.

For example, if a hot Stanford post-grad trips, your average person will find him/her more attractive, while if an attractive hobo trips, your average person will think less of him/her (observers also think less of people they rate as having middling value). In both cases, the effect is increased if someone berates them for their screw up (e.g., the observer will think even more of the Stanford post-grad and even less of the hobo if they see them trip and subsequently see them being berated).

This effect is much stronger in the way men perceive female attractiveness than in the way females perceive male attractiveness. This must contribute to the perpetual archetype of the clumsy female scientist sex interest. At any rate, this would be a great trope to play up when dating—if you can pull it off.

The Kawaii Effect

There is an emotional state for which no English word exists that is useful to understand in order to fully take advantage of the way our partners emotionally process time spent together. The closest English words we have for this emotional state are "squee" or "cute"—but each of these words is often used in other circumstances, making them not really useful here. The most accurate word describing it is "kawaii," which is Japanese for lovable/cute/adorable.

When you have a strong emotional attachment to someone, things they do that are slightly unusual and quirky—but characteristic of them—create a very strong, short burst of positive emotional reaction. TV shows will often attempt to tap into this by granting a few token "quirks" to characters, like having them put their hands to their chin when saying something, sitting in a weird way, playing with scissors, or talking in an odd pattern.

The interesting thing about this emotional reaction is that it inverts when a relationship is going poorly or, in the case of media, if you do not find a character endearing. Things that elicit this squee reaction when you have a strong romantic attachment to someone will elicit an equally strong negative reaction that feels like annoyed disdain.

This effect is one of the core reasons why it is difficult to turn a negative relationship positive. Each day around someone you hate makes you hate them more. However, this dynamic also gives you an easy way to maximize the positive emotional state felt by people who like you.

Protean Signals

Proteans are subtle, subconscious flirting signals. A classic example would involve a woman touching her hair when first meeting a man. Before regarding these signals as surefire signs of interest, consider that one study observed that (in general) women tend to exhibit these behaviors when they first interact with a stranger, and that these signals only become indicative of true attraction *after* a prolonged period of interaction.

Still, if you really want to try to learn these and related nuanced signals of interest, such as behavior mirroring, go for it. We will only mention them as an area of potential further research for you, as we believe they are too subtle and not statistically relevant enough to be genuinely effective in seduction play.

Friends and Groups

This classic tactic is statistically proven to work: If you surround yourself with less attractive people, you will look more attractive. Another related effect, "the cheerleader effect," causes people to see individuals as more attractive when part of a group.

Use of Metaphoric Language

Women find men more physically attractive after the men have paid a compliment, either to the female's possessions or appearance, using metaphoric language (as opposed to literal language). In other words, it makes a man more attractive to say: "You have the elegance of a ballerina" but not: "You look elegant."

The positive effect of metaphoric compliments appears to be stronger when the compliment is paid to a woman's appearance as opposed to her possessions. Interestingly, compliments on appearance using novel metaphors were preferred by women in a relationship during the fertile phase, but by single women during the luteal phase (when a woman is infertile). In *The Pragmatist's Guide to Sexuality,* we discuss how a woman's ovulatory cycle affects her arousal patterns and what we might be able to learn about early human mating habits from this in detail.

Waist-to-Hip and Chest-To-Waist Ratios

A woman's waist-to-hip ratio and a man's chest-to-waist ratio, with a lower ratio being better in both cases, is a key determinant of attractiveness. You can, therefore, make a significant positive impact on your attractiveness by altering these ratios, either through clothing, weight loss, and/or strategic muscle development.

Notes from the Research:
- Surprisingly, a few studies have shown that men value positivity in a woman's attitude way more than you would expect. While niceness may not

matter much, positivity certainly does—at least in women.
- Research coming out of Michigan State University's Close Relationships Lab suggests that similar personalities among relationship partners do not necessarily correlate with high relationship satisfaction. Instead, traits such as niceness, low anxiety, and introversion appear to have more influence on relationship satisfaction.

MOTIVATING YOURSELF

The hardest part of securing a mate, be it for sex or a long-term relationship, is working up the motivation required to get out there and reach out to people when every single interaction you initiate bears a risk of rejection and thus to some extent invalidation of your self-worth. This invalidation of one's self-worth is incredibly painful and yet an inevitable part of dating. There are a number of mechanisms that make putting yourself on various markets easier, which we will explore in-depth below.

Realistic Expectation Setting

One reason why rejection hurts people so much is that they have totally delusional expectations regarding how much dating is actually required to secure a high-value partner. We have met many women in their thirties who want to find a husband and complain about not finding a good partner—and yet they only go on one date every couple of weeks. This is akin to someone sending out one job application every couple of weeks and not understanding why they are still unemployed.

Even crazier, we have heard some claim that they tried active dating—dating in which they hunted for partners and initiated interactions, typically on online dating websites—but stopped because they had a few bad experiences and are now just waiting for someone to find them randomly. This is akin to giving up on a job search after a few bad interviews, concluding that the "right" /

good boss will scout them randomly. Sure, such instances are possible, but we would hardly bet our entire futures on the initiative of a complete stranger who may or may not have means of discovering us.

Dating with the intention of finding a well-matched, healthy, long-term relationship is not naturally fun. This sort of dating is **a job**. Dating just enough to find the experience of dating itself pleasant is like being a professional author who only writes when they fancy writing—rather than to meet a deadline for publishing a book. Sure, dating—and writing—are sometimes loads of fun, but if you really plan to complete a complex project, be it finding the right partner for your entire life or finishing a book, you must come to terms with the fact that sometimes, you simply must push through.

If you are looking for a high-quality, long-term relationship, aim to go on at least four dates a week and expect the search to last for (at least) two years. Before meeting Simone, Malcolm went on five dates a week for three years. If that sounds difficult, improve your time management skills. Learn how to manage back-to-back dates. Carefully budget and schedule your time. Manage partners with a CRM system (we personally use Streak; it works with Gmail and offers a powerful free version that integrates directly into your inbox). We inhabit the 21st century and must play by its rules to win. If you want to find the best possible match in your geographic region, you must process people at scale with the assistance of technology.

Don't expect to fish for a partner; hunt for one. If you must fish, do so with dynamite.

Speedy rejection of suboptimal candidates plays a critical role in helping you achieve the level of throughput necessary to find an optimal partner. Don't waste a third date on a prospect that you know to not be marriage material if your goal is to find a husband or wife.

If you are a male looking for sex, expect a one-in-one-hundred payout when you are inexperienced (i.e., for every 100 targets contacted, you should expect rejection from 99). Once you become experienced, you can easily get this number down to one in four, which is about the success rate an inexperienced woman looking for sex should expect.

If you are a woman targeting women, note that your success rate will drop to nearer to that of a man targeting a woman with the same experience but till a bit better (25 failures for every one success). With time, this success rate will slowly ramp up, hopefully easing into one-in-four odds. (This often comes as a shock to women who try the poly scene if they are used to only dating men.)

If you cannot deal with the fact that regular sex with new (unpaid) partners will require thousands of rejections, work on your self-esteem before you burden the sex market with your emotional baggage.

Leveraging Point-Based Motivational Systems

Simone used two point-based systems while dating to make the disagreeable process somewhat more palatable. One point-based system leveraged competition with peers to motivate her to get out and date; the other helped her cull suboptimal candidates.

For the first, Simone created a scoreboard at her workplace in which she and other single-and-dating colleagues marked and tallied up points (won for various dating achievements such as a first date, a date lasting longer than four hours, a second date, etc.) and competed to get the highest score. While Simone rarely wanted to head out on a date, she *did* want to win, so in many cases that scoreboard made all the difference.

Point-based systems designed for dating motivation should be tailored to reward you for finding what you are looking for; however, they also need to reward you for the negative inevitabilities of dating. You should win points for rejection, particularly bad dates, and dumping someone just as much you should win points for scoring a second date with someone you really like. These systems will make the negative aspects of dating sting less and thus encourage you to expose yourself to rejection in ways you would never otherwise consider.

The points-based system Simone used to determine whether someone was or was not worth a second date involved five questions, each of which would be given a score of 1-10:
- How excited were you to see this person?
- How much did you enjoy any physical contact?
- How much did you enjoy the conversation?
- How much would you like to see them again?

- How much do you think they would like to see you again?

Anyone scoring above 35 out of 50 is a viable candidate. Anyone scoring under 20 is a clear "next." People who yield middling scores might be worth further investigation, but only with an extremely critical eye.

You may decide to use different criteria. The important thing is that you carefully, intentionally, and consciously evaluate each target and drop those that are clearly not worth your time. When you hesitate to pass over a sub-optimal match, perhaps not wanting to hurt someone and/or their feelings, keep in mind that by failing to reject someone in an act of cowardice, you are not only wasting your own very limited time but also wasting theirs.

Leveraging Social Reinforcement

If you still struggle to go out and meet people but know you need to, focus on social reinforcement strategies. You may, for example, agree to report your progress to a friend every week (or hire someone on Upwork to demand weekly reports). Tell this person your goals and promise to call them once a week to report in on your progress towards achieving them. Even though this person may be a total stranger, your promised action (combined with how stupid you would feel paying a stranger for nothing, should you decide to hire someone) will create enough cognitive dissonance to get even the most gigantic coward out on the market (we say this having been *terrible* dating cowards when we first started on our individual quests).

Getting Back On the Market

So you got dumped. So you are going through a divorce. So your partner died. You loved this person and they were a huge part of your identity. How long is it appropriate for you to stay off the market?

Most relationship advisors treat people going through these tough times with kid gloves, recommending time for grief and other emotional indulgences. Pragmatists acknowledge that emotions can present important signals that should be felt and acknowledged. Pragmatists *also* accept that emotions result from scars on our cognition left by evolutionary pressures that may not align with our goals. Emotions should never be in the driver's seat of your mind. Using emotions to justify strategically poor actions is the height of narcissistic degeneracy. Keep our perspective and biases in mind while digesting our advice.

With that said, the best time to get back on the market is fairly obvious: You should stay off the market no longer than the minimum socially acceptable length of time within your societal context.

Gauge what your peers would accept as a respectable cooling off or mourning period (ignoring, of course, the one stick-in-the-mud who insists you should live in mourning forever) and mark the end of this period in your calendar. The day your mourning period ends is the day your new dating campaign should launch.

Plan your dating campaign in private while waiting for its official launch date. Prepare your dating profile content and photos if online dating will be part of your strategy (though do not bring it live). Should you turn to a matchmaking service for help, pour over reviews and pull a few anonymous quotes so that you can engage the service the moment it is appropriate. Get in shape. Focus on bringing yourself to a state of tip-top mental and physical health. Refresh your wardrobe. Binge on YouTube videos offering male or female grooming tips to see if your hygiene and preening habits need a refresh. Consider organizing a party or celebration on your campaign's launch date to make things fun (if you are embarrassed, you don't have to tell friends why you are celebrating).

If you have trouble moving past the loss of a partner, it is likely because you incorporated a relationship with them into your self-image. This is not something that will change on its own; you must actively change your self-image to release this person's hold on you. Chapter three of *The Pragmatist's Guide to Life* addresses this topic in detail. Do not waste your life consumed with negative emotions that lead to inaction—this is not what a dead partner would want for your life, assuming they were worthy of your devotion in the first place. Endlessly mourning a lost partner will only extend the negative emotions associated with the loss of this partner.

BREAKUPS: A GUIDE

An ability to break up with suboptimal partners early plays a crucial role in the process of finding a good lifelong partner. While there are many societal conventions about the best way to break up with someone, these only matter in so far as they apply to any negative, stigma-related blowback you may get for breaking these social conventions (being villainized by breaking up with someone via text, for example).

Pragmatically speaking, there are only three factors to consider when selecting a breakup method:
1) How and for how long will the breakup affect your partner
2) How and for how long will the breakup affect you
3) Whether the method you are choosing will be so emotionally difficult to execute that it will significantly delay the breakup (even a cruel but easy method, like ghosting a partner, is better than staying in a bad relationship you know you plan to end because you cannot bear the emotional pain of breaking up through a conversation)

Your goal when choosing a breakup method should be to leverage knowledge of you and your partner to choose the method that minimizes suffering and maximizes the recovery speed of all partners involved.

High Taxation Breakup Methods

High-taxation breakup methods are best for those with a strong, healthy relationship, a partner they care about, and a high level of emotional self-control.

These methods include:
- The Public Breakup
- The "Let's Stay Friends" Breakup
- The Slow Ghost Breakup

In The Public Breakup, you take your partner to a public place because you fear they may freak out or try to forcibly extend the length of the conversation. Focus on public places tied to fairly short sitting times, so you won't have to stay at for a long time to finish the breakup. For example, you may take your partner to a coffee shop where payment for drinks is made upfront instead of a restaurant that typically serves five-course meals. Also consider public places that evoke emotions likely to prevent your partner from fully engaging in the breakup as it is happening (such as a rollercoaster ride), which can take the emotional edge off things... or make the situation worse, depending on their personality.

The Let's Stay Friends Breakup is the "best-case scenario" breakup and the default choice for anyone who is emotionally mature and cares about you. A good breakup—like a good firing—is one that the person should see coming from a mile away. A good breakup will not spring out of nowhere.

In this method, during normal hangout time (e.g., going grocery shopping, cooking dinner, etc.) you casually tell your partner that you do not think there is a future together, but that you like them as a person, and that you want to end the sexual aspect of your relationship, but are happy to help them secure their next partner. Yes, this might sound weird, but nothing does a better job of lowering the resentment of a breakup than quickly and successfully setting an ex up with someone new. Securing an immediate rebound for your exes has the side benefit of preventing them from obsessing over you.

If you are afraid that the person will not stay friends with you after the breakup (or vice versa) your fear may have a strong foundation. The reality is many people only take the time necessary to maintain the burden of friendship with someone because they get an externality from the interaction like sex or status. If you don't stay friends without the externality added, you almost certainly would have made terrible long-term partners so it is odd that this fear could prevent a breakup.

The Slow Ghost Breakup is the best breakup method for partners with whom you are not particularly close to, but with whom you occasionally have sex. Such breakups involve slowly increasing the time between any rendezvous (maybe delay one for a couple weeks, then push the next back a couple weeks, and finally just call it off). The Slow Ghost Breakup method is nice because it allows you to dump a partner without their actually realizing what is happening or feeling like they are definitely being dumped until long after the dumping really happened, which significantly blunts the emotional impact (depending on the ex's personality and level of obsession with you).

A slow ghost is totally different from ghosting someone. In a slow ghost, the target rarely is that close to you to begin with and becomes acclimated to only hearing from you maybe once a month before you cut off communication entirely. Ghosting involves quitting, cold turkey, someone you are seeing a few times a week—the emotional impact of the two is not remotely comparable.

Low-Taxation Breakup Methods

These breakup methods are best utilized in three scenarios:
1. You find yourself delaying the breakup because you lack the emotional maturity and willpower necessary to go through with it.
2. You expect your partner to become violent, but quickly calm down during the breakup (if you expect a partner to become violent and hunt you down after a breakup, consult a professional before doing ANYTHING).
3. You expect your partner to attempt to manipulate, coerce, or otherwise persuade you not to break up with them when you attempt to do so. While a partner who loves you might do this, one who cares about you never would.

A very common low-taxation method involves ghosting: Just blocking the other person and removing methods of contact, hoping they get the message. We generally advise against this method because it can be too vague—especially if your partner is a little obsessive (it can lead to their hunting in manners that are at best not fun and at worst extremely dangerous). Worse still, ghosting might lead an ex to think you are in danger or are having an emotional breakdown, which may lead them to rope in friends, family, or even the police to help. A ghosted ex would be completely justified in doing this. When someone you see on a regular basis just disappears or changes behavior patterns out of nowhere, the correct response is to try to help them. This method can be emotionally easy in the short run, but it typically causes more pain than the saved emotional weight of the breakup is worth.

Even more common among low-taxation breakup methods involves breaking up via text (or email, letter, voicemail, etc.). In this method, you deliver a clear, concise breakup to your partner in a way that does not require you to see the pain in their face or hear the hurt in their voice when they internalize the news. This method furthermore removes any serious risk of debate and is excellent if you feel like you would ultimately talk yourself out of a breakup if forced to do so through a live conversation.

Breakup Traps

There are a few things to avoid when breaking up:
1) Do not leave any doubt about whether or not you are actually breaking up with someone.
2) Do not say specifically *why* you are breaking up, especially if it is something a partner can leverage to turn your breakup into a negotiation (e.g., "you have not been nice to me lately," can incite the response, "I am sorry; I have been stressed lately and will start being nice from now on.") Such negotiations can turn you into the bad guy for not

giving them the chance to fix their behavior after being alerted to it.
3) Never tell someone you are leaving them for someone else (unless you are breaking up with an emotionally mature partner with whom you want to stay friends). This may cause your ex-partner's anger to be unfairly directed at your new partner.
4) If you genuinely plan to stay friends, set your next meeting as friends during the breakup. Should you fail to do so, it can be too emotionally taxing to set a time to meet up later, which creates tedious "it's been so long, it would be weird now" situations.

If you are a woman and find breakups to be uniquely painful, take solace in this: Research has found that while women experience more short-term physical and emotional pain after a breakup, they tend to recover faster and more fully.

Sometimes breakups are not as clean as one would like; this is OK. One study found that 25% of participants had sex with recent exes. Counterintuitively, this ex sex did not seem to have any harmful psychological effects or increase distress about the breakup, even though you might assume that post-breakup coitus would make it difficult to get over the split.

CONCLUSION

Now that you have thoroughly perused our "mental library" on relationships, had some pre-existing ideas challenged, and maybe even become a little (or extremely) offended, it is time to wrap things up. The conclusion to this book will give you a peek into our lives with an emphasis on the things that people normally do not share and examples of how a unique relationship model can be crafted using two individuals' personal ideologies. As such, it will also give you a peek into our larger ideological agenda.

A relationship is a living manifestation of its participants' combined beliefs and ideologies. It is impossible to discuss a long-term relationship without discussing what the partners want from their lives and why. Opening up about this kind of stuff obviously puts us in quite a vulnerable position vis a vis our readers, but we think this is a helpful exercise and appreciate your getting this far.

We have what would be called a "Goal-Oriented Relationship." This means everything about the way we structure our relationship is designed around hacking the human condition in pursuit of a shared goal: A fight against the loss of sentience.

Humans evolved to be able to communicate ideas with other humans, test them, and move forward with the best ideas, be they philosophical, scientific, religious, or about relationships. This ability lies at the very core of sentience. It is why our consciousness exists at all. Dogs feel sadness, joy, and love, but only humans (so far as we know today) can test one idea received from another individual against those they already hold and independently and internally decide which is best.

Though humans evolved this brilliant sentience, they have yet to evolve the necessary mental capacity to prevent simple thought viruses from quickly spreading throughout populations. These viruses have existed since the first cities were founded, but now, with our increased interconnection as a species, they have amassed virulence and volume they have capable of destroying a person's very ability to consider competing thoughts, leaving the individual nothing but a ghoulish husk stumbling through life on autopilot.

The miasma of idealism and tribalism spreading through our species' collective consciousness is suffocating sentience—smothering people's ability to consider new ideas. The effects of this pall upon the human condition are evident to anyone who is willing to take an honest look at the world. We are not the only ones who can see this creeping fog snuffing out sentience; we just seem to be the only ones who see it and do not presume the solution to this threat involves their own team's memetic set, an idea that only exacerbates the problem. They tell us:

> *"The cure for bigotry is political correctness."*
> *"The cure for liberalism is conservatism."*
> *"The cure for religious extremism is Rationalism."*
> *"The cure for social justice warriorism is the Red Pill."*

We have become a society that attempts to immunize itself against memetic viruses with even more virulent

strains of other viruses. Like ants infected with the mind-controlling fungus *Ophiocordyceps unilateralis*, a fungus that eats their brain while leading them to climb to a high leaf to spread the deadly spores as far as possible, once a human has lost the capacity for free thought—the capacity to entertain new ideas that conflict with what they already believe—the virus that has erased their sentience compels them to broadcast itself in any way possible, whether it be via YouTube, reddit, or in a university lecture hall.

When challenged, these viruses drive their hosts, chittering husks of wasted human potential, to mindlessly attack those expressing opposing views like a shrieking zombie. The internet gives these attacks the ability to sting. Should you dare to say something that challenges any of the world's various mental zombie hordes, you may find yourself living through an uncannily-cinematic nightmare as one of the horde spots you, shrieks, and begins the chase, thereby rallying others nearby to create a deadly mob entirely focused on your destruction.

While there is no personal benefit to be gained from fighting back against the tide, there are vast fortunes to be won by giving in and allowing one's free will to be swept up in exchange for the validation of a powerful tribe. If you think there is some intelligent cabal of global elite that lives free of this infection, you are dead wrong. From Stanford's Graduate School of Business to the University of Cambridge's historic halls, invite-only venture capital events in Silicon Valley, secret societies made famous by conspiracy theorists (that we contractually can't mention by name), secret political fundraising parties, and almost every bastion of elite culture—liberal or conservative—we have seen nobody more constrained in their thought than those who have risen highest, perhaps because they are the biggest targets and experience the greatest pressure to conform. There is no backup plan that elites have for the world. There is no association of wealthy billionaires with machinations in place to set things right. Without concerted intervention from normal people, sentience will be snuffed from existence by tribalism.

In biology, viruses can be used as vectors. You can insert DNA you want to deliver to a patient into a virus so that the virus can rewrite the way the patient's cells work. We believe The Pragmatist Framework is the "DNA fix," as it were, that the human brain needs to maintain sentience in the face of the unfurling mental pestilence.

Given our shared ideological vision and deep concern about humanity losing sentience, you may now better understand our chosen relationship style as well as our motivation to write these books (to promote a framework for approaching ideas and challenges that is uncorrupted by tribalism).

All this is to say that relationships can be so much more than an accessory in your life that helps you secure various baubles, be they children, career advancement, happiness, personal validation, social status, company, sex, safety, or financial security. A relationship can enable you not only to achieve feats unfathomably out of reach to individuals but also to become so much more than yourself. **By using relationships to step out of a personal identity and into that of a marriage, family, clan,** dynasty, or diaspora, you can transcend space and time in ways that even immortals would envy.

We would also be happy to help you build your own goal-oriented relationship. Tell us what you want from life, as well as whether you want a monogamous or non-monogamous relationship, and we will connect you with any other readers who have a similar vision and lifestyle preference (assuming we know or have been similarly contacted by a good match—it's doubtful, but we will give it a shot because you took the time to read this far).

If you want to make our day, please take the time to write an Amazon review. Reviews make it profoundly easier for us to share this book with a larger audience. New ideas are rare, and people open themselves to attack by sharing them, so novel ideas rarely spread without help. Please help us share fresh concepts and perspectives by—through your review—granting the social validation required to open more people's minds.

Appendix

As most authors do, we ended up discarding about three out of every four chapters of this book's unpublished manuscript. Some chapters and subchapters that ultimately made the cut are either relevant only to a sliver of the book's audience or incredibly boring (but comprised of critical scaffolding behind Pragmatist relationship theory). This content was moved to the appendix and organized in the order in which it would have appeared in the book.

The first few appendices present "quick start guides" focused on specific goals or life stages (think of them as alternative intros to the book for targeted audiences that want specific questions answered). These are followed by appendices containing more detail on certain subjects addressed in the book's main chapters.

> For those who wish to work with a live person to take a deeper dive check out:
> Pragmatist.Guide/RelationshipCoaches

HOW TO "GET LAID" AS A YOUNG ADULT

The strategies that help a 40-year-old man pick up partners in a bar are not going to work for a senior in high school, and yet most of the people writing books on "how to get laid" are writing about the strategies they use and developed as adults.

Many of those reading books on sexual strategy are engaging with the idea of dating and sex for the first time. The sexual strategies optimal for a virgin with little life experience (who is likely targeting fellow romantic and sexual novices) are totally divorced from the strategies that are appropriate for a grizzled pick-up artist.

This chapter is explicitly written for individuals who are:
- Over the age of 17 but under the age of 25
- Sexually inexperienced (having slept with under two people)
- Primarily looking to have sex and/or dating with people like themselves

If you are over 25, have more sexual experience, or are targeting people much older than yourself for sex, this chapter will have zero relevance to you; turn instead to the chapter on Lures on page 19.

While dating and sex are fairly easy to obtain when you have the process down, not having perfected the process on your own in no way indicates a lack of intelligence. In fact, while studies show that intelligent people have higher libidos, studies also show they have sex at lower rates and start later in life (well, maybe, some studies have shown it is actually *scholastic achievement* and not intelligence that negatively correlated with time of first sexual encounter, but the two-track moderately well).

IMPORTANT: As this section is written specifically for younger individuals, we have a few upfront warnings:
1) *Understand the age-of-consent laws in your state and all neighboring states. Depending on the state, these laws can be extremely counterintuitive. In some states, a couple may be dating and legally allowed to have sex one minute, but then after the stroke of midnight on one of their birthdays, sex between them legally becomes rape, only to become legal again a few months later when the second party's legally relevant birthday comes around. Do not screw with these laws no matter how "in love" you are with someone. We understand that every opportunity to have sex when you are young feels like a once-in-a-lifetime thing, trust us when we say there will be plenty of other opportunities and the risk often is not worth the fleeting reward.*
2) *Check out the laws related to pornography in your state. In some states, you can legally have sex with your boyfriend at certain ages, but if he sends you a photo of himself naked, you can now be charged with child pornography, and he can be charged with the distribution of child pornography. At these ages, knowledge of the laws in your home state and states you have visited is almost as critical as a solid*

understanding of birth control and STI transmission.
3) *People will tell you to avoid crazy partners. Don't take this warning lightly. Even if you use protection with a woman who happens to be unstable and she takes your condom from the trash and uses it to get pregnant, you are still legally 100% responsible for that baby. In the same vein, getting an effective restraining order against a guy you thought was just a pity date can be very hard and take a long time.*
4) *Consent is a concept well worth understanding, but it is somewhat inherent to the strategy presented in this chapter (for obvious reasons). How you (and society, for that matter) define consent is irrelevant. What matters is how the law defines consent in your state, how your local college rules define consent, and most importantly, how your partner defines consent. Make sure you speak with any potential sexual partner about this concept. As a bonus, a philosophical discussion with someone about the topic of consent presents a great way to pick up on hints that they may be interested in you sexually—but more on that later.*
5) *Exercise basic sanity when it comes to dating. Don't get in a strangers car, don't go to an isolated place that someone else has chosen on a first date, don't get intoxicated around people you do not know well, don't let someone else mix your drink, don't give someone any picture of you they could blackmail you with, etc.*
6) *If you are in this age range and thinking of trying to seduce a partner more than five years older*

than you . . . don't. It doesn't matter how relatively mature you are. If that person is responsible and mature, they will turn you down, which means you will only have a chance at success if that person is a danger to you. Dating older people at a young age filters out people who aren't "crazy," dangerous, or predatory.

7) *We generally don't discuss topics to which we have nothing unique to add; hence, we won't be discussing things like safe sex, how to have sex as a virgin, how to have anal if you haven't tried it, how to give a blow job, etc. Suffice to say this is one of those things in life where you can't just "wing it" from what you have seen on TV or in porn. Google how-tos on the above topics if you plan to try them, definitely Google safe sex even if you don't plan on having sex, and if you do end up having sex use a condom.*

8) *If you are a creep trying to use this section to pick up people in college or for other nefarious purposes, it won't work. We would not publish any advice that we thought could be leveraged by older people looking to sexually engage younger or even underage individuals. The techniques discussed in this section are specifically designed for individuals who are both sexually inexperienced and still discovering who they are as a person—they will be clunky and ineffective for someone with significant life experience. They also focus on high throughput approaches, so they are way more likely to get you caught and publicly exposed.*

It pains us to even remember dating in our younger years. Some of what we say about our youth could be used against us in the future. Worse, this section in general is quite sensitive as a topic, but having been there and done that without a guide, we feel the benefits of this information to others outweigh the costs associated with sharing it. A large portion of the population is going to start looking to experience sex starting around the age of 18. This is particularly true because our society ties so much of a young person's self-worth to their ability to secure sexual partners (or at least the sexual interest of others). Allowing young adults to figure this stuff out on their own or copy techniques not appropriate for their age range is likely to lead to tragic results.

It really is crazy that we would risk our reputation by including such a potentially perilous chapter in our book, but slightly less crazy than the fact that good guides for this stuff don't exist. We are not black and white people. We understand that putting this kind of information out in the world could lead an individual to try something sexual before they are ready. Even with that sobering fact in mind, the research is pretty clear: Pretending that people in late high school and college are not sexual beings leads to much higher rates of teen pregnancy, higher transmission of STDs, and lower psychological wellbeing.

It is all well and good to teach young guys they must respect consent, but teaching young men about consent *without teaching them how to get what they want while still respecting consent* will lead a portion of the population to disregard consent entirely. It is great to teach young women to demand their partners wear condoms, but should they not understand the market dynamics for men and women their age and lack crucial communication tools, many first-timers will cave when their boyfriends say they don't like using them.

That's one of the core tenets of Pragmatism: Accepting the world as it is. While the trend appears to decrease in lockstep with sexual education, between 40%-60% of people, have sex before they graduate high school (studies and countries yield varying results typically in that range). Failure to provide young men and women with a guide on this subject may lead some to reinvent the wheel in unpredictable ways out of desperation—or source seduction advice from sexually frustrated 30-year-old pick-up artists that really only works well for those picking up drunk chicks at bars.

What makes the sexual strategies appropriate for people at the start of their journey so different from those who are further along?

Someone in their mid-thirties attempting to seduce their preferred gender is largely playing a game of arousal. Their goal is to get someone aroused enough that this emotion overcomes their better judgment. This is categorically not the case when you are young. When both partners are still sexually inexperienced, getting someone to the point at which they are willing to sexually experiment is a game of inspiring vulnerability through the creation of a personal connection and an environment of safety and genuine trust. This is true regardless of gender or sexual orientation and explains why strategies developed *by* middle-aged people *for* middle-aged people, like those pushed by pick-up artist communities, are so clunky and dangerous for young adults to implement. Using pick-up artist strategies for sexual novices is akin to using a guide to playing soccer to a game of basketball merely because both games use balls and nets.

If you are at an age where you are just beginning to experiment with your own sexuality, many of your peers have not yet passed that threshold. Once you recognize this in an individual, they should be taken totally out of consideration without even the slightest hint of hesitation. Sexually engaging with someone who *may* not be ready is just not worth the risk.

This does not mean that next week the prospective partner who you wrote off because you thought they were not ready won't make a terrible decision to move ahead with someone else before they are ready in an act of poor judgment (e.g., they were drunk and a popular classmate was hitting on them), but even if they do, that type of sexual experience is not the type with which you want to be associated. The not-quite-ready person will likely regret the experience. We can't emphasize how much you won't want to be a part of that terrible memory.

This caveat highlights another core deviation between sex as a youth and sex as an adult: Assuming a position in someone's Hall of Regrettable Decisions after a drunken post-office-Christmas-party one-night stand is very different taking top billing in someone's memories as their first sexual partner and having them regret it. That shit will haunt you for life. Many pick-up artist guides written by middle-aged men are like trail guides to a location that has since been sown with land mines that focus on all the types of pretty birds you will see on your hike If you actually care to navigate the region, first and foremost, you need a guide to how to not step on mines because those things will screw you up.

Because most seemingly eligible partners are not actually ready, securing sexual partners while young is also much more of a numbers game than it is in middle age. The game must be played far more conservatively because your hormones will be yelling at you to dash through any opening you think you might have. Just because a person doesn't fight back, just because someone does not actively say stop, and just because you don't "go all the way" doesn't mean you are not raping another person. This is super hard to keep in mind when your hormones are at 130%. Sexually inexperienced people often suck at saying no and have a horrendous track record when it comes to speaking up the moment a boundary has been crossed. Any sexual strategy you implement needs to account for that.

Sexual strategies implemented while young should never feature a single target as a goal. There is no guide in the world that will teach you how to get the singer of your favorite band or that quirky girl who sits behind you in Spanish to sleep with you. Yes, there is always a possibility that things work out with that one person you have a crush on, but you are profoundly more likely to end up that creepy person who can't pick up on the fact that this target has no interest in you.

While relationships at this age are fundamentally about finding people with whom you feel comfortable experimenting, keep in mind that it's hard to open up to someone with weeping, popped blemishes on their face, bad smells, or overpowering perfumes emanating from their mouths/clothing/skin, or repugnant buildup on their teeth. Bathe daily. Go easy on the perfume (or skip it entirely, focusing on scent-free antiperspirants instead). Exercise daily. Practice good oral hygiene. Watch your weight. Wear clothes that fit you. (Despite what the ads tell you, perfumes and colognes statically do not help you get laid . . . well kind of. Studies show they do increase attractiveness of people wearing them both in person and in pictures, so it is not the smell that increases attractiveness but increased confidence.)

Should you have at least moderate social intelligence and cover your bases on the hygiene front, you will be in a strong strategic position, regardless of any extra hotness or popularity you may bring to the table. Should you still believe you are too objectionable for anyone to date, skip to: But Whatever I Do, Nothing Works on page 413.

Finally, we can dig into the details: You are young, you are inexperienced, and yet you are determined to have sex, and no one is going to talk you out of it. Where do you start? Step one toward becoming someone to whom others can open up involves honing your social skills and confidence in social situations to a sharp edge. You must learn to engage strangers in conversation effortlessly and without hesitation.

Engaging and Talking to People

The first ten people who turn you down won't be turning you down for sex; they will be turning you down for a conversation because you either failed in your engagement strategy or at your "chat." This is by far the hardest skill to master in the tree of skills that lead to sex. The easiest place to practice is through online engagement, but if you really want to push yourself, find a place with constantly cycling strangers and practice introducing yourself and engaging them in conversation (Malcolm used to do this on weekend trips to Boston, on the subway, or at a local mall).

DO NOT (we repeat: NOT) pick a familiar environment with a limited pool of people for practice (e.g., never do this with your classmates, co-workers, local hobby group, etc.).

Your goal in perfecting this skill is to get to a point at which you can walk up to a random stranger, engage them in conversation, and have that introduction and resulting conversation be smooth and compelling enough that 10% of the time this stranger is asking for your number (not the other way around). The goal is not to secure sex or a date, just to stay friends and continue chatting. Should you be practicing in an online context, try to get to 30%, as you won't have the same drop off levels of people who sincerely have somewhere else to be.

This is emotionally hard to do. Talking to a stranger requires an enormous emotional hurdle. Learning to effortlessly clear that hurdle is the core purpose of this exercise. If you cannot clear that hurdle, remember: It is not really something you *can't* do, it is something you *won't* do—something you have chosen not to do because you don't see the ultimate goal as being worth the pain. If you knew you would die in 30 minutes, if you didn't engage someone, you would find a way to make it work. However, if someone gave you a choice between talking to a stranger and having a nail stuck through your hand, if you are anything like us, you would probably choose the nail. We get that it's hard, whether you are willing to push through is up to you.

While sex is a good motivation to learn this skill when you are young and horny, there are far greater reasons to perfect your ability to walk up to a stranger and engage them in pleasant, interesting conversation that compels them to want to engage with you further. Perfecting this skill will make earning lots of money and advancing your career significantly easier when you grow up. The same skillset Malcolm developed to get laid at ages 18-19 was tapped to raise millions of dollars from ages 24 onward.

This is not a step that can be skipped or half completed. If you want to achieve your apparent goal (sex) or even just ever become an adult with whom people enjoy interacting, this is a step you will have to pass. Developing this skill is going to SUCK. You know how people say all you need is confidence? Ever wonder how people actually *get* that confidence? This is how. If you are starting with no foundation, perfecting this skill will easily take five hours of dedicated work a week for up to six months.

Escalating Conversations

Once and only once you are good at engaging strangers in conversation, experiment with transitioning to topics or activities that push past the boundaries of the conversation by broaching topics people don't discuss with those they don't know well. Don't focus on anything sexual at first; your goal here is to learn how to get people to indulge in breaking social conventions with a like-minded compatriot. If you have been successful, targets will be excited to break social conventions in a safe environment around someone they like. If your conversational partner becomes at all uncomfortable, you have failed either at step one, at the transition between steps, or in your choice of social convention to break. Disengage and start again with someone new until you master this ability.

One way to easily break social conventions is by getting your target to talk about a topic that would get them ostracized from normal social groups (such as offensive views). Discussing taboo topics with someone inspires them to create a personal narrative in which they feel safe around you—otherwise, they wouldn't expose themselves in such a way.

One skill that may take some time to master is judging what social conventions your partner is eager to break in conversations when contrasted with the social conventions *you* are eager to break. Discussing offensive topics with someone requires a good read of them (e.g., you can't just engage a target on offensive views you hold; you have to engage them on socially offensive views they have hinted they hold).

Instead of focusing on taboo conversation topics (or in addition to discussing taboo ideas), you may explore taboo actions. For example, you may sneak into somewhere innocuous like school after hours, the woods at night, or an abandoned church, and have a picnic together. The effectiveness of this tactic can be increased by adding elements the target could subconsciously contextualize as romantic (like sneaking into your high school's auditorium after hours and have a picnic in the center of the stage while setting up flickering LED lanterns around you—this also has the advantage of strongly signaling to them your ultimate intentions and gives them a choice to turn you down if they ultimately would have anyway).

Taboo actions bring with them a higher potential cost (potential injury, arrest, etc.). There is often a reason such sites are taboo, and you should expose neither your partner nor yourself to material risks. We merely mention this as an option for adolescents who already do stuff like this. *(Again, we cringe so hard at decisions we made in our youth—but we have to expect you to think like we did when we were young and not like we do now.)*

The method with by far the highest success rate is to coax your target into opening up about deep philosophical insecurities. Inspiring someone to talk about why they think they exist and their purpose in the world takes vulnerability and openness to a level no other method might (plus it is super safe). Despite the relative safety of deep philosophical insecurities over (1) socially offensive topics and (2) socially taboo acts, these are not things one talks about in polite society. *The Pragmatist's*

Guide to Life's Step One can help you a lot with this kind of conversation.

While discussion of deep philosophical subjects presents by far the most effective of all tactics discussed, it requires more cognitive engagement and preparation. You will have to educate yourself enough to speak competently about cognitively engaging topics without leaning on fancy words or the names of famous thinkers. Should you approach this path, remember your objective is not to show how clever you are but to inspire your target to engage with their own philosophical views and think through them with you. Handle the philosophical views of your target in a non-judgmental but curious fashion that helps them recontextualize elements. Doing so reassures this person they can be comfortable being open with you.

In fact, let's double click on that last point. When you start getting strangers to engage with you in conversation, you will subconsciously use the conversations to try to get the stranger to see you in certain ways—as smart, knowledgeable about things they don't know about, deep, emotional, mysterious, popular in your local social circles, etc. Being able to pass the escalation stage requires quashing those instincts and instead focus on being a better canvas for your conversation partner to paint who they are—then taking that image and finding the parts of who they think they are that they are afraid to share with the world.

Flirting

Flirting comes after engaging and non-sexually escalating with a target, but before any actual sexual (or even somewhat sexy) engagement. While many books recommend looking for excuses to touch a person or brush up against them, we do not recommend this pathway—especially pre-college. Frankly, in the current cultural climate, physically touching an individual in a way that could be construed as sexual without explicit consent isn't worth the risk. There are two strategies to work around this hazard, both of which can be implemented at any point after an individual clearly feels comfortable breaking social conventions with you.

Keep in mind that your first attempts at flirting have a near 100% chance of being socially awkward. This is why we so heavily advocate against honing these skills among your peers (rather than in totally separate social contexts, such as neighboring cities).

If you feel confident that a potential partner likes breaking social conventions with you but are not yet sure of their sexual interest, see if they are willing to wear something of yours. This could be anything from a cap to a jacket, glasses, or something you made (this strategy is more effective if whatever personal item they decide to wear is unique enough to be "iconic" to your image and easily recognizable by others as yours).

Do this through offering it to them with a statement like "you would look cute in this; try it on," or "you look like you are getting cold" while you two are in private during a playful conversation you are clearly both enjoying (e.g., they are laughing a lot). If your target takes your personal item off immediately, it is a strong sign they are

not interested. Do not push things forward. If the target leaves the personal item on, but then takes it off right before anyone who knows you both socially sees you, it is ok to move forward in being explicit about sexual topics, but do not expect a public relationship. Should your target leave your personal item on in the presence of others, it is a sign they might be interested in an eventual public relationship, as it could inadvertently signal to others that your target is already intimate with you. Your target's choice to continue sporting your personal item around peers demonstrates how comfortable they are with having that message sent.

This strategy only works in college or high school, as those are the only times in your life where a potential dating pool and a wider acquaintance pool are going to have a huge overlap.

Anthropologically speaking, getting a sexual target to sport a personal item of yours would be classified as a mate-guarding tactic. Other classic mate-guarding tactics involve putting your arm around your partner, something we would not recommend until kissing is routine. Mate guarding behaviors are things most people do subconsciously or through cultural traditions like the exchange of wedding rings. Mate-guarding tactics are meant to signal to an individual's social set that they are not on the market and highlight the person or people to whom they are attached. Such strategies are easily implementable by both men and women and a useful escalation technique because they can be turned down or accepted non-awkwardly (especially in comparison to a straight-up proposition) and are far less risky than skin-on-skin contact.

If you absolutely must move forward with a skin-on-skin contact escalation method, use a strategy that allows you to do so with consent. A method we used to see people leverage was to ask a target if they wanted a massage. This allowed them to ask for consent to touch a target in a plausibly non-sexual context—but to be honest, neither of us ever found a way to use this method effectively, so we can't recommend it to others.

Another skin-on-skin escalation method that could be used—**but which we do not recommend**—involves finding a quiet, isolated moment to speak with the target, looking at the target, allowing a pregnant pause to develop in the conversation, putting out both hands, and asking if the target feels comfortable holding them. Should the target decline this hand-holding invitation, do not move forward. If they clasp your hands, just hold them for a moment while looking into your eyes, squeeze their hands. If the target squeezes your hands back every time you squeeze, you have a fair sign they would not object to a kiss on the mouth. Being turned down for asking to hold someone's hand is less awkward than being turned down for a kiss. However, odd invitations to hold hands are SUPER socially awkward and not the path we would recommend—we only really mention this tactic as an alternative for those who are insistent on leveraging the non-consensual touch or kiss strategies common in older books that are way too dangerous to implement for modern adolescents.

Side note: In general, if you find yourself holding hands with someone through some other means and whenever you squeeze their hand, they squeeze back in the same pattern this is the universal sign for let's get somewhere private and kiss. This was even true in countries Malcolm hitch hiked and did not speak the language, we have no idea why this is such a universal sign for "let's make out," but it appears to be. To test this, squeeze the persons hand and see if they squeeze back, if they do then squeeze their hand twice in a row and see if they give you a double squeeze back, typically this is followed either by a flirty look from them or intentionally looking away from you while starting a hand squeeze pattern of their own. If we had to guess why this works so consistently it is that somewhere deep in the "human code" hand squeeze pattern exchanging is subconsciously as intimate as making out but doesn't carry the same social stigma.

We ultimately recommend skipping traditional verbal or tactile flirting entirely when you are interacting with people who have little experience with relationships. Flirting as a relationship escalation technique is really only appropriate for more experienced individuals, as it works in two ways.
1) In the middle-age dating market as a way of covertly saying: "Hey, I'm down; are you down?" which is a boorish engagement strategy when someone is still figuring out their sexuality.
2) The flirting arouses your target so much they sexually engage with you based on an in the moment arousal pattern. This is very likely to drive someone to engage with you against their own better judgment, which, as we have explained, is not a desired outcome when hooking up with other sexually inexperienced people.

Flirting can also be used just for the sake of flirting. Once you become more comfortable with the witty banter involved, flirting can be quite a fun little game. That said, we strongly recommend against this with less experienced individuals, as it can easily be misunderstood and lead to hurt feelings or worse.

Broaching the Topic of Sex or a Relationship

Only after you have gotten good enough to walk up to a stranger, engage them in light conversation, transition to deep conversation, and get them excited about breaking social boundaries with you, should you even begin to try to learn how to engage someone sexually.

If you make it to this point, well done: In addition to unlocking access to far more sex than the average person by mastering this process, you also gained a skillset that will make getting a six-figure job by your mid-twenties a realistic endeavor (and the less attractive you are, the more robust that skillset will be, so if you are not naturally attractive, lucky you). If this claim seems farfetched, consider the nature of this skillset, which features an ability to confidently walk up to a stranger, engage them in conversation they find stimulating, and inspire them to trust and want to engage more with you. This is the same skillset people use every time they raise money, bring in customers, hire employees, run for office, etc.

Make sure you actually reach this point before attempting to push forward. We cannot stress this enough: Do not rush getting to a stage with someone at which the subject of sex or a relationship is broached. Make sure you have totally perfected the other stages first. Up to this point, everything was training. You were playing with paintball guns. The moment you explicitly bring up something sexual with a target, you switch those paintballs for real bullets, entering the realm of stuff that can permanently destroy your life and reputation.

Your first goal in this exercise is to get your target comfortable talking about sex with you. Most people want to talk about their sexuality, but they have very few people in their lives with whom they can discuss it (*The Pragmatist's Guide to Sexuality* will be of high utility to you here). Every exercise up to this point is meant to teach you how to become a legitimately safe outlet for someone's intimate thoughts and secrets. Don't betray the trust your target has built in you. If a person is hesitant to discuss these topics with you but is OK breaking other social conventions with you, CONGRATULATIONS: You just made a friend. Don't press further. There are only two reasons this may happen; both mean "stop:"
- The target sees where this is leading and is not interested in you sexually
- The target is not comfortable engaging their own sexuality yet

To put it simply: Your only goal at this stage is to determine whether your target is comfortable talking about their sexuality with you, nothing more.

Moving to The Idea of Sex

Note: It is possible and fairly easy to reach this stage without ever having kissed or touched each other in an arousing fashion.

Once you have been talking about sex with your target for a meaningful period of time, you may strategically drop, in a non-threatening way, that you would be open to trying one of the things they mentioned. This works especially well if the sexual act in question is something your target thinks no partner would be interested in trying with them—hence the utility of knowing what sexual taboos they secretly fantasize about.

Getting a person to feel comfortable opening up about scandalous, philosophical, and private topics creates intimacy and allows you to move to more explicitly sexual topics like: "What weird things have turned you on in the past?"

Suggestions like: "Well, would you be interested in trying X with me? I have fantasized about that too" become far less jarring once someone has spent time talking about other forbidden-feeling topics. Sexual propositions become even less intimidating if sent in written format after discussing other scandalous subjects, as without vocal intonation or body language to read, your target can easily reject you while pretending they thought you were kidding around. If someone "misreads" a proposal to escalate a relationship as a joke, they are turning you down in a socially nice way. When someone turns you down in this manner, don't re-frame your proposal more explicitly, as doing so will create needless social discomfort. By pretending to misread your proposal, your partner is attempting to do you a favor and maintain a platonic friendship with you. Do not sabotage this kindness.

In addition to pretending to interpret a proposition as a joke, a target's choice to breeze on with the conversation indicates they are not interested. There is no problem with a target not being interested. In fact, if your target reacts in these ways, they are showing you respect by not drawing attention to the rejection. If you handle your rejection with grace, you will come away from this conversation very likely to get a referral to someone else who might be interested. Your former-target-turned-friend wouldn't have made it to this point if they didn't consider you a friend—a friend with whom they feel safe talking about sex and a friend they can trust to push boundaries. Just never cross these boundaries.

Learning how to go through these steps online before practicing in person has many fringe benefits. Rejection stings much less online, but it still stings enough to help you acclimate to the feeling and not fear it. As an added benefit, you can run multiple online "dates" simultaneously. Practicing different conversation pathways with three or four people in different chat logs on the same night increases your learning rate by 300%-400%. As an added bonus, you can go back and review chat logs to see where you made a mistake with the perspective of hindsight, which will enable you to identify and learn more nuanced patterns.

If you accept that your first thirty or so attempts to "get good" are going to end in failure, it doesn't matter if the pool from which you are sourcing is worldwide rather than regional. Practicing with a cute guy from a rural town in Germany is fine because you are probably going to fail early on anyway. The conversation pathway you develop that gets you to the point at which someone says: "If you ever come to Germany, I would love to have sex" is the same conversation pathway that will be effective for an individual who lives 30 minutes from you. The potential leads in your geographic area are limited, whereas those in other countries are practically unlimited, which is why we don't discourage practicing in an online setting so long as you know better than to meet strangers online in person. (Just to be clear: Meeting in person with people you've met online is dangerous.)

Getting References

When you are young and still engaging with other people who are new to exploring their sexuality, you will have some sexual strategies open to you that cease to work as you age. One of the most dramatic of these involves "references." It is fairly common for a group of close friends to recommend having sex with someone when said group is still exploring their sexuality together, but very rare post-college. This is why we so strongly recommend engagement strategies designed to deepen your relationship with other people without ever pushing over the line with them. This obviously does not work with everyone; it depends on the type of friends a person has and the individual's openness and personality, but so long as you are able to maintain positive interactions with potential partners, both those who turn you down and those with whom you sleep may refer new potential partners to you.

This is one of those areas in which applying pick-up artist techniques developed by 30-year-olds to your early sex life can be disastrous. These techniques are often developed without any worry of burning leads if they do not end in sex. This is incredibly self-destructive advice to give to someone in late adolescence.

Pick-up artists aren't providing bad advice with malicious intent; they simply have no way to know about techniques that are effective in late adolescence. People who have no trouble getting laid in late adolescence don't grow up finding the thought of sex with hundreds of strangers terribly appealing and certainly don't obsess on the topic enough to write books about it or skulk around on message boards. This is why you won't see tactics specifically useful at these ages discussed within pick-up artist communities.

For boys looking for either female or male partners, maintaining positive friendships with a target is absolutely critical, as the easiest way to gain new sexual partners is through referrals from former targets and sexual partners who know that you respect boundaries and make for an engaging friend. It is not surprising that girls (and guys) of this age range looking to experiment sexually would recommend a clean, safe, discreet, respectful guy who is honest and outside their core social circles.

The same often works for girls: If you make it clear to a guy that you are clean, safe, discrete, respectful, and looking for other partners, most young guys will enthusiastically recommend you to their friends. The downside for females is that, while a guy will rarely care if a girl goes to brag to her friends that she slept with him, girls can be sensitive if a guy brags about sleeping with *them* (as guys within this age range love to do). Perceived promiscuity in women carries some inconvenient societal baggage that the majority of young women would prefer not to lug around.

Young women keen to avoid promiscuous reputations among their peers should focus on targets that are clearly independent of their normal social circles. It may be safer to source male sexual partners through geographically and socially distant female friends with similar sexual tastes than it would be to source male partners directly. Such female friends will likely be aware of discrete, trustworthy males and any discovery of your efforts to court them (these other women) as friends are less likely to get you labeled as promiscuous.

To be successful at securing referrals, you need to be more than just "inoffensive" in your interactions with others but actively exciting, unique, and engaging. These are all characteristics you can develop through practice, though it takes longer for some people to cultivate these features than others. People don't recommend vanilla ice cream to their friends. Having a specific, unique personality makes a huge difference. See the fourth chapter of *The Pragmatist's Guide to Life* for more guidance on developing a compelling public persona.

As to why this pathway closes off as one ages, there appear to be two factors at play:

1. Sex as a conversational subject loses its luster and sparkle as adults age, and the novelty wears off.
2. The types of friend groups that share this type of information with each other largely either dissolve or become stagnant and stop interacting with new people as everyone ages.

In sum, while the opportunity lasts, it pays to be *extra* to ensure every potential target with whom you interact—regardless of the ultimate outcome with that particular person—walks away from the interaction satisfied with and intrigued by you. If others feel they will look good by referring you to their friends, rest assured they shall do so.

Warnings

If you have horrible hygiene, dress like a slob, or have an ass-hat personality, a 0% success rate will stay 0% no matter how many people you engage. That said, we still recommend this strategy, as if you have a minimum baseline of social intelligence, you will eventually pick up on whatever it is that turns targets off. If you don't feel you have that minimum baseline of social intelligence, we encourage you to flip to the chapter entitled: Whatever I Do, Nothing Works on page 413.

Working to build up a large number of sexual partners is hazardous, and not just for the obvious disease-and-baby-related reasons on which you have no doubt already been briefed.

Even if you are 100% well-intentioned toward and respectful with every individual with whom you are intimate, once your number of sexual partners gets near a hundred, even a 1% failure rate to read what a person wants (and yours will be much higher) means someone will be hurt by your sexual campaign.

Even if you never step on that particular land mine and, on the aggregate, generate more positive than negative emotions in others, the interactions that will take up most of your mental capacity for decades to come are the negative ones that you think you may have caused. Trust us: Ten years from now, you will not reflect on all the awesome sex you got by sleeping around indiscriminately, but rather on all the people you may have hurt—and the higher that number goes, the more it will eat at you.

The best way to protect yourself against this risk is to either minimize your sexual partner count, or, at the very least, avoid sexual partners who react to situations in unpredictable ways (the type who will sneak into your dorm after midnight wearing edible underwear then tell you they never consented to your eating it). If you cannot predict a person's intentions and mental state, do not expose yourself to the risks associated with courting them, no matter how thirsty you are. Even a 0.1% chance that someone will perceive your interaction as non-consensual is not worth the risk. This is why you should immediately disengage yourself from anyone who seems mentally unstable and anyone who likes to play hard to get. Consent is extremely difficult to read in these groups, which is why you should never play hard to get yourself. Smart people will merely avoid those playing hard to get. There are other fish in the sea.

If you successfully execute on this advice, you will learn two things:
1) Sex is ultimately quite boring and routine. Sex with random people is certainly nothing to take pride in. Bragging about sex is like bragging about being able to read; the only people who do it are people who just learned to read (honestly, the same can be said for bragging about almost any category of success—people only brag about things they did not expect to get). Sometimes we feel like puberty is this magic curse placed on humans that can only be broken by realizing that neither sex nor attractiveness are really that important, but in the weaker-minded of our species (like ourselves) said realization can only happen when these two things stop being a challenge.
2) Constantly attempting to secure new partners and maintaining multiple relationships will teach you a lot about yourself and other people. Sadly, this information comes at a cost. Learning requires failing and failing in a relationship means accidentally hurting people. If you are in a large number of relationships in your youth, you will hurt people (no matter how well-intentioned you are), and that will haunt you.

But I Hate Being Rejected!

Learning how to respond to rejection with dignity is a critical skill that does not come naturally. To start, focus on learning how to not be apprehensive about being rejected by recontextualizing each rejection as a small win (bear in mind that each new rejection helps you develop a thicker skin and each rejection symbolizes one step closer to your ultimate goal). Learning how to successfully ask for something is a breeze once you learn how to not worry about rejection in the first place.

Next, learn how to be rejected with dignity, both in general and when asking someone out. Develop a classy response to rejection that does not make things awkward—one that gives up on the hope of future sexual interaction with the other party for at least a year and does not lead you to bear ill will towards the party that rejected you.

Focus on the wide and colorful number of ways you might be rejected. A rejection may manifest as anything from your target changing the subject to a somewhat flimsy excuse. Anything other than a "yes" is a rejection.

SECURING A LONG-TERM RELATIONSHIP

Even more than finding a consenting sex partner, the key to securing a solid long-term relationship (or spouse, should you want to make it legal) lies in your ability to generate a large pool of leads and process them at an industrial scale. In biology, one of the most common methods for finding an antigen (a molecule that fits perfectly into another structure and thus binds to it) is called high-throughput screening. Scientists using this method test hundreds of thousands of molecules against a structure to see which variations yield the strongest connection. The simplest reliable strategy for finding a long-term partner works through a similar process, thus the term—high-throughput screening—we have given this strategy.

While "brute forcing" your way to a good long-term partner by setting up an industrial-scale processing operation within your life may be seen by some as "unromantic" or inelegant, this is not an area of your life in which you can afford to take risks. Long-term partner selection (or failure to secure a long-term partner) will have a profound impact on your life.

Choosing a bad partner is one of the single worst decisions a human can make in their lifetime. Decades can be lost to toxic partners, a series of short-term relationships that never last, or a non-committal partner just using you as a placeholder.

A favorable life partner will do more to help you achieve your goals than wealth, fancy college degrees, popularity, etc. Goodness, if you don't have money, one of the fastest ways to become wealthy even involves securing a (wealthy) long-term partner.

Our high-throughput screening method presents the tools and mindset needed to build your own unique processing operation meant to vet whatever characteristics you decide are important in a partner. This processing operation will enable you to quickly build relationships intimate enough to harvest the personal details required to vet an individual. While reading the entire guide will provide you with the information necessary to build a processing operation customized to your needs, we will provide two template strategies—one for males, one for females—demonstrating limited examples of how the book's general principles might play out in action.

Male Template Strategy

Your first goal should be to go through as many leads as you can, as fast as you can, while obtaining enough information on the nuances of each target's personality, background, and motivations so that you may determine whether or not they are a good candidate.

To find a high-quality long-term relationship, assuming a worst-case scenario, expect to be processing at least five targets a week for half a decade with short interludes of dating for a few months to test the viability of serious candidates. While it won't take everyone this long, especially for more "vanilla" people who can easily find compatible partners, you should key a length of time about that long into your life plan and not expect to start looking for a wife or husband at 32 and be married by 35.

While five dates a week may sound like a lot, both of us hit that number. A dedicated search for a long-term partner will take up about as much of your time and emotional investment as a dedicated hobby and is not the same thing as casual dating. The key challenge faced by men leveraging a high-throughput strategy involves cost: Generally, people expect men to pay for all or part of a date, which means financial planning plays a crucial role in your process. The financial burden of high-throughput dating is lighter should you be looking for another guy as a partner or should you be the type of guy who wants a progressive partner, as insisting on going Dutch can weed out bad fits on the first date (if you want a progressive partner, insisting on going Dutch will scare away more conservative individuals before having to even waste a second date on them).

How can you counteract the financial hardship? Let's outline a strategy that may be appropriate for a cash-strapped college student:

At the beginning of a week, buy finger foods and snacks in bulk (such as nice cheeses, crackers, nuts, and drinks) and divide them into kits that get broken into for each date. Utilize these purchased-in-bulk meals to put a picnic together on the day of each date; this will vastly cut down the costs of the dates and the preparation time needed. Then use the "taboo location for picnic" strategy. To implement this taboo location strategy at scale, scout a number of safe locations and thoroughly playtest access plans for each. It is critical to clean up well and be respectful when using a strategy like this in order to maintain access to said taboo locations. If you are uncomfortable utilizing taboo locations, you can look for other small taboos to break, such as taboo times (e.g., an early morning tea with a view of the ocean).

This taboo location strategy is primarily designed to get the target to build a "partners in crime" story about your relationship—something that most people want. This framing helps targets develop a personal narrative in which you two are well matched while also acclimating a target to pushing boundaries with you.

As an added benefit, by framing targets' interactions with you as engagements in which they expect to push boundaries, you can quickly cull those who do *not* want to push boundaries and save time and money on a date never had. Nevertheless, keep in mind that such a strategy could also accidentally filter many perfectly sane women who are afraid of sexual assault. You can try to fish for such concerns and, should they be present, look for alternative free locations that are more crowded (like a beach, a park, or a bluff).

During dates, focus on getting the target comfortable enough in interaction to openly divulge the information that is of the most interest in vetting someone for a potential long-term relationship. This checklist might include:
- Religious and philosophical beliefs
- Desire for children (and optimal number of children)

- Goals in life
- Level of ambition
- Career (versus stay-at-home parent) ambitions
- Conversational skills
- Sexual predilections

After each date, log this information into a makeshift customer-relationship management system (spreadsheets work fine), along with information on the general course of the date to ensure you do not mix up this targets' details.

To ensure that individual relationships could be escalated through the traditional male gift-giving ritual so common in Western society without breaking the bank, look into buying large quantities of low-quality gemstones from wholesale industrial providers. Loose, poor-quality gemstones (even higher-prestige options, such as sapphires, rubies, and pearls) can easily be purchased in bulk for $25 each, but convey a much higher social value due to a general understanding about how much jewelry containing them usually costs (which is a significantly inflated price). The ritual in reference is the exchange of romantically themed gifts such as flowers, expensive chocolates, or jewelry as a sign the relationship had escalated (this is discussed further in the subchapter: Implied Contract Escalation on page 88).

Loose, low-quality, uncut gemstones come in handy with relationship escalation rituals not just because of their relative low cost when contrasted with their perceived value, but because they help the target build a narrative in which they would eventually use this early relationship gift in a marriage band. Giving these gemstones creates a scenario in which you can mine targets for nuanced information about how they expect a marriage to work far earlier in your relationship than would otherwise be realistically viable. (Just as going Dutch on meals can serve as a means to weed out more traditional women, the same can be done by leaving out the gift-giving ritual.)

The point of moving your relationship timeline forward as fast as you can and at scale is to more quickly cull bad candidates. While it may feel like rushing things, the only three aspects of a relationship you are accelerating are:
1. Time taken to extract information used to judge whether or not to marry someone (e.g., don't delay talking about how many kids your target wants and find out quickly if they have emotional control problems)
2. Time taken to develop a level of comfort with the individual so that their "true underlying behavior patterns" reveal themselves
3. Time taken to cull an individual when it is clear they are not a good candidate for a long-term relationship.

Being able to quickly enter a relationship with someone, recognize they are not an optimal match, and move on to the next candidate, increases your odds of securing an optimal long-term relationship that ultimately benefits everyone.

It is easy to decide that this whole process can be dropped by asking more questions faster; however, this isn't this case. Some key details will not be revealed (accurately, at least) without relationship escalation.

Many individuals hide their true selves, and the manner in which they plan to behave after your relationship passes certain thresholds. Mere questions on a first or second date will not shed light on these details.

Malcolm has dated plenty of women who seemed totally normal until the relationship got serious. Had Malcolm allowed these relationships to take years to reach that point, he would have never met Simone. As clinical and cruel as our methods sound, methods that reduce time spent with poorly matched partners are more humane—both for you and your various long-term relationship candidates. Be a Pragmatist. Drop the social conventions and the narratives we want to tell ourselves and focus on the true purpose of a task, which, in this case, involves finding a long-term partner and eliminating distractions that obscure the path forward.

We don't expect you to copy the template strategy provided, but we present it as an example of how you might think through the challenges of vetting long-term relationship candidates at scale—and affordably—yourself. Your goal is to quickly and inexpensively enter a relationship and rapidly escalate to a point at which you can determine whether someone is a bad long-term match. Identify the bottlenecks you will face in this process, be they monetary or temporal, and then invent creative "out of the box" solutions to circumvent or industrialize them. It is extremely unlikely that someone in the first fifty candidates you interview will be your best possible life partner.

Female Template Strategies

If you are a female targeting males, the above section was likely frustrating, as it was written from a male perspective. What can you do to quickly gather the necessary information on a male to vet them while simultaneously making them fall for you?

Women are in a worse position when it comes to securing long-term relationships because of a conundrum unique to their gender. Women will likely run into a large number of males who pretend they are looking for a long-term relationship when they are really looking for casual sex because average quality males have more value on the long-term relationship market than on the sex market. Simply put, an average guy can get a hotter female partner if he pretends to be looking for a long-term relationship and not just sex. Men don't have to deal with this issue, as there just aren't a lot of women who pretend to want a long-term relationship with a man in order to secure sex from him.

Not only must you learn quickly how to determine whether an individual is a viable long-term relationship target, but you need to determine if they want a long-term relationship at all!

A core advantage you have as a woman is that it is possible to execute high-throughput dating at restaurants without breaking the bank if you are ok with manipulating social norms to your advantage by getting most of your male targets to pay or by going Dutch. On the other hand, unlike a male strategy, if you take the picnic route and save money by bringing basket snacks and meals to scenic locations, you will need to select public rather than private (and taboo) places due to the risk of sexual assault. One affordable high-throughput strategy for women involves dates at a public park/wharf/beach with a thermos filled with alcohol (to add social boundary-breaking and loosen dates' tongues) and a snack of the target's choice (or something that signals something about you, like a portable multi-tiered afternoon tea setup).

Note from the Research:
- If a male date does not call you back within 24 hours of your first date, one study suggests there is only a 12% chance he ever will. Nevertheless, this study didn't look at texting patterns, so it may not be as relevant anymore.

To quickly vet candidates while developing a sense of intimacy, we suggest philosophical, religious, or life goal-related conversation topics. If you feel uneasy when engaging in these sorts of conversation topics, we strongly suggest our first book, *The Pragmatist's Guide to Life,* half of which is basically a guide to discussing and thinking about these topics in relatable vernacular.

While a topic like religion can quickly end a date and thus has a social stigma against it, it would only end a date that would have ended in a sub-optimal long-term relationship and successfully breaking said social stigma assists in building a sense of camaraderie. Remember that a "failed" date is often a win for you: A guy who thinks negatively about you because you wanted to discuss ethics or life plans instead of making out is likely a low-quality long-term relationship partner. Alas, philosophical topics alone will not fully filter out guys looking just for sex—they are more for determining whether they are a good match.

While the tactics described above are meant to bring you to a point at which you can harvest useful information from a target, they do not solve the problem of males who pretend they want long-term relationships when all they really want is sex—a problem that is exacerbated by the fact that someone who only wants sex has a motivation to lie about what they are looking for in a long-term relationship to mirror what they think you are looking for.

Thankfully, this problem lends itself to a solution. Specifically, **someone who is primarily interested in sex will mirror exactly what they think you are looking for in a long-term relationship with their answers, while someone genuinely looking for a long-term relationship will be honest.** Someone who clearly shares goals that deviate from your own—but that might still work with your life plans—is being honest.

It is also possible that a genuinely perfectly matched partner will mirror *all of your goals and values*, being so suspiciously perfect that you accidentally throw him out. Should you want to get a second opinion on a target's seemingly too-good-to-be-true interests before tossing him aside, consider interviewing his friends and/or family, plus looking for other behavioral patterns that suggest his stated goals and values are genuine. If a target touts his financial conservatism and shares alleged desires to save up and buy a house: Check his spending (revealed through monthly rental costs of similar units in his apartment building, some back-of-the-napkin calculations of his daily food and beverage expenditures based on some days spent with him, etc.) and take a quick look at average salaries paid to the position he holds. If the math suggests he is barely living paycheck to paycheck, you can rest assured his supposed fiscal conservatism is anything but. A guy who is responsible with money will make an infinitely better long-term partner than a guy who irresponsibly treats you to nice things or who has a slightly better job.

You might also weed out those only looking for sex by gauging their interest in public relationship declaration. Being officially in a relationship—especially on a social media platform regularly used by your target—makes it extremely difficult for them to discreetly secure other partners without the other targets knowing they are with someone. Someone who only wants sex is therefore more likely to decline publicly announcing their relationship with you—at least in social contexts and on social media sites where their peers mix. The catch with this tactic is that it takes far longer to vet candidates if you use the public announcement strategy (it's better to get to "no" well before one would even think of a public relationship).

Honestly, this predicament is grating to say the least because there are no realistically implementable, foolproof strategies for navigating it. Some women completely divorce sexual access from long-term relationship vetting, basically saying: "Look, I am going to have sex with you whether or not you are actually interested in a long-term relationship, so there is no reason to mislead me on that front," but even this strategy would often not be effective, as guys who pretend to be looking for long-term relationships get so stuck in their ways that even when they no longer need to lie to secure sex, *they still will*.

The antithesis of this strategy, saying you will not have sex no matter what until marriage, is also uniquely ineffective. This is because there are many women who claim this but really seem to mean, "no sex unless I am horny on the third date or after." Guys accustomed to sleeping around have heard this gambit a thousand times and have become trained to not believe it, whether or not the claimant is being genuine. This tactic is therefore useless at filtering these guys out, unless it is paired with enough sexless dates to convince them you are legit, and this would be too much of a time drain to be implemented at scale.

Honestly, your best bet is to parse out common stated philosophical beliefs or physical/behavioral tells indicating someone is dishonest about their long-term relationship plans. Such sleuthing pairs well with a dating conversation strategy that focuses on breaking social conventions with a target through deep philosophical conversations. Deep philosophical conversations also have the side benefit of confusing men who are implementing the above strategy and will often lead them to choke up and agree with all of your philosophical beliefs, thereby betraying their true intentions.

SECURING A HUSBAND

As we went about our research, we came across many studies that could be considered relevant to those specifically searching for a husband. This is great news, seeing as while men are relatively easy to secure for sex, they are in high demand in long-term relationship markets. Knowledge, on this front, is power.

Age Considerations in Husband Searches

Women in their twenties would be well served by targeting men aged 28-36 with steady jobs. Most men will not commit to a long-term relationship until they have been living and working independently for at least two years. A robust 80% of men with a high school education will not seriously consider marriage until the age of 23. Men with a college education expect to get married between the ages of 28 and 33, while those with a graduate education shift that age range to 30-36. After the age of 37—and again after age 43—the probability that a man will commit to a long-term relationship (if he isn't already in one) drops dramatically.

As they must also compete with women in their twenties, women in their thirties are at a unique disadvantage when looking for husbands. They may benefit from diving into age ranges that 20-something women would not consider at such high rates—such as men 40 years old or more. Of men over the age of 40, the only group with a high likelihood of committing to a long-term relationship are those who are divorced or widowed as well as those who are more religious. Of men over 50 getting married, 88% marry divorced women. By this age, women are wizened enough to be systematically playing the market arbitrage game, looking for men who are low value in superficial traits and high value in those they specifically care about—if you can learn to play that game in your 20s you will be able to secure a vastly better long term partner for you.

Women targeting the over-40 crowd will be well served by being laid back and kind. While younger men statistically value the women they end up marrying based on virtue, talent, or accomplishments, 62% of men who got married over the age of 40 cited "niceness" (congeniality, agreeableness, a relaxed, and low-maintenance attitude) as the primary trait that attracted them.

Helpful Husband Hunting Tactics

Leverage Peer Pressure

A target may be uniquely good husband fodder if his friends and siblings are coupling up. Men with friends and siblings who are married are more likely to get married. More specifically, 60% of newly married men had a friend who married within the last year, and men without any married male friends were found by one study to be three times more likely to say they were not likely to marry.

Pop the Question

Do not be afraid to propose marriage. If your suggestion is initially rejected, be congenial and merely mention that it means a lot to you—you may enjoy favorable results. Of men who initially rejected the marriage proposals of their eventual wives (mostly by saying they hadn't thought about it yet or that they were not ready), one third had forgotten the event happened and the two thirds that remembered mostly did not see the event as a big deal. Of men who rejected the idea of getting married in a conversation, a large portion nevertheless proposed within four months of saying they were not ready.

Consider Moving On After 22 Months And No Engagement

Most men who *do* propose will do so by the 18-month mark. After 22 months, the likelihood that a man will ever propose begins to diminish—and at 3.5 years, it begins to diminish rapidly. For couples who have been together for seven years without a proposal, the odds that one will ever occur are near zero. Given women's short windows of arbitrage (the ages during which they have a strong advantage on the market, but are also in a life position in which getting married makes sense), it is not worth dating a guy for over two years if he doesn't propose, assuming marriage is her goal.

Some cultures seem to have internalized this dynamic and applied interesting interventions. We have heard that in some traditional Chinese towns, a man can be fined for dating a woman for an extended time without proposing then leaving her as compensation for taking up some of this window.

Make Sacrifices

Given that women are typically at a disadvantage when seeking husbands, those who make more sacrifices in order to win often see better results. Consider making sacrifices with your location, job, and hobbies.

Women who do get married are three times more likely to participate in masculine activities in which they had no real interest and twice as likely to have made lifestyle sacrifices like changing jobs or moving to meet eligible men. Perhaps surprisingly to some, women do not often secure their partners by acting overly sexual: Only seven out of 2,000 men report their wife was in a sexy outfit when they first met.

SEX AND DATING IN A WORLD WITH SOCIAL DISTANCING

As this book was being formatted for publication, COVID-19 snowballed into a global pandemic, causing worldwide lockdowns and presenting a fresh and fascinating challenge to the dating world: How should someone adapt high-throughput strategies to societies that restrict human interaction? The best approach depends on your objective.

I Want Sex and Dating

If you are looking for no-strings-attached sex with strangers, a world in which every social interaction involves heightened risk will be limiting—though not because social distancing impedes the seduction process. In fact, convincing a partner to have sex with you using the Sexual Exploration Lure through written interaction is both easier and more expedient than picking someone up at a bar or meeting someone through serendipitous social interaction. At one point, Malcolm A/B tested a number of different engagement strategies when looking for sex with high-quality partners; none came close to written interactions within instant messaging systems. No-strings-attached sex with new people is not difficult to secure in areas encouraging social distancing per se (outside of those that literally won't allow you to leave your house).

Casual sex becomes difficult in such scenarios not because of social distancing, but because the potential consequences resulting from casual sex—be they death or long-term organ damage—filter out a portion of the population that might have otherwise been interested in one-night stands. When you filter people concerned with their own safety out of the sex market, the risk you take on when engaging with the remaining market explodes. Crazy partners can screw up your life. If you insist on no-strings-attached sex when all "responsible" people are bowing out, you are much more likely to end up with a whacked-out nutter butter.

Fortunately, our anecdotal experience indicates that the COVID-19 pandemic has not been a death knell to the sex lives of our friskier friends. In fact, many tight-knit poly communities seem to be adapting to the situation well—if a bit recklessly (too reckless for our risk tolerances).

The primary challenge faced by intimate social clusters that continue socializing during periods in which socializing bears risks is that the team is only as strong as the weakest link. If just one person in a polycule (a poly relationship network) decides to lower their guard and meet with additional people, *everyone* in the polycule hurts. Many poly networks we know were among the first to get COVID-19 during the pandemic. Some members of these networks were so hooked on social interaction that their idea of "self isolation" involved merely *talking* about being careful while nevertheless meeting and spending time in close quarters with three separate social groups in a given day. On the other hand, the few groups we know that cohabitate in isolation from members outside their group home have held up quite well. Should dangerous diseases become a part of daily life, cohabitating polycules with strict ground rules and that leverage technology to track their members may present the safest solution for individuals who have a predilection for romantic variation. (Though this would likely nullify the purpose of polyamorous relationships for many.)

I Want a Monogamous Long-Term Partner

We wish we had the luxury of dating and looking for marriage partners in an environment that required social distancing. A world unburdened by interpersonal interaction presents a transparently easier, less expensive, and more efficient dating and marriage market.

When flippantly meeting in person is an option, it becomes an expectation. Social norms demand in-person liaisons before most people become willing to open up and escalate relationships. However, when social norms can't be met, they are bent. There are voluminous benefits from being able to date and get to know people without having to meet in person.

The ability to become acquainted through written exchanges early in a relationship minimizes time wasted before you can delve to "deep" topics—the types of topics most relevant to vetting someone as a long-term partner. Not only does communicating through typing give a person time to think through what they are about to say, but it also allows them to think in a fashion less encumbered by social signals and posturing. Anecdotally, both of us have found that people are more willing to talk about philosophically-engaging topics when they can do so in a written format—plus they're more comfortable being explicit about sexual topics. Such increased openness makes it possible to more quickly establish compatibility with a partner when it comes to less vanilla aspects of your sexuality.

Bear in mind that written exchanges are the form most virtual dates take, so you can rest assured that socially-distanced courtship does not doom you to the endless, awkward Zoom meetings most people assume distance dating entails. Unlike awkward video calls, written correspondence can be utterly enthralling (there's a reason why so many romances in the pre-internet era were sparked from love letters). If you have never had that feeling of becoming entranced in a written chat that had you glued to a screen, anticipating every response until you pass out from exhaustion at five in the morning, you are missing out.

We would go so far as to encourage partners in a long-term relationship to occasionally take vacations from interacting with each other physically and instead interact through instant messaging or long-form diary entries. You will be shocked how communicating through different mediums can unlock aspects of an individual's personality that remain occluded when you limit yourself to verbal communication.

Another beneficial aspect of "forced distance" dating is that it seems to intensify and extend new relationship energy—that feeling of excitement and anticipation you get early in a relationship. This can explain why new relationship energy lasts much longer and feels more intense in long-distance relationships. We theorize that new relationship energy is a product of anticipation created by gaps in a person's knowledge about their partner, which can feel more profound when you must operate without the convenience of in-person social cues.

Better still, not having to meet in person makes it easier to cultivate multiple relationships simultaneously, making it possible to dramatically increase your throughput of potential partners and find your optimal match more quickly. Dating through text communication creates forced pauses during which a partner has to think through what they are going to say next (assuming you are engaging in deep issues). These thoughtful pauses enable you to run multiple conversations concurrently, which in turn helps to weed out suboptimal matches as you will organically gravitate toward the most intellectually engaging exchanges. Any increase in potential partner throughput and suboptimal partner rejection decreases the length of time between now and the point at which you find that perfect match.

Finally, women are in a dramatically better position when looking for a long-term partner through a dating market that impedes the possibility of easy sex. The market dynamics of in-person dating enable men to secure higher-quality females by pretending to be interested in dating or a long-term relationship when they really only care about sex. Women are dramatically less likely to encounter these motivational impostors when dating in a world of social distancing.

How do I go about getting people to engage with me online?

❈ The Pragmatist's Guide to Relationships

While you can take the obvious route through dating websites and apps, these are not necessarily your best options. Back when Facebook let users send messages to anyone, Malcolm sourced many of his romantic partners through cold messages sent to people on Facebook. While such an approach would now require that a person of interest accepts you as a friend before you can contact them, meeting someone through Facebook is not dramatically harder than it used to be. The same can be said for sites like LinkedIn.

Meeting a new person online is no different from meeting a random person on a subway train or at a bar . . . except you know more about them than whatever their appearance and public behavior implies, so you can conduct far more thorough pre-date screening tests (deciding you can only meet someone online on dating websites is like deciding you can only meet potential partners in-person at speed dating events). As with in-person meetings, you can choose to be upfront with your intentions or ask your target to set up a call or chat time to talk about a topic of mutual interest (on a train, this might mention a book you saw someone reading, whereas on LinkedIn you might strike up an exchange about a target's listed areas of interest).

How do you reach out to random people online without looking like a creep? Learning how to contact people online out of the blue requires practice and failure—more failure than you would endure were you to engage people through more familiar avenues. That said, once you become skilled at chatting folks up online, your success rate will be as high or higher than it is with in-person dating. Remember how awkward it was to ask people out in your teens? Well, buckle up, bucko, because you are going to have to go through that all over again—that is, if you haven't already taken time to learn how to meet random people online earlier in your life. On a positive note, it won't be as bad this time around because the sting of rejection hurts much less in written form and you will develop a thick skin more quickly given your ability to amass online rejections at an astoundingly higher rate.

When dating must be exclusively virtual in its early stages, more care will need to be made to prevent the relationship from escalating without having an extremely clear idea of what the person looks like, plus confidence that they are who they say they are. Most people who catfish others online do not consciously intend to mislead their victims. We all want to post pictures that paint us in the best light possible, however doing so on aggregate can obscure deal breakers from potential partners' view. Let's say a person has really messed up teeth. They likely are not going to not smile in pictures, leading their dates to be in for quite the surprise the first time they lean in for an in-person kiss. This kind of unintentional catfishing is something we all do to some extent.

While it helps to have access to a profile on a social network like Facebook, on which a potential partner has lots of friends (who will tag this potential partner in likely-less-flattering photos that *they've* chosen to post), the only real way to ensure everyone has an accurate view of each other is to escalate communication to video calls as soon as sexual innuendo or mentions of dating arise (though even this isn't foolproof and can obscure common deal breakers—like a person perpetually smelling of cigarettes). No matter how into a person you are, if they avoid video calls, it is probably in your best interest to break things off immediately—the probability in such cases that a potential partner is being honest with you in this age of technology is so low as to be negligible.

Even in the scenario we are proposing, in which a global pandemic makes in-person interactions dangerous, relationships kindled online won't stay virtual forever. Even in worlds locked down due to viral spread, there is room for safe, long-term, in-person relationships with people you trust. In such a world, it makes sense to move in together when dating gets serious. In many ways, kicking off serious dating with close cohabitation and forced isolation presents an optimal means by which you can quickly determine whether or not someone would be a good fit for a long-term relationship. Such a scenario would certainly get you to "no" faster than biweekly in-person meals at a restaurant.

Being obligated to develop new approaches to life in the face of changing world conditions should be exhilarating. The type of person who can see a changing world as an opportunity to discover and develop even more efficient strategies will consistently outperform those who classify turbulent world conditions as an excuse to indulge in procrastination.

BUT WHATEVER I DO, NOTHING WORKS!

If you find yourself thinking: "But whatever I do, no one wants me," the problem is you.

If you find yourself thinking: "But everyone I date treats me poorly," the problem is you.

If you find yourself thinking: "I am so ugly and pathetic, no one will ever want me," then get a dog and for the love of all things wholesome, take good care of it.

If what you want is the validation that comes from being loved and wanted, then a dog will give that to you—you don't need a human for that. Wasting another human life on something as trivial as feeding your desire to feel needed, appreciated, and loved is narcissistic in the extreme.

There are two general categories of people who just can't seem to catch a break: People who have no chance because of factors outside their control, and people who have no chance because they are unwilling to alter who they are, however flawed and suboptimal they may be. We will address each category in turn.

People Who Just Don't Have a Chance

We live in a world that has somehow managed to delude itself into the belief that everyone can get what they want from a relationship if they just implement the correct strategy. We accept this pleasant fantasy because we desperately want to believe in the potential for an equal society.

Humans are not born equal. Life is not like a video game in which, because you have only one point in attractiveness, your avatar has more points to spend in intelligence. Instead: looks, intelligence, height, motivation, and wealth are all highly correlated (we mean this scientifically and not subjectively—statistically speaking, hot and tall people are more intelligent and wealthier). This sucks, but it's a statistical reality.

No matter how ugly and poor a person is, they can still get whatever they want from a relationship so long as they are smart and motivated. That said, not all people are smart and motivated. Any relationship guide claiming to be able to help unmotivated, intellectually challenged people is telling a cruel lie and doing these people an honest disservice.

Some children are born to great disadvantages. Some kids starve to death before their fifth birthday. This book isn't going to change this reality, but at least it can avoid making the world worse by not acknowledging it. Telling people that everyone is guaranteed a satisfying relationship so long as they follow a few simple steps is as willfully ignorant as telling people that anyone can become a billionaire should they merely work hard enough. The world isn't fair, and pretending it is only makes things worse for those who struggle the most.

If you are that guy who has sent thirty unprompted dick pics and has gotten thirty immediate rejections yet still holds out hope that dick pics are a viable sexual strategy or if you are that gal who thinks that if you just stand in the corner at enough bars for long enough, eventually your future spouse will sweep you off your feet: You simply lack the social intelligence required to engineer a successful relationship or a productive sexual strategy. All we can say is we are sorry, and the world isn't fair.

Note from the Research:
- Before making the above assertion that those who send dick pics are idiots, we researched dick pic sending behavior to see if perhaps those who chronically send unsolicited pictures of their penises aren't idiots, but rather exhibitionists. It appears that a portion of men sending unsolicited dick pics actually expect their action to be part of a successful strategy because of a severely underdeveloped theory of mind and inability to take the perspective of those receiving these unsolicited photos. Specifically, these men are trying to mirror the manner in which *they* most want to be approached by a woman. These men would *love* for women to send unsolicited genital pics to them, and like a cat bringing a dead mouse to the foot of a human's bed as a gift, feel confused when the gift's recipient appears horrified. The hilarious irony here is that dick pic senders see the world through a lens or true gender equality—they genuinely believe that women will want to be treated and think the exact way they do.

People Who Fail Because of Who They Are

A tragically large number of individuals are unwilling to accept that their failure to secure sex, a long-term partner, or a happy relationship results from a personal character that they can—but are apparently unwilling to—change.

Every human has the potential to deserve love and happiness. But have you ever heard the phrase: "You get what you deserve"? Some people expect more love and happiness than their efforts, self-reflection, and self-control can earn.

Being the source of your own problems doesn't necessarily indicate you are mean or ill-intentioned. We know nice people who repeatedly end up in horrible relationships, and all we can say is: "Well, it sucks, but we get why it keeps happening to that person." If this statement shocks you, make more friends. You will eventually meet that person who, while being perfectly innocent, sees all their relationships end or turn toxic for reasons that would be obvious to them were they capable of self-reflection.

The good news is that personal failings can be fixed. If you want help on that front, read our first book: *The Pragmatist's Guide to Life*. We will even give you a free digital copy if you send a short description of your last relationship to Hello@Pragmatist.Guide. The bad news is that taking the steps outlined in *The Pragmatist's Guide to Life* requires sustained effort and motivation, which will be thoroughly unpleasant, assuming you are the kind of person who does not enjoy making themselves better.

DEFINING HUMAN RELATIONSHIPS

Whenever we first tackle a topic, we do our best to define it. Here is our best crack at delineating what exactly a relationship is:

A relationship forms when **participants believe that through collaboration they can differentially benefit from a partnership.**

Let's break that down:
- **Collaboration**: This can have a wide range of definitions, both sexual and non-sexual. Two people who non-sexually cohabitate to raise a child are, by our definition, in a relationship—as are two people who mutually decide to have a one-night stand and never see each other again. While our use of the word collaboration means that bosses and employees, as well as friends, are also in relationships, this book will focus on relationships that include some form of sexual engagement, cohabitation, or a shared public identity.
- **Participants:** Anyone involved in a relationship is a participant, and there can be one, two, three, or more participants in a relationship. A participant may also be one individual in a relationship with a group, such as a man who is dating a married couple.
- **Benefit:** We define "benefit" as the maximization of an individual's objective function (the thing or things they have chosen to attempt to maximize in

their lives). An objective function may revolve around anything from personal pleasure to the pursuit of fame, the service of God, or the wellbeing of one's children. Individuals who do not have an objective function typically aim to optimize whatever gives instant pleasure or reinforces a self-identity they have developed over time (such as that of being a good, loving husband, a ruthless alpha male boss, a shrewd mom who would do anything for her kids, etc.). For a more detailed explanation of objective functions or how human autopilot works, consult our first book: *The Pragmatist's Guide to Life*.
- **Believe:** We include this word because beliefs are not always correct. One of the most common strategies implemented to secure a sexual partner (and sometimes even a spouse) is to attempt to manipulate a target's worldview to reflect an inaccurate reality, causing them to overvalue the relationship.
- **Differentially:** This means that the participants believe they benefit more from the partnership than they would benefit from other mutually exclusive partnerships available to them (multiplied by their perceived ability to successfully enter said alternate partnerships). This can become quite complicated when the differential benefit comes from a negative modifier. For example, someone in a holistically negative, abusive relationship may fear their partner will kill them if they leave the relationship, which may lead them to conclude that they believe they differentially benefit from staying with the abusive partner (by not being murdered). We expand

upon this concept in detail in this book's chapter on abuse.

- **Partnership:** Partnership typically exists as some form of social contract (either implied or explicit) that is occasionally verbally confirmed. We strongly recommend making the contracts that govern the terms of your relationship as explicit as possible, or you may end up with, "I didn't know that being your boyfriend meant I couldn't kiss other girls" situations. We explore this concept in the book's chapter on relationship contracts.

More simply put, we are all looking for the same things from a relationship: A mutually beneficial partnership with one or more people. (Well, most of us are—we suppose sociopaths don't care if a partnership is mutually beneficial.)

FACTORS AFFECTING DESIRABILITY

The factors that raise a person's desirability (both aggregate and individual) can vary dramatically and are worth investigating. In this investigation, we will focus on factors that can contribute to both individual desirability and aggregate desirability, as well as how such factors can be exploited to your advantage within the marketplace.

Gold has value because the market values gold. Whether or not you individually value gold, and whether or not gold has any inherent moral, functional, or philosophical value, is irrelevant. If the price of gold is higher in Syria, this does not mean Syrians are gold-mad fiends, or all Syrians want gold; it is merely a market fact: The price of gold is higher in Syria. Such facts are worth discussing because they reveal arbitrage opportunities that can be exploited.

Our statements like: "Additional wealth increases a male's aggregate desirability more than a female's aggregate desirability" are therefore devoid of moral judgments or any other implications aside from what the statistics show. Please keep this in mind when reviewing seemingly harsh statements.

A quick refresher:
- Aggregate desirability: A person's aggregate value on a specific marketplace *(e.g., The average price of a fish at a marketplace)*

- Individual desirability: A person's value to a specific other person (e.g., *How much you, personally, would be willing to pay for a fish*)

Physical Attractiveness

While some basic physical features indicating genetic fitness—such as facial symmetry—are universally seen as attractive, there is a wide array of deviations in which physical features are considered attractive between markets. Physical attractiveness, therefore, presents an excellent opportunity to identify and exploit arbitrage opportunities.

Suppose you are deathly pale. This would vastly decrease your aggregate physical attractiveness among a Jersey Shore subculture, but vastly increase it among a goth subculture. Thinking about aggregate desirability in this specific context makes it clear that it is often worth thinking about the tools you have at your disposal and what subcultures value those tools most. Goth aggregate desirability rank is going to be different than Western societal aggregate desirability rank even though Western society contains the goth subgroup.

In general, when we use the word aggregate desirability without a modifier, the modifier we are implying is western society, as that is the population to which most adults turn when attempting to calculate their own aggregate value for the purposes of making decisions about who is "in their league" (e.g., when trying to decide if they could do better than their current partner) and thus the rating that influences relationship stability the most.

If you have a physical trait that has little positive or negative effect on your aggregate desirability, but that is a specific, strong turn on for a small portion of the population—lots of freckles or heterochromia (having eyes of two different colors)—you can exploit this. If you secure a partner that has an attraction to this trait, it will be easier to ensure your individual desirability to that partner stays higher than your aggregate desirability.

Should you have some feature that significantly *negatively* impacts your aggregate desirability on a societal level, but that a few small communities find to be very attractive, you can get a leg up by targeting those communities. There are, for example, people who find severe obesity or being quadriplegic very attractive. Playing specifically into these communities can allow you access to partners of a quality that would be extremely difficult for you to find on the open market.

This tactic has two downsides:
1. It can be very difficult to sexualize something of which you have been conditioned to be ashamed. Life will be hard if your life partner adores one of your top points of shame. To reduce that discomfort, consider re-framing your ideal self-image in a manner that embraces that feature, which you once saw as a flaw.
2. These communities don't filter out "creeps" as aggressively as other social groups, leading to a feeling that they attract creeps even though that isn't really the case. It is not that creepy individuals

have these proclivities more often, but that creeps are more likely to be open about their interests. People rarely voluntarily make a sexual kink community their primary social circle; thus, those that do are more likely than average to have been expelled from most other communities.

Kink Preference

Typically an individual's kink preference only affects individual desirability because it is not broadcasted publicly. A masochist would have a higher individual desirability to a sadist, but a sadist would typically not know someone is a masochist because that isn't the type of thing people signal publicly.

Kink preferences can affect aggregate desirability in some scenarios. A woman who likes anal or a man who loves cunnilingus may have higher aggregate desirability in some markets. The tricky thing is signaling this to the market in a way that doesn't cause more harm than good to aggregate desirability. Kink preference, therefore, really only comes into play in the poly dating scene and within specific kink subcultures where sharing this kind of information is more normalized.

Contractual Perks or Downsides

A person may be able to raise their individual desirability with a prospective or current partner through the terms in their relationship contract (the "rules" of their relationship). Rather than written documents, these contracts are typically just a set of expectations as to the "rules" of the relationship and are talked about in detail in this book's chapter on relationship contracts.

For example, a woman might increase her individual desirability in the eyes of a man by creating a relationship contract in which he is not out of bounds when sleeping with other women. A man might increase his desirability by creating a contract in which there is an expectation that he does all the chores. The ability to alter your relationship contract to increase your value to your partner should not be underestimated as a tool to increase relationship stability even if society rarely flags it as an option.

In rare instances in which a subculture publicly broadcasts expected relationship contract terms, one's acceptable terms can have an impact on aggregate desirability. For example, a polyamorous couple looking for a unicorn (a single, bisexual female willing to be in a relationship in which she has lower status than the primary female) has a legendarily high aggregate desirability within polyamorous communities, as few people are interested in being that kind of third wheel and unicorns can become therefore they are in short supply. Of course, this opens the doors to significant arbitrage if you either enjoy or don't mind the dynamics of a "unicorn" contract allowing you to secure partners well "out of your league."

Personality + Trope

Some people have a unique predilection for certain personality types. If your partner likes your personality type, you will enjoy higher individual desirability and thus a more stable relationship.

Personality, as expressed within cultural tropes, also affects aggregate desirability. Tropes are personality archetypes we have in our collective social consciousness—a cultural shorthand for a group of personality traits. A great arbitrage play is to embody a trope that has little real-world representation but for whom a fair number of individuals harbor a strong sexual preference. When Malcolm first started dating, he attempted to embody the "preppy" trope of what girls generically considered hot—something that all the other guys were doing. Then he switched to the nerd archetype, and his difficulty in securing partners dropped dramatically. This was due to the large portion of girls finding the nerd archetype "hot" and few physically attractive guys embodying it (at least back then—this has changed dramatically in the past decade).

Mental Attributes

Mental attributes can range from innate intelligence to mental stability or a sense of humor. Preferences for different mental attributes vary across subcultures, allowing opportunities for arbitrage. Interestingly, some subcultures appear to value low intelligence in females that, because it can be easily faked by an intelligent female, leads to interesting market dynamics.

Emotional, Hormonal, and Instinctual Factors

A person's individual desirability is often modulated by the emotional and hormonal processes they trigger in other people, intentionally or otherwise. These processes range from "love at first sight" (which is not the same emotion as love, studies show it's closer to lust contextualized differently) to new relationship energy (NRE) and HLA (HLA is human leukocyte antigen, which has been shown to have some effect on who people find attractive, though the research on HLA does not support the massive effect some people want to pretend it has).

These factors are most relevant right at the start of a relationship and are experienced as "new relationship energy" / limerence. In longer-term relationships, these factors are experienced as love. Either way, they almost always increase your individual desirability to a specific partner with whom you have interacted physically.

Availability

An individual's availability and willingness to emotionally and sexually engage with a partner affects both individual and aggregate desirability, but not always in ways that you would expect.

On an individual level, you can increase your desirability by making an effort to actively engage with a prospective partner on an intellectual, emotional, physical, or/and sexual level. While doing this watch for and react to "bids for attention," be they overt (like asking to go on a walk) or covert (like silently pouting). However, having a highly available partner is not every individual's preference—thus, you should attempt to determine an individual's preferred relationship style before increasing your desirability in this way.

Unexpectedly decreasing availability can have a profound, deleterious effect on relationship stability. This often comes with the natural decline or increase in sexual and emotional availability common in many due to natural hormonal changes (triggered by age, relationship status, children, etc.), which instigates friction in relationships and can profoundly affect the extent to which each partner values their significant other.

Where things get weird is how availability impacts your aggregate desirability. A phenomenon called **mate-choice copying** causes individuals to find a target who has already been chosen by another person to be more desirable. While this phenomenon is seen in many species, it is particularly strong in humans. Studies have found that a man wearing a wedding ring will be flirted with more often than a man without one, and the presence of an attractive partner increases a man's perceived desirability. This phenomenon is seen more in human females than in males (but it honestly hasn't been studied much in males—we suspect it exists but is counteracted by men's aggregate preference for chastity).

Mate-choice copying appears to be a primarily female mating tactic aimed at simplifying the assessment of a man's suitability for long-term sexual relationships. Supporting this hypothesis, studies show that lack of experience increases copying behavior in women (e.g., a woman with less sexual experience will strongly prefer an already "taken" partner on the aggregate).

Mate-choice copying becomes a problem when it begins to snowball—males who are successful with women have an easier time with other women, which in turn makes them yet more attractive to other women. The fact that mate copying impulses are strongest among inexperienced women (this has been shown experimentally) causes the classic high-school stud conundrum, in which a few guys have an artificially inflated value in high school: A perception among the school body that all the girls like a guy causes many girls to like him more. Simultaneously, mate copying makes it much harder for a young guy who is *not* successful in the sexual marketplace in high school to break in.

What we perhaps find most fascinating about this behavior is that for a portion of the population, it appears to have no upper limit to how it modifies attractiveness. It is hard to say how big that portion is, as there has been no research on the subject that we are aware of. The effect can be seen when you get large groups of inexperienced women, all demonstrating interest in the same male, as is often seen with famous musicians (think an Elvis, Justin Bieber, or boy band performance). What is cool is we can trace this behavior back to even the earliest days of film in performances, like those of Frank Sinatra. The behavior is even recorded in historic texts, with the phenomenon appearing around generals and musicians going all the way back to the Renaissance.

Perhaps the stimulation caused by mate choice mirroring creates a snowball phenomenon in which each woman sees the increasing desirability rating for the male among her large group of peers and thus up modulates her affection displays in turn, leading her peers to up modulate theirs. This snowball of stimulation can literally reach such levels that people will begin screaming and crying uncontrollably then pass out.

There is no corollary phenomenon involving male groups frothing at the mouth and passing out over females, which lends credence to the experimentally supported evidence that mirroring affects females more than males (not that males won't cheer for famous females, but there is a pretty clear distinction between this snowball phenomenon and normal crowd admiration). The fact that mate-choice copying appears more in inexperienced women also explains why the bands most frequently cause a snowball phenomenon target preteen girls (boy bands, etc.). *We need to clarify here that we think the normal mechanisms meant to prevent mirroring from snowballing aren't in place in only a small percent of the female population, but that when you expose someone to a large enough crowd of women, that small percent without the normal regulation mechanism feed off of each other.*

Note from the Research:
- One study we found suggested that the effect may be inverse in men. In this study, men who saw a woman with other men judged her as being less desirable than if she was depicted alone, while, unsurprisingly, women judged men as more desirable when they are around other women.

Chastity-Promiscuity

The effects of perceived chastity on aggregate desirability vary profoundly between cultures, genders, and sexes. Among the majority of heterosexual individuals looking for long-term partners in Western cultures, a high level of chastity among women is typically seen as a positive modifier (depending on the age of the individual), and medium levels of chastity are valued among males. Some studies show the negative modifier to attractiveness associated with promiscuity is equally strong among both men and women. We expect this is the case for high promiscuity but are not sure if we "buy it" at low/medium levels, such as two or three partners.

On the other hand, promiscuity can be a positive modifier for men and women's aggregate desirability in short-term relationship marketplaces, as it lowers the perceived investment required to achieve sexual payout.

In other words, in females, chastity increases their desirability as a potential long-term partner but decreases desirability as just a sex partner due to the implied increased time investment to gain sexual payout from a chaste individual.

Chastity versus promiscuity has a sizable impact on individual desirability and may also trigger a sexual preference modifier ("I find slutty girls hot") or a situational modifier ("I need someone who is sexually experienced to show me the ropes"). We dive into the statistics associated with chastity in some detail in the chapter on chastity, exploring how it affects societal perceptions of desirability, neurochemistry, and relationship dynamics.

Wealth

The effects of wealth on desirability are obvious, but the consequences of said effects on society may be more insidious than one would imagine at first glance. A high level of wealth modifies a male's aggregate desirability if he can effectively signal his wealth, whereas wealth might even run a risk of reducing aggregate desirability for women in many markets (and the statistics back this up).

At a societal level, this has two important consequences:
1. Once a man has acquired a high level of wealth, he is more likely than a woman to spend it on things that a prospective partner may see and recognize as expensive. This may help to explain why more single wealthy men buy and publicly

display expensive luxury cars than single wealthy women (93.6% of Ferraris are bought by men, 84.4% of Maserati buyers are men, and 80.3% of Porsche buyers are men—even though women buy 62% of cars overall). You see this effect in cars because a car is the highest ticket item you can own that can be shown to someone without taking them back to your residence, and hence cars can signal a person's wealth as early as the first date.
2. A woman could increase her aggregate desirability a *little* were she to have half a million dollars to her name, but her wealth-based-gains pale in comparison to those made by men. To an average male, half a million dollars is everything it is to a female, but it can also be used to give him a much larger value boost in the sexual marketplace. This means that unless we can get men on average to value the wealth of female partners more and women to value wealth among male partners less, a marginal increase in wealth has more value to an average man than an average woman. This is likely a contributor to men choosing higher-paying jobs with lower work-life balance on average at a higher rate than women (leading to uncomfortable statistics, like 93% of workplace fatalities being male).

Fertility

In most cultures throughout time, fertile men and women have a higher aggregate and individual desirability (see King Henry VIII and his wives as an excellent example), but in modern Western culture, fertility is only really relevant to individual desirability in someone who wishes to produce offspring with a long-term partner. Interest in bearing and raising children also falls into the category, as a woman desperate to get pregnant often has slightly lower aggregate desirability on the casual dating market, whereas a man who really wants to start a family has slightly higher aggregate desirability on the long-term relationship market.

Physical Alteration

In modern western society, physical alteration through surgical or other interventions generally lowers aggregate desirability. That said, both present time and history are full of examples of groups who view significant physical alteration, such as tattoos, foot binding, neck extension, the use of gauges, or forehead flattening, as a means of significantly raising aggregate desirability.

Individuals who have undergone significant surgical alterations will have arbitrage opportunities if these alterations demonstrate dedication to a subculture, and the individual is hunting for a partner within said subculture. Things like tattoos and piercings can be used to demonstrate dedication to a subculture through the sacrifice of lowering one's estimated value in mainstream society and thus raising their value within a subculture (think of a goth with significant piercings or someone in a gang covered in tattoos).

At a societal level, the negative modifier associated with physical alteration is usually tied to both the extent of the alteration and the quality of the alteration. Something like veneers or a facelift typically has a low effect. Augmented breasts typically have a medium effect. Sex reassignment surgeries typically have a profound effect. All these effects can be heavily modified by the quality of the work.

On an individual basis, the extent to which physical alteration changes attractiveness varies highly. For some people, it is a deal-breaker, while for others it is irrelevant or a positive. The attractiveness gains possible through cosmetic surgery can more than make up for any negative effect of having undergone alteration. Even on an individual level, a guy who thinks "fake" boobs are gross may prefer larger breasts enough to still prefer a surgically altered breast.

Note from the Research:
- One study showed that while men expect tattoos will increase their desirability, they do not. More specifically, men with tattoos ranked themselves as more attractive, but females did not prefer tattooed males when the tattoos were digitally added to images of shirtless men. Women also ranked men with tattoos as worse prospective partners and parents in the study.

Children from Previous Partners

An individual with children from a partner to whom they are no longer attached has lower aggregate desirability across almost all cultures; however, the negative effect hits women harder than men. In contrast, having children with a partner typically significantly raises your individual desirability in that partner's eyes (this is tied to social stigmas and the financial convenience in your partner also being the parent of a child you share).

This double whammy of lowering your value on an open market, but increasing your value to your partner has a huge effect on relationships pre- and post-kids making them much more stable—which is useful because having kids also increases stress levels, which could otherwise drive more couples to break up after having their first child. (In other words, after a couple has kids together both of their desirability to other people goes down dramatically but the logistical simplicity of staying together typically increases for both of them. These two things happening at the same time helps increase the stability of a relationship at an otherwise stressful time.)

Beliefs About the World

It would seem obvious that alignment of beliefs affects a person's individual desirability in the eyes of a partner, but personal beliefs can also affect an individual's aggregate desirability. To take an extremist example: A neo-Nazi has a lower aggregate desirability than someone who is not a neo-Nazi. In general, a more conservative or men's-rights-focused worldview improves a woman's aggregate desirability, because these beliefs are less common in women, and a more liberal and feminist view improves a man's aggregate desirability.

Something that lowers one's aggregate desirability on an open market but improves a person's individual desirability when they find a match creates a very stable relationship. Were two neo-Nazis to meet each other, the rareness of that belief system and how undesirable they each are on the open market would create a relationship better than most others they could hope for. As neo-Nazis typically hang out in communities of neo-Nazis, the effect is somewhat muted as they likely judge their aggregate desirability against their social group.

Sources of Recreation

The effects of preferred hobbies and recreational activities on individual desirability are obvious. Most will gain more from a partnership with someone who enjoys doing the same things they do—though there are some who would prefer to maintain their own separate domains, and it is helpful to parse out such preferences when vetting relationship candidates.

Hobbies can heavily impact aggregate desirability. For example, a woman who likes playing first-person shooter video games and watching football or a guy who enjoys shopping may have a leg up with partners of the opposite gender. Ownership of pets also falls into this category and has a significant impact on individual and aggregate desirability; thus, pets are sometimes used in partner acquisition strategies.

Opportunity Cost

Since the generic societal relationship contract is a monogamous one, being in most relationships precludes—or at least significantly impedes—one's ability to source other partners. If you know that you are in a place in life with a large pool of potential partners that are easy to meet (college, for instance), any relationship that eats up time you have to source within that pool will have a negative value modifier attached to it.

For example, when Malcolm was at Stanford Business School and starting to date Simone, he made it clear how severe the opportunity cost was to him. Stanford's GSB presented a pool of pre-vetted, intelligent, high potential earners he would only have access to for two years—he would only pass up access to a pool like that for someone he was extremely likely to marry.

Status

The perceived aggregate desirability of an individual—in other words, their status—can directly affect the individual desirability of that person among those who care deeply about how others see them (thus the archetype of the trophy wife). In other words, people who value association with prestigious things will put a uniquely high premium on partners that society as a whole puts a high premium on.

Signaling

Sometimes an individual will gain value from another by using a relationship with the other person to send a message about who they are. A Christian, for example, may choose to date a Muslim in order to demonstrate to either themselves or society that they are not biased by religion. Alternatively, an individual may only consider dating people within their own race, social group, culture, or class to signal their devotion to racial/group/culture/class purity.

One of the strongest effects of signaling can be seen with self-signaling, which prevents long-term relationships from dissolving. Someone who wants to see themselves as a good husband, good mother, family man, good Catholic, etc. may place a uniquely high individual desirability modifier on a relationship because ending the relationship would damage how they want to see themselves. While this effect can raise individual desirability to almost absurdly high levels within some religious groups due to the negative stigma these religious groups cast on divorce, more often this effect is felt when a person just doesn't want to believe that they "wasted" the last fifteen years of their lives and therefore refuse to leave an ill matched-partner because doing so would require admitting their own mistake in choosing that partner and continuing to stay with them for so long.

THE FOUR CORE MARKETS

The unpleasant shock of realizing that your value (your aggregate desirability) is much lower on one market than another is a tale as old as time. We all know the attractive woman who has no trouble getting guys to sleep with her but can't find a guy willing to date her in public—or the guy who opened up his marriage with the expectation he would be able to go on a sexual rumspringa only to realize that no one wants to sleep with him, while his wife picks up a new lover every time she stops by a bar.

People looking for no-strings-attached sex look for totally different traits in a partner than those looking for someone to marry. There are different markets for every type of relationship you may seek, and your aggregate desirability may vary dramatically across these markets.

The four core markets are:
1. The sex market
2. The casual dating market
3. The long-term relationship market
4. The non-monogamous market

The Sex Market

This is the market for those seeking short-term sex and short-term sexual intimacy. The sex market is radically different from the other three which, while not perfectly aligned, feature some sense of parity. The majority of people on the sex market are really looking more for the short-term intimacy associated with casual sex or validation granted by an ability to easily secure sex. Statistically speaking, few people of any gender ever actively search for emotionless sex.

Men are incredibly undervalued on the sex market. The aggregate desirability of a man on this market is vastly lower than it is on other markets, and the aggregate desirability of a female on this market is astronomically higher than it is on any other market. As a result, many men who are only looking for sex will pretend to be on other markets, and many women who are actually looking for more serious relationships pretend they are only looking for sex.

This can be an effective strategy for men wishing to secure sex, but it is rarely an effective strategy for women keen to secure a long-term or casual dating relationship. This problem can lead to an enormous negative cognitive effect on a woman when a man using her for sex convinces her that they are actually casually dating.

The relative value difference between genders on this market is not an issue of mere perception and has been studied fairly extensively. In the often-cited paper, *Gender Differences in Receptivity to Sexual Offers*, men and women asked strangers if they wanted sex. Not a single female ever agreed to a male's request, whereas 75% of males in one study and 69% of males in another agreed to the requests—this is even more striking when you consider that in the same studies, when men and women requested a date, there was almost no gender difference at all in response rate (about 50% for each). These findings imply that the men observed in this research were more willing to go to a stranger's house for no-strings-attached sex than they were to consent to a date with a stranger! *(If this feels familiar, we mentioned these studies briefly when describing the Easy Lure.)*

Follow-up studies have worked to find out just how high value an individual needs to be to get women to agree to no-strings-attached sex at a similar rate to men. While men would agree to no-strings-attached sex with celebrities like Jennifer Lopez at about the same rate as they would a stranger, once you get to the level of a celebrity like Johnny Depp, women will finally consent to no-strings-attached sex. In experiments like the first—but featuring incredibly attractive individuals—83% of men agreed to sex with a stranger, but this time, 3% of women did. To dissect this data another way: While women have an easier time on the sex market, a woman who is astronomically high in value (like a celebrity) is not of much higher value on this market than a woman who is merely moderately attractive.

The sex market is also unique in that a single individual on the market can pair with a large number of other individuals. A single man on the sex market can sleep with five females in a week, and vice versa. Moreover, it is not uncommon for an individual—especially a man—to value the number of his sexual conquests over the quality of those partners. Thus unlike in other markets, it is not uncommon for a man of high desirability within the sex market to sleep with a woman of low sex market desirability if he assumes there will be no cost in doing so. This leads to the Lazy Eight dynamic, in which a woman who is between a One and Seven (in that crass system people use to rank aggregate desirability) assumes that she is an Eight, merely because she was able to secure an Eight on the sex market (a market in which she is already overvalued).

The "Lazy Eight" problem can easily ruin a person's life. By setting unrealistic expectations, it can render a person unable to secure a viable long-term partner and tempt them to repeatedly seek emotional validation on the sex market.

This is not to say that people with low aggregate value on the sex/dating/long-term relationship market are of lower value as human beings. Intrinsically, wood is no "worse" than gold and honestly has more utility, but this does not change the fact that people pay less for wood than they pay for gold. We live in a society in which people—especially women—are led to believe that their value as an individual equals their value on the sex or dating market; thus, there are inevitably large numbers of people who seek personal validation on the sex market.

Fortunately, both of the aforementioned market failures are fairly easy for women to avoid. If you are trying to find a guy who is actually on the dating market and not just pretending to date while really just looking for sex, inform prospective male partners that you have a rule whereby you do not have sex with someone until you have dated them publicly (as in you are seen as being in a real relationship on social media platforms, and/or within social circles, frequented by that partner and their peers) for at least one month. This rule will weed out cads and make it easy to know when you are actually dating people who are genuinely participating in long-term relationship and casual dating markets. (For more tactics on this front, see the chapter Female Template Strategies on page 396.)

Women employing these tactics must come to terms with the fact that that the male partners they succeed in securing will be of lower aggregate value once they filter out people using them for sex. Moreover, a male being filtered out by this method will not just quietly walk away; he will likely argue with you or insult you in one final gambit.

Despite what romance novels tell us, people do not randomly choose lower-value mates for long-term partnerships. When people *do* buddy up with lower-value mates, it is because they are not monogamous, they were tricked, or for some reason, they value something about that mate that the rest of society ignores (typically due to a kink). **You can easily weed out a large category of people who are pretending to be on the dating or long-term relationship market, but who are really in the sex market, by asking yourself: "Would a stranger think this person is well out of my league, and if so, do I know specifically what they value so much in me?"**

Counterintuitively, the sex market is rarely voluntarily entered by straight men. This is because a man's value is so low on the market that it is unusual for men who are not in the top 20% of the market to enjoy *any* interaction within it. It is not uncommon for a man's first honest interaction with the sex market to take place after he enters an open relationship and has to explain to potential partners that there is no real possibility of a casual or long-term relationship early in their interactions.

The sex market is also the primary destination of those looking for kink-based interactions, such as hotwifing or husband trading.

If all of this seems rather depressing, keep in mind that your value on the sex market is not judged based on the same characteristics as other markets. Research shows that when searching on the sex market, people do not value characteristics such as intelligence or personality much and instead focus mostly on physical attractiveness.

The Casual Dating Market

Casual dating is different from dating in pursuit of a long-term relationship in two ways:
1) You may ask someone on a date who has a trait you would see as making it impossible to seriously consider them for a long-term relationship (like marriage).
2) You do not immediately break up with someone as soon as you realize it is highly unlikely that you will be spending the rest of your life with this person.

In general, the casual dating market is the sandbox in which those with monogamous leanings play while racking up major milestones they want to hit before they would seriously consider marriage or another form of a long-term relationship. In this role, it is a very useful marketplace for having practice relationships that can teach a person many of the skills they will leverage in subsequent, more serious relationships. While it certainly has its utility, the casual dating market also features its fair share of dangers and limitations.

In addition to playing this "practice relationship" role, the casual dating market features:
- Players who have recently left a serious relationship (and want to "acclimatize to dating" before seriously beginning to look for a new one).
- Individuals who are simultaneously ideologically opposed to long-term relationships and polyamory, but who still want the new relationship energy that comes with dating.
- People want to fulfill the societal expectations that come with dating without getting tied down by long-term partners.

New relationship energy, often referred to as NRE, is a term used to describe the unique mental, emotional, and physical thrills one experiences when in a new, passionate romantic relationship, only just beginning to discover a partner, and not yet sure how things will turn out or what will happen next. New relationship energy is highly addictive and, in our experience, the most pleasurable emotional state emerging from human sexual interaction after love. New relationship energy far outpaces any pleasure that can come from an orgasm (in that an orgasm just feels physically pleasurable, whereas new relationship energy provides an intense, deep sense of psychological satisfaction—after your fifth time orgasming in a day, you are quite bored of it, but your fifth time drawing a sketch of someone with whom you are experiencing new relationship energy is just as magical as the first). New relationship energy has also been shown to have very addictive qualities, functioning on similar neural pathways to painkilling medication. New relationship energy leads people to make even dumber decisions than love does.

One major problem with the casual dating market involves the large number of people who "fake" being on it. As it is in between the sex market, where *men* are disadvantaged, and the long-term relationship market, where *women* are disadvantaged, a large number of men who really want sex will pretend to be in this market as well a large number of women who really want a more serious relationship. The second major problem with the market can be seen with its degradation after the age of thirty or so. Most individuals who are "catches" and interested in casual dating eventually get locked down, whether they want to or not, or transfer to the polyamory market, leaving an increasingly dry fishing pond for the average casual dater as they age.

The greatest hazard of the casual dating market involves settling into relationships without consciously intending to do so.

Imagine you end up going on a few dates with a woman or man you like. You neither find their personality or appearance actively offensive, so you fool around and have sex a few times. A few months later, you are having sex regularly. Now this person is asking to be "official" with you, posting photos with you online, and introducing you to their friends and family.

Should you resist these mate-blocking and relationship-solidifying behaviors, you will lose a source of sex (and it's not like anyone else is lining up), plus you find it pleasant to spend time with this person, and you look forward to seeing them on nights and weekends—it is so *nice* to not be left alone and feel like someone is there for you.

Months turn into years that you spend with this person. You have gone through some hard times together. They lost their house at one point, and you ended up moving in together to save money. You even are beginning to feel like you really love this person sometimes. Then, one day they ask to get married. You know they are not a perfect match—not what you dreamed about as a kid—but getting back on the dating market would be hard, and you have been with this person seven years now. Figuring that this must be "as good as it gets," you say yes. Now you are cursed to live your life trapped in mediocrity. Merely because breaking up with this person was never "convenient" or easy, you are doomed to live and die in the relationship equivalent of a beige office cubicle.

This horrifying trap consumes the lives of millions of people every year and is totally preventable. In fact—**if you are over 23 and date someone for just three months, you are more likely to still be dating the same person in four years than not** (this comes from a great study done by Facebook's data scientists—see: *Flings or Lifetimes? The Duration of Facebook Relationships*).

There are a few strategies you can employ to prevent this from happening to you while still engaging in the casual dating that will help you hone your skills for an eventual, intentional long-term relationship. When dating in high school, create a rule for yourself whereby you will not extend any relationship formed while in high school into college. You must communicate this intention clearly to your partners early on in your relationships, saying that if you really do end up bonding, you will find each other again after college.

It is easy to set this rule given the salience of the trope of the high schooler who follows a boyfriend/girlfriend to college, only for that partner to summarily dump them or cheat on them once exposed to a much larger, more vibrant market. In other words—given the salience of certain cultural stereotypes among high school relationships, telling a high school partner you plan to leave them when you start college, as a rule, is less likely than it otherwise might be to cause offense and thus allows you to safely experiment with casual dating at that age (well, hopefully it won't cause offense, but then again high schoolers love indulging in emotional reactions).

You can employ a similar set of rules during college or during any other phase of your life in which you know you will be leaving a location in a set amount of time (e.g., "while I can date you the relationship has to end in six months when I move/join the military/start my new job/etc."). That said, if you are looking for a marriage partner with whom you will have kids, college is probably the best time to start searching for this person given universities' large pools of single, pre-vetted candidates with similar educational attainment and socioeconomic status.

Do not underestimate how long it will take you to secure a suitable long-term partner. We estimate that if you dedicate an average of two hours a day to finding your optimal long-term partner starting in college, the process will take you a total of eight years. Do not be that person who plans to get married at 31 and neglects to begin looking for a partner until they are 26. As we discuss elsewhere in this book (see page 163), your market advantages shift significantly throughout life. What may have been easy three years ago can become nigh impossible (and vice versa) depending on age and gender.

Once you decide you have reached a point in life in which you are ready to begin systematically searching for a long-term partner, give up casual dating—unless you have chosen to join the non-monogamous community. Dump partners the *moment* you realize they are not people with whom you would like to spend the rest of your life.

Every day, month, and year you spend on a relationship with someone who is not an appropriate match for you involves foregoing hundreds—if not thousands—of opportunities to meet your optimal partner. Every second you put off an uncomfortable breakup with a suboptimal long-term partner increases your risk that such a breakup will never take place. If you find it hard to dump someone today, just imagine how hard it will be next year. The key to securing an optimal long-term partner involves breaking up with someone as soon as it becomes clear they are not a viable long-term candidate for you.

The Long-Term Relationship Market

You are on the long-term relationship market if you are dating with the intention of securing a long-term relationship—also known as an LTR. While on this market, a person will only date people with whom they can imagine spending the rest of their lives. Participants acting in their best interests will end a relationship the moment it is clear this will not happen.

More than any other, the long-term relationship market deprioritizes physical attractiveness while prioritizing features like education and wealth. While it goes against conventional wisdom, attractiveness (in so far as it does matter), affects the value of men in the long-term relationship market more than it affects the value of women. One study showed that while unattractive men were less likely to secure a university-educated woman, a woman's attractiveness did not affect the rate at which she could secure a university-educated male. This is an interesting trend as *more* attractive males are statistically shown to invest significantly *less* in their relationships than *less* attractive men.

The long-term relationship market is also unique in that it heavily favors males—especially after a person reaches their mid-thirties. Because of this, many males falsely signal that they are in this market in an effort to secure better partners than they could in other markets, just as many women really looking for long-term relationships will signal that they just want sex.

The Non-Monogamous Market

Non-monogamous relationship models are rapidly growing in popularity. Searching for a partner while in a non-monogamous relationship or pairing up with a partner who is non-monogamous themselves gives birth to unique market dynamics, which only really kick in when you are looking for something more than sex from additional partners—otherwise the market dynamics are nearly identical to sex market dynamics.

Certain individuals' aggregate desirability can vary wildly in these markets. The non-monogamous market participant with the highest value by far is the polyamorous unicorn: A single bisexual female not interested in being a primary partner in a relationship. If you fall into that category (or can pretend to be in that category), you will be able to secure astronomically better partners in this market than you can in any other market.

The non-monogamous market is unique in that it has not yet settled on well-known cultural norms and differs vastly among different cities and age groups. While in some cities the market is to a great extent comprised of vast, often co-living, ideologically motivated polycules (groups of people in a relationship with each other), the non-monogamous market in other cities is managed in a top-down fashion by a hierarchical cabal of matriarchs who choose which individuals are allowed into the metroplex-wide polycule—though these matriarchs may not contextualize their positions this way. In yet other cities, you will find a few core polycules dominating the market like an infighting aristocracy.

As fascinating as these communities are, they are evolving too quickly to pin down. Participants in these communities seem unaware of the geographic differences among non-monogamous communities. Between the cities in which we have lived recently: Seoul, Lima, Edinburgh, London, San Francisco, Dallas, and Miami, we can say that while these communities share a common literature and identity, they have evolved independently and are only superficially the same; hence, it is difficult to make sweeping statements about the market dynamics of each. For example, some of the markets we have seen place a strong positive value modifier on being a bi male, while others do not seem to care.

That is not to say that there is no research that elucidates some interesting aspects of the community. Some research suggests that men are valued more for their attractiveness in non-monogamous markets than in other markets, and that male social status and resources matter considerably less among non-monogamous markets than they do in any other market outside of the sex market.

One commonality among all non-monogamous markets is the importance of virtue signaling to an individual's aggregate desirability. While we hope the community can get over its obsession with ethical virtue signaling, the obsession makes sense given that most non-monogamous market participants grew up in societies in which promiscuity has been categorized as fundamentally unethical. Since no one wants to believe they are a bad person, it is only natural for people to practice a behavior seen as unethical by some to seek out and build evidence of their ethical goodness or even moral superiority.

ON CITATIONS AND STUDIES

Despite using science as our primary standard of evidence (the type of evidence we value above all others), we will rarely cite specific studies in this book.

It is all too easy to believe oneself to be a dispassionate lover of "science" and "rationality," only to lean on studies like a crutch, cherry-picking findings, and conflating rationalization with rationality. It is a bad habit of countless writers and random commentators to make an outrageous claim, then cite a single study to back it up, putting the burden on the reader to look up the study and analyze its methodology, try to determine how it was funded, and look up the history of the researcher to determine whether the results are credible. We strongly disagree with this way of communicating.

If you see a statistic in a book and believe that statistic more because it comes with a study citation, we encourage you to rethink how you engage with information. We want to do our part in fighting against these sorts of dangerous mental shortcuts.

When we make a claim you find to be dubious, the last thing we want you to do is read the same couple of studies that lead us to our conclusion—especially if a subconscious bias could have led us to cherry-pick those studies. That is how bad information gets spread and pop-science comes to dominate. Our goal is to create new methodologies for relating to and interpreting data.

When you want to sanity check something, we urge you to go online and dig into the topic. Ask yourself why we drew the conclusions we drew given the information available to us, then draw your own conclusions.

We understand this approach runs contrary to the manner in which many were taught to engage with science and ideas, but we ask you to give it a try. You may find our approach surprisingly empowering. If you give this way of writing an honest try and still hate it, just shoot us an email at Hello@Pragmatist.Guide letting us know. Should we get enough of these emails, we will include fastidious (rather than occasional) citations in future books.

In addition to consulting research on relationships when writing this book, we reached out to around a hundred professional relationship therapists to sanity check the new theories it espouses. The number of therapists who read the entire book in detail is debatable, however we incorporated the feedback each therapist sent, with the major criticism being we are too harsh in our views on when a relationship is doomed.

WHY PEOPLE CHEAT RATHER THAN LEAVE A RELATIONSHIP

An individual will leave a relationship if they believe there are better, *mutually exclusive* options available to them. This is why married individuals have a higher risk of divorce when the adult gender ratios of their office present more members of the opposite gender (such office environments give them the impression that there are many better options). However, it is important to note the options tempting partners away from an established relationship must be mutually exclusive in order to increase the risk of relationship dissolution.

Not all people have the same view of when a relationship is mutually exclusive. Someone may, for instance, secretly marry a separate partner in another country and maintain a separate family with that partner. To most, this would qualify as a mutually exclusive relationship possibility—one that a normal person would likely leave their first family to pursue—but to some people (perhaps due to extreme wealth and/or a career that involves frequent, regular travel between two places), such opportunities are *not* mutually exclusive. To these people, it is *fine* to have two families.

This dynamic can be used to predict when someone may choose to cheat on a partner rather than leave their relationship entirely.

The most common barrier to cheating for most people involves the struggle to simultaneously believe "I am a cheater" and "I am a good person." This is why once someone has cheated once, they are extremely likely to cheat again (300% more likely, to be exact). After someone cheats the first time, cheating again becomes very low cost (outside the risk of getting caught), as they have already come to terms with the cognitive dissonance of internalizing that they cheat on partners.

If you started your relationship with someone as "the other man" or "the other woman" with whom your partner cheated on an existing partner, be aware that your present partner will very likely cheat on you, as they no longer have to fight the cognitive dissonance associated with cheating. After all, cheating granted your partner their current loving relationship with you, did it not? How bad can cheating really be?

What to Do When a Partner Cheats

After someone cheats on you, what do you do?

There are six ways to maintain a relationship with a cheater:
1. Alter your relationship contract to open your relationship, making sexual relations with others permissible. This may seem like a strange reaction as it "rewards the cheater," but it is also by far and away the most viable way to maintain the relationship. Even with the below alternate strategies, it is highly likely your partner will cheat on you again or just leave you.
2. Through heavy surveillance, increase your partner's perceived probability of being caught should they cheat again. If the odds of being caught are near 100%, your partner will be less likely to attempt cheating, even if the punishment is fairly moderate. This is a feasible strategy, but not a smart strategy, as it will almost certainly degrade the relationship over even a short period of time and vastly increase the likelihood that your partner will cheat over any period during which

they are not monitored. If your partner *really* wants to sleep with other people, they may also be pushed by this strategy to merely terminate the relationship.
3. Decrease your partner's opportunities to cheat. Consider a wife who doesn't let her husband eat alone with a woman or drink at mixed-gender events without her present. In an increasingly equal society, such a strategy is seen as abusive and almost absurd to maintain.
4. Increase the perceived cost of your partner being caught cheating. If you do not immediately leave a partner who cheats, you must keep in mind that you have almost certainly lowered your partner's perceived cost of cheating, hence the crucial thing about implementing this strategy is that any punishment you threaten must be something you are genuinely willing to execute, and cannot involve breaking up with your partner (as you have already shown an inability to follow through with that potential ultimatum). Potentially effective threatened punishments include threats of releasing damaging information to your partner's family or promising to release incriminating information about the cheating partner to the police or national tax authority (note this behavior is illegal in many jurisdictions). If you are going to threaten harsh punishment for cheating, you must also come to terms with the fact that the odds are well over 50% that your partner will decide that, given their high likelihood of cheating on you again, your relationship is not worth maintaining, so they will break things off. Some studies also show that when people are warned of clear

punishments for infractions, such as fees for coming late to pick up children from daycare, they are more likely to commit those infractions—perhaps because they have been aware of the price and they still find their crimes worth it.
5. Renegotiation of the relationship contract in some way other than just opening up the relationship could conceivably lower the possibility of cheating. This would likely be done through marriage counseling or "open discussion." That said, we would not recommend this strategy as it is very likely to allow the cheater to displace responsibility ("I only cheated because X"). This strategy furthermore fails to change the underlying dynamics that caused the cheating but instead reinforces them. Really, the only way this ends up being effective is if the act of the discussions themselves increase partners' attraction or dedication to each other.
6. Getting your partner to agree to be surgically neutered. Few are likely to consent to this, but it can help to combat a desire to cheat in the future. It's a crazy idea, but probably effective.

Cheating will *not* be halted by a slap on the hand and expectation that the relationship can go back to normal, free of cheating. The cheating partner will almost certainly cheat again. Why? Because now they have strictly less motivation *not* to cheat. If you do not leave your partner after they cheat and the world does not fall apart, was the cheating such a bad thing?

Any strictly monogamous relationship in which there is even a slight probability that your partner will want to sleep with someone is at extreme risk. The paths to repair the relationship after a cheating incident are extremely limited. It is far more efficient to create a relationship contract that states sleeping with another person would hurt your feelings but is within the rules as long as each partner informs the other partner of each dalliance in advance. This type of contract clause increases the cost of sleeping with someone else (as they will need to tell you first, knowing fully well that they are hurting you) without making them choose between your relationship and cheating. While someone still may attempt to hide their dalliance to avoid hurting their partner emotionally, doing so has a higher personal emotional cost, as it may be difficult to believe one is a good person and yet unwilling to adhere to such a simple, low-effort rule honoring a committed partner.

Men and women do not respond the same way to cheating behavior. This is likely a product of men historically assuming the role of breadwinner in our culture and women traditionally acting as sexual gatekeepers, which has led men, on average, to value a partner more for sex and a woman to value a partner more for resources. This has historically meant that sexually unsatisfied men can easily acquire more sex just by cheating, whereas for a sexually unsatisfied woman to fully benefit from another man, she must leave her current partner. This has contributed to making men more likely to cheat within a long-term relationship while simultaneously making them less likely to leave a sub-par partner. This is backed up by several studies on cheating behavior across men and women. In one study, 56% of men who reported to be cheating also reported being in happy marriages, whereas only 34% of cheating women reported their marriages to be happy.

Other Factors Contributing to Cheating

A study of eight million Ashley Madison users revealed that both men and women are more likely to have affairs when their age ends in the number nine; however, this effect is much more pronounced in men. Presumably, this is driven by a surging desire for validation as we approach symbolically meaningful age milestones. Weird ages are not the only time-associated factors increasing the odds that a person may be cheating: The so-called "seven-year itch" is really a thing. Both men's and women's odds of cheating increase approximately seven years into a relationship. Both men and women's odds of cheating decrease after this seven-year mark, but male odds of cheating begin to rise again after the 18-year mark.

Older age, in general, seems to be a factor contributing to cheating—at least these days. Americans aged 55 and older are now more likely to report having extramarital sex than Americans under 55. This is a reversal of trends observed as recently as the year 2000, when older Americans reported having less extramarital sex. Today, most people who cheat are 50 years of age and older (21%). Only 8% of people between the ages of 18-29 admit to ever cheating.

Infidelity appears to be more common among people who have specific types of oxytocin and vasopressin receptor genes. Vasopressin is a hormone related to social behaviors, including trust, empathy, and sexual bonding. A whopping 40% of instances of infidelity in women and 62% in men have to do with genetics.

Other genetic factors, such as intelligence, are also associated with higher rates of cheating. Both smarter men and women cheat at higher rates, though smarter women cheat at disproportionately higher rates, especially if their intelligence has not led to the achievement of a high level of educational attainment.

Cheating is not always sexual. Emotional affairs also exist, with 5% of men and 35% of women having admitted to having an emotional affair. Those self-reported percentages (at least among women) are far higher than the 20% of people who admit to having a physical affair. We suspect the larger number of women having emotional affairs is either a product of women being more emotionally aware of what they are doing or women "getting more out of" emotional affairs than men.

Women cheat more now than they did in the past (or at least are more comfortable disclosing their cheating behavior in surveys). Rates of women cheating have increased 40% over the last half-century. Furthermore, 90% of women who cheat on their husbands do not report feeling guilty—instead, they say they felt entitled to their extramarital activities due to perceived failures on the part of their husbands. Of these women, 65% report enjoying sex with their lover more than their husband, and 70% claim their lover is the "opposite" of their husband.

Almost 70% of cheaters cheat with friends. Cheaters also tend to have more sexual partners than the average person: A median of 12 throughout their lifetime. Those who like spending more time in social contexts may be more likely to cheat, as at least one study we came across found extroverts are more likely to cheat.

SEX IN A LONG-TERM RELATIONSHIP

How do those in a long-term relationship keep their sex lives healthy, vibrant, and fresh? How do partners avoid the dreaded "dead bedroom" in which they almost never have sex?

The first key to understanding how to preserve sex in a long-term relationship is to understand that the core desire for sex in a long-term relationship is driven as much by a desire for personal validation as it is driven by a desire for pleasure.

Most human action and emotion is driven by attempts to align our positions in the world with our ideal selves—the internal models we have created describing who we are or who we want to be. Our internal models, especially those tied to sexuality, are mostly socialized into us at a young age, but can be altered (see *The Pragmatist's Guide to Life* for detailed explanations on how).

A young man's sadness resulting from the fact that he is still a virgin at 25 has nothing to do with an arousal impulse—nor is it really tied to any innate emotional impulse. That sadness stems from his internalizing that in order to be a happy 25-year-old male, he must be virile and desired. If this young man did not hold this belief, he would not feel sad. Instead, he is sad because the difference between his ideal self and his current self, as recognized by his subconscious, produces a negative emotional state.

This emotional state may drive the 25-year-old to attempt to have sex with someone in an effort to better align his actual self with his desired self-image. We refer to the process of matching one's actual self to one's desired self-image as validation.

While sex with a person does cause slight effects on happiness that cannot be secured through masturbation, these effects are insignificant when contrasted with the reported distress of dead bedroom relationships. A dead bedroom is not soul-destroying due to any shortage of orgasms. There is an abundance of methods, products, and tools that facilitate top drawer orgasms and require nobody else's participation. Dead bedrooms torture those who begin to see themselves as no longer sexually attractive or desirable. Those with dead bedrooms stop getting validation as sexual, desired, beings.

The cessation of sex in long-term relationships differentially affects men and women. In general, Western men who are single or casually dating gain social validation from the number of attractive women with whom they sleep. Once western men are in long-term relationships, their validation is gleaned, to a great extent, from the continued desirability of their long-term partners and whether their partners still want to have sex with them.

A man loses that source of validation when either his long-term partner is no longer desirable on the open market or when this partner no longer appears sexually interested in him. A relationship can involve long periods of no sex at all due to something like forced long distance, but still be immensely validating to a man if he always feels desired by a desirable partner. A man who has sex three times every six months, but who feels that his partner is envied by others and extremely sexually interested in him is far less likely to feel sexually unfulfilled than a man who has sex daily, but feels his wife isn't so interested in it or that she is not "hot" anymore.

To men, dead bedrooms are largely not about the sex, but rather a man's self-assessment of his own virility and sexual desirability. If actual sex were the issue, we would see more similarities between dead bedrooms and long-distance relationships that don't involve sex, yet communities that support these two groups of individuals could not be more different

We are NOT saying that a wife should always consent to sex with her husband. Heck, sex when one's heart just isn't in it could leave some men feeling *more* invalidated than they would feel if they didn't have sex at all. It is merely important for women with male partners to know that both the sexual interest they express in their partners, plus their overall desirability to the general population, will likely play a huge role in the average male partner's validation, and that validation will have a profound effect on his happiness.

In women, validation is gained more from being desired by people they respect and admire (assuming one has succumbed to Western society's socialization). This sense of validation can be lost when a woman loses respect for her partner or feels as though her partner no longer desires her. To the average western female, sex itself is trivial from a personal validation perspective. Sex with a partner who she does not respect has no validation value, whereas being desired by a partner she admires but with whom she cannot have sex, while frustrating, is still validating.

It is a failure to secure validation that the accusation of being "used for sex" emerges. Women commonly claim to have been "used for sex" by someone when said sex fails to grant the validation sought from the interaction—often because of a post-sex realization that the sexual partner had very little desire for them specifically or that they did not respect this sexual partner. We find the phrase quite humorous because it is used by those who do not get what they wanted from sex, but lack the lucidity to recognize that they, too, were hoping to use someone for sex but to gain validation instead of an orgasm.

At a young age, we are conditioned to believe that to be happy and fulfilled, women must be desired, and men must be virile. We subsequently spend the rest of our lives, attempting to fulfill these roles. Unlike with sexual arousal impulses, it is not any stimulus itself that leads us to feel happy when validated. Nothing is innate about these emotional outputs; they result from the analysis of measuring sticks that we built for ourselves. Most sex we have is motivated by an attempt to fulfill these self-images and not merely about orgasms or arousal; masturbation is just fine at fulfilling those particular desires (well . . . almost, there are admittedly some neurological differences between the effects of masturbation and sex).

Once we accept the importance of validation in long-term relationship sex dynamics, we can address that need far more adequately. To maintain a healthy sex life in a long-term relationship, you must make sure that **either** all partners have divorced themselves from societal socialization **or** that:
- Female partners feel desired by a partner they personally admire.
- Male partners feel desired by a partner they believe would be desired on an open market.

This distinction may seem nuanced but can play a big role in how relationships actually break down. For example, a male socialized in Western society can still gain sexual validation from a partner for whom he has lost respect so long as the partner is still "hot" and respectable to his social group, whereas the average woman cannot. Alternatively, if a female admires a partner and that partner desires her, she can gain validation from this even if her friends think the partner is gross. This is something much harder for a male to do if socialized in our society.

Recall that average male sex drive decreases with age and declines significantly along with testosterone when a man is in love or in a pair-bonded relationship. We emphasize that this is on average and not necessarily in *every* human—some men even supplement testosterone to counteract these changes. At any rate, this shift in male sexuality can often confuse women into believing that a man isn't interested in her anymore. This shift might even lead some men to believe that they are simply less attracted to their long-term partner, specifically rather than being less attracted to everyone as their hormone levels change.

Female sex drive also fluctuates in various circumstances (which are far too diverse to succinctly summarize here, as they shift from a midlife pique to pregnancy, to menopause). These fluctuations can also be misinterpreted as a lack of interest in a way that makes a man lose the validation he gleans from the relationship.

Sex is an activity that requires time and physical effort. If a person is exhausted and overworked, sex drive drops. Stress and exhaustion-induced loss of sexual interest frequently occur after people have children—without money for childcare, dead bedrooms become very difficult for new parents to avoid. That said, a dead bedroom in which it is clear to both partners that each still finds the other sexually compelling (and is simply not acting on that attraction due to exhaustion) is quite different from one in which one or more partners feel as though another partner has lost sexual interest in them, specifically. We would go so far as to say a relationship in which partners are not having sex because they have children and full-time jobs is not nearly as emotionally taxing or crushing as a relationship in which partners have frequent "duty sex" that is devoid of strong passion and attraction.

Reminder: The science is unambiguous on this point: In human males, being in love with someone lowers testosterone production and tanks their sex drive.

Researchers have confirmed the obvious: That confidence, attentiveness, physical attractiveness, frequency of classically romantic dates, oral sex willingness, willingness to try new things, and prioritizing a partner's pleasure over one's own correlate strongly with continued sexual satisfaction in a relationship. The only research we found in this subject that piqued our interest (by making a novel point) was a study that found a strong correlation between talking through joint life goals on a regular basis (looking for alignment) and mutual sexual desire—so be sure to read *The Pragmatist's Guide to Life* with your spouse to ensure good sex. ;)

If a mutual sexual interest in each other is so important, what must we do to maintain it?

One factor contributing to the dead bedroom phenomenon involves some people assuming that the standards of attraction are lower once they are in a long-term-relationship. These people assume they can "let themselves go" a bit, put on a few pounds, stop putting so much effort into exercise, outfits, foreplay, and grooming, and generally work less hard to be charming, confident, engaging, and considerate. The reality is that between the Coolidge effect (a decrease in attraction to individuals with whom you have had sex before) and the decrease in testosterone-driven sex drive when someone is in love, the amount of effort required to keep the level of sex constant in a long-term relationship is dramatically higher than the effort required in a short term relationship.

Similar to the age-old question of: "How can I lose weight without diet and exercise?" we hear people ask: "How can I maintain my partner's desire without constantly improving myself?" The real answer to maintaining a partner's desire is to improve physical (and societal) appearance over time and work hard to increase your partner's admiration for you. Perpetually improve the things your partner values most—be they looks, prestige, emotional control, knowledge, status, or anything else. Long-term partners have an advantage here, as they have had ample time to determine what their partner finds to be most attractive and endearing. Maintaining a partner's attraction and affection is difficult and clearly not feasible for everyone. We live in a society that seems to have trouble accepting that some people are going to fail despite trying their hardest.

The fact that many fail and ultimately find themselves living with a dead bedroom is fine. The best solution to a dead bedroom problem may be to accept it and come to understand how you can work around it. After all, polls show that 57% of people living in a sexless marriage report that, aside from sex being absent, they feel they have the ideal partner. A relationship may still be worth having even without the validation that comes from feeling desired and satisfied by a partner. Besides, relationships can be renegotiated in a manner that allows one or more partners to use outside partners to satisfy both sexual urges and, more importantly, desires for sexual validation (though this is admittedly not possible in all relationships, especially those in which the very fact that one partner is searching for validation outside of the relationship is invalidating to the other partner—life doesn't always have a win state).

Note from the Research:
- Only about 25% of women consistently orgasm during vaginal intercourse, 20% seldom have orgasms at all, and about 5% cannot orgasm period. We say this here because some men who are not very sexually experienced see their long term-partner not orgasming during sex as invalidating—a sign she does not like them or find them attractive.

Bonus Tidbits from The Pragmatist's Guide to Sexuality:
- It has become trendy among sex therapists to divide sexuality into responsive arousal and spontaneous arousal. What this division is used to clarify is that some people very rarely "spontaneously" become aroused and instead only become aroused after they are sexually engaged by their partner, but the sexual interaction they end up having is still rewarding and feels good to them. This style of arousal appears to be more common in women than men, and through this delineation, therapists have an easier time getting individuals who fall into this category to get comfortable having sex more often and not feel like there is something wrong with them.
- Libido may be depressed by outside factors. It appears humans have an inhibitory system that lowers arousal potential when exposed to environmental cues (specifically cues to suggest

now would not be a good time to have a kid, such as a baby in the next room, stress, uncertainty about the future, etc.). Sometimes a person's libido can appear low due to exposure to one of these stimuli or their inhibitory system otherwise being overactive in relation to one stimulus that is not that hard to remove from their environment. This is also one of the reasons a couple's sex life dies down after having a child.
- The two above points taken together yield the trope of taking wives and girlfriends out for a nice, romantic date in a luxurious-feeling environment before having sex and emphasize the importance of foreplay.

COMMON MARRIAGE CONTRACT THEMES

The easiest way to design a marriage contract is to start with one of the following themes and build terms around it. To choose among these themes, focus on the "point" of your marriage. Specifically, what are each of you trying to gain by entering this partnership, and how can the relationship be designed to maximize that benefit?

Common themes include:
- **Religion:** Marriage may be based on a religious dogma. If you decide to follow this path, do not make the common mistake of assuming that your society's traditional, conservative relationship template will line up with what your religious text asks of you. A marriage template that is based on the Bible, for example, would certainly not resemble a traditional, conservative relationship. Thus, if the Bible is your template, you should read the Bible instead of copying your peers' and parents' conservative marriages.
- **Complete Equality:** These models are focused on maintaining absolute equality in a relationship and are typically created to satisfy political ideologies of what a marriage should be (as opposed to terms that logically maximize the benefits of the partnership, something equality-themed relationships almost never do). Equality-themed contracts are susceptible to tit-for-tat terms and requirements, which can lead to resentment and instability whenever one side feels like the other is

benefiting more from the relationship, and yet the other side disagrees. Because of this, equality-themed contracts are only optimal for partners who harbor very strong political ideologies that value equality over efficacy in a relationship.
- **Family:** Family themed contracts are meant to maximize benefit among the relationship's children or an extended family unit. Societal appearances are often very important in these relationships and thus they are designed to appear very traditional and anti-scandalous from an outsider's perspective. Family themed relationship contracts can nevertheless be pretty unique depending on what you are attempting to maximize in your children's lives or for your extended family. A relationship based on maximizing the perceived status of the family will look quite different than one built on maximizing the individual happiness of the family even if they superficially look fairly similar.
- **Individual Happiness:** In this model, each individual agrees they are entering marriage because doing so will make achieving happiness easier. The contract terms of the marriage are typically far more laissez-faire than other models and can often be described as "roommates with sex and love." These relationships lead to significantly less emotionally close marriages than other options, but this lack of closeness also lowers conflict. Happiness-oriented marriages are also more likely to be polyamorous than other marriages.
- **Combined Good:** These relationships are designed to maximize a shared objective function (the thing

each partner wants to maximize with their lives). In these models, individual proclivities are often sacrificed or deprioritized in the face of larger goals and values, which can lead to a dehumanization of the participants. This model is both stable and effective so long as all participants maintain aligned objective functions and keep those objective functions above their own personal happiness.

- **Transactional:** Transactionally themed relationships involve individuals with different objective functions using the relationship to maximize their individual objectives. A woman may marry a man to protect her family's business because his family is wealthy, while he marries her because he finds her physically attractive and intellectually stimulating. These marriages can be stable so long as both parties are transparent about what they are using the relationship to maximize, and the contract is built along those lines. It is important to not trade a depreciating asset for an appreciating asset in such a relationship, or it will become unstable over time.
- **Master-Subordinate:** Master-subordinate relationships are defined by an easily understood hierarchy. One partner is in charge, and the other's goal is to act as their subordinate. While aspects of this model exist in many other models, this kind of marriage is unique in that its core focus is to allow the subordinate to live a life unencumbered with the stress of the responsibility of owning their decisions, while the master gains a feeling of control (along with immense responsibility). While we often think of these

relationships as being primarily "kinky" relationships, they don't have to be. These relationships can be quite stable and happy if well-matched but are frowned upon by our larger society so they are normally hidden (we suspect they are not as unusual as one might think).
- **TradCon:** A TradCon relationship is a traditional conservative relationship (a TradCon relationship with reversed gender roles or gay partners is still a TradCon relationship). The TradCon model is quite different from the societal template, which is more of a combination of TradCon + equality relationship models (a horrifying Frankenstein of a relationship contract that does not work, as the TradCon model is almost directly antithetical to the equality model). Instead, TradCon relationships attempt to emulate the idealized concept of marriage as it was perceived in America in the 1950s-1960s. TradCon relationships are tricky, as they can work fairly well if thought through, but are rarely well thought through. Relationships built on TradCon contracts are uniquely susceptible to dynamics that doom the relationship's long-term viability and put both partners at significant risk. The biggest hazard inherent in TradCon relationships is the asset depreciation problem, in which the home maker's reliance on their breadwinning partner increases while their aggregate desirability decreases, but the inverse happens to the breadwinner.
- **NeoCorp:** The NeoCorp marriage model is a newer version of the corporate family model, which was pervasive before being replaced by the single-breadwinner model of the early to mid-

1900s (which is now emulated by TradCons). This model prioritizes the family unit as the predominant player in the relationship with the family unit or "household" conceptualized as being like a "corporation" or "little empire." When creating a contract around this model, define the goals of the household and remember that its interests always trump those of its individual players. The NeoCorp model often includes employees and confidants as members of the household (most households include a "staff" that are thought of as part of the family unit) and should be written in a way that anticipates that peculiarity.

Note From The Research:
- While on the subject of TradCons, it is worth bringing up that couples who share housework have higher divorce rates than couples in which the woman does all the housework (Just in case you were wondering: Couples in which the man does all the housework have the highest divorce rate). We are not sure how much this really validates the TradCon approach as a superior relationship model, because more conservative people are less likely to get divorced, meaning this may be a matter of correlation without causation. We have, as an aside, seen studies claiming both more and less sex is had when husbands do more chores, but not enough on either side to say there is a consensus.

GUIDE TO AVOIDING CRAZY

There is truth to what they say: "Don't stick your dick in crazy and don't let the loon in your poon."

The increase in life quality that can come with early identification of what will become systemic bad behavior ("crazy") in a partner is monumental (by "crazy" we are not referring to mental health issues under treatment, but rather generic craziness—we address mental health issues in the false red flag section, mental health issues under treatment are usually not a big deal). The damage that an unstable and malicious partner can inflict upon your life includes (but is not limited to):

- Extreme stress resulting from mental abuse
- Miserable years spent in a bad relationship
- Physical torture
- Depression
- Bankruptcy
- Rape
- 18 years spent paying for child support for a child created without your consent and that isn't biologically yours
- Jail time resulting from false claims against you
- Loss of friends and family due to forced isolation
- PTSD
- Death
- Death of loved ones

When you have a person who has decided to make your torment a permanent hobby of theirs, your life can become very challenging. This is doubly true when they have convinced themselves that their actions are somehow morally just.

No matter how hot someone is, no matter how rich they are, no matter how high their status may be, it is never worth the risk to hook up with a potentially "crazy" person—someone who shows any signs of mental instability, severe immaturity, or who threatens you in any way. The momentary pleasure you may glean from an encounter will never justify subsequent months spent looking over your shoulder, potential incarceration, physical harm, and reputational and/or financial damage. Stop, think, and internalize just how much harm a person can do if they decide to dedicate even just a couple hours a week to making your life miserable. Think through the significant monetary and emotional cost of neutralizing a threatening, unstable person with whom you have had some sort of sexual encounter.

Be warned: Even someone who does not act "crazy" in public and among friends can have a different internal ruleset governing appropriate behavior with a sexual or romantic partner. Mentally unstable partners can be surprisingly difficult to identify.

We will help you spot individuals prone to behavior patterns that can be deleterious to your wellbeing, with a focus on behavior patterns you can't easily predict. What follows are some tactics you may use to identify "crazy" early on.

We have organized red flags into two categories:
1. Signs that even a single sexual encounter with this person could ruin your life.

2. Signs that a date is bad material for a marriage.

How to Avoid Dangerous and Unstable Sexual Partners

Because the negative consequences of sexual engagement with dangerous and unstable partners are so extreme, it is best to err on the side of caution when you are unsure as to whether a target is or is not a potential threat.

In general, and erring on the side of caution, avoid the following:
- People who associate their identity with their sexuality
- People who are visibly unstable
- People addicted to hard, highly addictive drugs
- Vengeful people
- Anyone way out of your league who makes the first move
- Desperate people
- People who do not like you or your kind
- Emotionally manipulative people

People who associate their identity with their sexuality

Those who strongly identify with their sexuality, whether that sexuality involves being a super manly heterosexual patriot, a flamboyantly gay force of nature, or a captivating BDSM dom, can be dangerous. Because sexuality is so core to how these people see themselves, *you*, as one of their sexual partners, must properly follow a complicated set of rules in order for *them* to feel secure in their identities. It can be nigh impossible to predict the nuances of these rules. The consequences these people deem appropriate for breaking them can be extreme.

In general, mentally sound individuals understand that sexuality is a garnish that sits on top of a person's identity. If you walk into a restaurant and a waiter serves a plate of nothing but maraschino cherries, that should be an immediate flag that something is seriously wrong in the kitchen.

Tied to this red flag are people who allow their politics to define their sexuality. An example of this might be someone so sex-negative they believe that certain otherwise-mainstream sexual positions are immoral because they are degrading to the participants. While these people might seem safe in theory, one can never know exactly what is going to set them off. When someone has non-normative views on sexuality, it is difficult to fully probe those views through limited and brief interactions. If you don't know the exact line across which something turns from an innocuous interaction to an extreme faux pas in someone's mind, you are likely to get in big trouble.

Imagine you are an explorer who has just happened upon an undiscovered tribe. The chief's daughter is clearly interested in you, but you actively avoid her. Why? You don't know the rules of this new, strange culture. You don't know if dancing with the chief's daughter will bond you in marriage or whether accepting a gift from the chief's daughter without sleeping with her is punishable by dismemberment.

Just as our imaginary tribe would likely assume that you know all of their unique rules, political extremists will assume you know their esoteric rules—and you may be very surprised by what they deem to be appropriate punishments. Things that might be a normal part of a sexual interaction for you might be seen as justification for extreme retaliation to them. Infractions may involve one partner reaching orgasm while the other doesn't, failing to have a written consent form ready, using one form of birth control over another, or telling this partner about a sexual fantasy of yours involving them. When you can't even predict what lines in the sand a person may have, it is not worth walking into that particular sexual minefield.

There is one exception to this rule: Most people involved in a polyamorous community have weird political views on sexual relationships. If the person hasn't been kicked out of a "sane" poly community, they are normally very safe for sexual interaction, so long as you know the rules of that poly community. That said, be sure it is a "sane" poly community, as some polyamorous communities have rules that are difficult to predict. Fortunately, these communities are fairly easy to spot and broadcast their craziness very loudly. If, for instance, senior members of a poly community demand you pay for things or otherwise attempt to extract money from you, stay away. Depending on the regional culture of your poly community, it may not have clear "thought leaders" making it harder to vet, but we might go so far as to suggest doing online checks of any clear leaders of a poly community with which you might become involved to search for potential warning signs.

People Who Are Visibly Unstable

We are *not* telling you to avoid potential partners just because they suffer from a mental illness. People with a wide variety of disorders, such as bipolar disorder, depression, OCD, or Asperger's can make spectacular partners, even in long-term relationships, so long as they don't lean on their disorders as excuses for personal failures (in which case you will find yourself in a, "it wasn't my fault; X made me do it, so I am actually the victim," dynamic whenever they do something shitty).

We merely recommend avoiding anyone exhibiting strange speech behavior (e.g., repeating the same things over and over, use of made-up words, rhyming words without meaning, difficult-to-understand speech), engaging in absurdly reckless activities (like provoking a law enforcement officer or hitting on a random homeless person during your date), or scarily narcissistic behaviors around service staff. This might seem obvious, but all judgment calls become difficult when a person is hot enough. Be aware that these warning signs often represent tips of very, very large icebergs.

People Addicted to Hard, Highly Addictive Drugs

In this case, we are referring to drugs like meth and heroin. No matter how "good" a person may be, certain addictions can make even the best-intentioned people do truly terrible things. An addicted partner's knowledge of your home and its contents is not… ideal in such scenarios. It is also not great if you come to mind as a blackmail target for someone with a serious addiction. There are very few effective methods for neutralizing an individual addicted to a hard drug that sees you as a potential source of resources.

Vengeful People

Avoid anyone who mentions having punished an ex for a perceived slight on the first couple dates. Anyone who does this is signaling to you what they do to people who cross them, which implies they are vindictive and likely to take the time and effort required to screw up other domains of your life after being dumped.

People Out of Your League Who Make The First Move

If someone way out of your league eagerly engages you, it is too good to be true. In such instances, you are almost certainly being subjected to some sort of scam and simply have not figured it out yet. The only exception here is if it is clear you have a really high individual desirability for some unique reason that is not valued on the market (for example, if you are an amputee and this person has a devotee kink—a kink for people with disabilities). If this is the case, high-value individuals will certainly signal clearly to you what that thing is.

Desperate People

Upon encountering a target who is obviously extremely desperate, you may think to yourself: "This will be easy; I am way out of their league, and no one will sleep with them anyway, so this will be a low-investment endeavor." You are almost certainly extremely wrong.

People far below your league often become very high-investment liaisons because they are uniquely scared that you will leave them or not follow through with whatever fantasy about your relationship they create in their minds. Desperate people are also much more likely to have very little relationship experience and thus can also act hurtfully without realizing it.

People Who Clearly Do Not Like You Or Your Kind

Sex with someone who you know to not like you—or sex with someone who is associated with a group or organization that does not like you (or your race, gender, social group, company, family, whatever)—is extremely risky. People do not randomly decide to have one-night stands with people they hate, despite what stories depict. Giving someone who hates you access to your life, body, and reputation is risky.

Emotionally Manipulative People

Avoid anyone who attempts to use some form of emotional manipulation to obtain sex. A common example of emotional manipulation manifests as someone goading you into consenting to sex with them by eliciting a sense of pity (i.e., pity sex). Anyone willing to engage in emotional manipulation to gain sex has demonstrated they are willing to attempt to emotionally blackmail you into sex. Any concession to this behavior is an admission on your part that their tactics are effective on you.

How to Avoid Dangerous and Unstable Long-Term Partners

Avoiding dangerous, unstable long-term partners is much easier than avoiding risky sexual partners and has a far more profound impact. To give you an idea of the damage that a risky long-term partner can cause, recall that it is common for abusive partners to threaten to murder their own kids if their abused partner leaves them (and some follow through on these threats).

What follows is a clear list of warning signs exhibited by hazardous long-term partners. Obviously, not everything on the following list of red flags indicates that someone is crazy enough to murder children, but each of the following characteristics nevertheless indicates life-destroying levels of danger.

Avoid with all your power:
- Partners who demand money or gifts
- Partners who would be vindictive in a divorce
- Partners who keep score and hold grudges
- Inherently suspicious partners
- Partners with significantly different worldviews/values/objective functions (especially if they act as though the mismatch is not a big deal)
- Partners who refuse to value emotional control (that is, control over their personal emotions)
- Partners who make threats or pose ultimatums

- Partners who actively seek sexual validation from others
- Partners who internalize negative character traits as core elements of their identities

Partners Who Demand Money or Gifts

Anyone who demands—or suggests that their affection is dependent on or given in exchange for—money or gifts, is a dangerous partner. A person poses a significant threat even if the gifts/monetary sums they demand are very small. The hedonic treadmill effect will only lead initially modest demands to escalate. If you rescue someone from poverty and give them a spectacular lifestyle, they will acclimate to it fairly quickly and expect more. Such partners will pressure you to make stupid business decisions that may ultimately lead you to lose everything.

At one point, a visiting speaker in one of Malcolm's Stanford Business School classes was asked: What is the number one reason why Stanford Business School grads lose their fortunes? His reply was that—by a long shot—wives and husbands drove his classmates' financial downfalls. They married people who pressured them to make dumb business and investment decisions because they were not content with what they had. These partners always left them after they lost their money and just married other rich people. They had no qualms about pressuring their spouses into making risky business decisions because the cost to them was lower than it was to their partner.

Stay away from those who measure their self-worth by their wealth or ability to signal wealth—unless they plan to be the individual in the relationship generating and accumulating that wealth and expect absolutely no contribution from you (though in that case, you yourself may be a status signal to them—a trophy wife/husband—and will be discarded the moment you cease to function as a flattering accessory, assuming they think they can do better).

Partners Who Would Be Vindictive in a Divorce

Do you think your prospective partner may be vindictive in a divorce? Would this person ever attempt to punish someone for leaving them? Someone who even subtly demonstrates this capacity should be avoided like the plague. Vindictive behavior is not acceptable, no matter how much someone may attempt to convince you it is. Taking time to hurt someone that could otherwise be spent on self-improvement or looking for the next partner indicates poorly ranked priorities in the extreme.

If you suspect your partner may be prone to vindictive behavior, even if everything else about them is perfect and you love them, we still strongly recommend you leave them over just this one sign. You will likely regret ignoring our warning if you maintain your current course with someone exhibiting these risk factors.

Partners Who Keep Score and Hold Grudges

Anyone who refers to past slights in current arguments is a liability. Someone willing to bring up your past wrongdoings in a current argument before you initiate a long-term relationship will likely escalate such behavior down the road (they will have more fodder with time, after all). Such behavior is uniquely toxic because it creates an environment of fear around bringing up grievances, specifically a fear that airing grievances will trigger defensive behavior in which an old fight is unearthed. Not only does this mean every argument you have becomes this argument *plus all arguments you have had throughout the course of your entire relationship,* but it also means perceived grievances often are not aired until after they have reached an explosive point.

Fortunately, the problem of grudge-holding and scorekeeping in arguments is easy to address as long as you can come to a point at which all parties agree that such behavior is unacceptable and sub-optimal and that the team must work together to end it. This is often a necessary discussion early in a relationship, as many people grew up around this kind of behavior and thus must unlearn it. Just don't commit to anything long term with a partner until they show both willingness and capacity to quit their grudge-holding and scorekeeping habits. We would go so far as to make this a red line for proposing to someone or accepting a proposal: No proposal should be accepted until you have trained your partner to permanently scrub this behavioral pattern from their life.

Partners Who Are Inherently Suspicious

Beware of anyone who is inherently suspicious of you, especially if they are suspicious of your cheating on them. There is no greater sign that someone is breaking the terms of your relationship contract than the demonstration of clear suspicion. If your partner ever secretly accesses your texts, phone, or email without your permission, consider it a severe warning sign.

An equally bad sign is if, during the normal course of your relationship, you need to access one of your partner's online/social media accounts (maybe they are overseas without an internet connection and would benefit from you handling their account) and your partner refuses to let you do so. This is just as much a demonstration of lack of trust as snooping (or a sign that they are hiding something from you). Some limits on partner account access are entirely justified—especially if one partner is prone to accidentally deleting information, forgetting which account they are logged into, etc.—but it is nevertheless a bad sign if a partner does not even allow supervised entry into their accounts.

While this isn't a big deal in short-term relationships, someone that does not trust you or who you do not trust is unlikely to make a strong long-term partner. The statement, "I am willing to commit to spending the next few decades with this person," and "but, I fundamentally don't trust them," are not congruent. **The voice in the back of your head telling you not to trust a partner with your email password should also be telling you not to trust them with the power marriage gives them over you.** In general, partners in a healthy long-term relationship should expect to have full access to all of each other's social media accounts, phones, email accounts, etc. You should be able to trust the good judgment and respect of any long-term partner you would accept into your life.

The exception: Privacy makes sense when you know someone is a good partner for you, but openly disapproves of some aspect of your life of which they are aware (maybe the type of porn you watch). Such cases are common and relationships can still function fine with them, so as a society, it makes sense to set up moderate expectations of privacy even within a long-term relationship.

Partners With Significantly Different Worldviews / Values / Objective Functions

If you and your partner subscribe to two different religions, or if your partner wants kids and you do not, you are already shouldering significant opportunity costs. A partner with congruent values and/or worldviews would likely help you maximize your objective function (the thing(s) you want to maximize in life) with far greater efficiency and ease than a partner whose values and worldview are different. A partner with different values and objectives in life may even actively hamper your ability to pursue and align with what matters to you most.

If your partner is aware that your worldviews, religions, values, or objective functions do not match well and behaves as though this is not a serious problem, beware. Such behavior indicates that they are willing to overlook and downplay large potential problems in favor of relationship stability. In such cases, be vigilant of other problems that this partner is downplaying.

In a worst-case scenario, your partner may assume that your philosophical mismatch will not be an issue because they expect you will eventually "come to your senses" and learn to see the world their way. A person who does not care at all about vastly different views, but otherwise cares about you, likely expects to convert you to their beliefs on a subject. These are issues that absolutely must be resolved before you initiate a long-term relationship with a clear plan of action.

All of this becomes 1000% more pertinent if a partner adheres to a religious tradition that believes in hell or some form of eternal punishment for not adhering to it—and yet they aren't constantly attempting to convert you. An individual who literally believes your soul will be tortured for all eternity, but who is willing to ignore that for the chance of a relationship with you, clearly does not care about you as a person; instead, they primarily value the chance at a relationship with you. Someone who values a relationship with you over your own best interest is a terrible choice for a life partner.

If you look broadly at relationship research, you will find that people are far more willing to date those of different religious leanings than they are to marry them, implying that if you are dating someone from a different religious tradition, the odds of the relationship ending in marriage are much lower than they otherwise might be. In the US, 85% of marriages are between people of the same faith, while 72% of unmarried relationships are.

Also, keep in mind that for certain religious traditions, in-group marriage is more critical than it is for others. If you look at the stats on this, Mormons and Sikhs have very low rates of marrying outside their faith, whereas Jews marry outside their religion quite frequently.

To clarify: **We are not saying that interfaith relationships do not work or should be seen as a major red flag.** What we mark as a massive red flag are relationships with people of different religious backgrounds who downplay it as a complete non-issue and a topic to be avoided—especially on important issues like how children will be raised.

Partners Who Do Not Value Emotional Control

Beware of anyone who does not understand that a failure to control their emotions is a bad thing. A person who sometimes explodes with anger or sadness and apologizes shortly afterward can be fixed over time through careful training and conditioning, but only if they are willing to label emotional outbursts as negative, unproductive, and unacceptable.

A person who yells at you over something and subsequently refuses to admit they were in the wrong to lose emotional control, even if they were right about what they were mad about, makes a very suboptimal long-term relationship prospect. If challenging your partner about losses of emotional control—whether those losses of judgment entail yelling or sobbing—means broaching a "touchy subject," either succeed in convincing this person that it is not appropriate behavior and gain their commitment to fixing it or do not enter a long-term relationship with said person.

Partners Who Make Threats or Impose Ultimatums

A person's habit of getting what they want through threats or ultimatums (e.g., "Do this thing for me or I will humiliate you/punish you/hurt you/deprive you of something/falsely accuse you of something") dies hard. Whereas we have found that some behaviors can be changed if an intervention takes place in time, we do not consider this red flag behavior to be worth the risk unless it can be fully erased before engagement.

Partners Who Seek Constant Sexual Validation from Strangers and Acquaintances

Beware of individuals who fish for sexual validation, such as men who boast about their number of sexual partners or women who frequently mention or solicit interest from others for no particular reason. If, for example, your partner's Instagram feed is comprised mostly of flirty, "sexy" pictures of them, you must acknowledge that this person has a nontrivial drive to secure sexual attention. Such people are not posting randomly; they are posting in pursuit of a certain emotion and trying to create a certain public image.

People seeking sexual validation are typically poor partners in long-term relationships for two reasons:
1) As we age, libido can change. This leads to different levels of sexual interaction throughout a relationship. If your partner gains a large amount of their personal validation from those sexual interactions, this can be devastating to them

emotionally and create very high odds of cheating.

2) As we age, our value as a sexual object decreases in the eyes of society. If sexual attention and validation comprise a huge source of self-worth for an individual, their "sex display" behavior will increase over time to a point at which it will become counter toward a productive adult life—or this person will have a major emotional breakdown and begin to define their self-worth based on something else. This could end up being something positive like "being a good parent," or it could be something negative. Whatever it is, the fact that you cannot predict it makes this individual a risky long-term partner.

Partners Who Incorporate Negative Character Traits into Their Core Identities

Anyone who self identifies with a negative character trait is worth avoiding. Those who take great pride in being sassy, being a drama queen, drinking too much, getting a little wild, losing control on occasion, or being prone to passionate rages are dangerous and make for dangerous long-term partners. Any attempt to improve such partners will be received as a personal attack, as these improvements would also require that these people shed an aspect of their identity that they treasure. These issues might be easy to overlook early in a relationship, but with time, the damage caused by a partner's apparently unassailable bad behavior will snowball.

A Call for Introspection

Be acutely aware that you are just as likely as a potential partner to exhibit any of the red flags listed above. Your present personality, behavior, and motivations may make you a terrible sexual and/or relationship candidate and a genuine danger to others. If you find you have trouble maintaining human relations over time or the majority of your exes dislike you, the most likely source of your problems is you.

The best place to begin troubleshooting is with your own personality and behavior. It would serve you well to re-read through the red flag behaviors listed above from a strictly introspective perspective in hopes of identifying toxic behaviors you can correct.

False Red Flags

We have all picked up many sets of "default red flags" from society that we are supposed to use to identify potentially dangerous partners. You may notice that while the red flags listed above have some overlap with societal defaults, some that you may have expected might be missing. Society has done a terrible job of judging how a relationship should be structured in the current age; this failure extends to societal labeling of potential red flags in partners.

Do not mark the following as automatic triggers to reject a potential partner:
- Partners who suffer from mental illnesses
- Partners who suffer from addictions

- Partners who exhibit controlling behavior
- Partners who do not conform to societal ideals
- Relationships in which one partner voluntarily surrenders power to another partner
- Partners who have strange kinks

Partners Suffering from Mental Illness

While we already mentioned this in passing, the mere presence of mental illness is not a red flag by any means. Pharmacological and psychiatric treatments have advanced considerably over the past half-century, making many previously untenable conditions entirely manageable. Mental illnesses are only really dangerous if an individual refuses treatment or is prone to flippantly going off their meds when life seems back on track. While working in psychiatry in his early career, Malcolm observed that this was always a huge problem with patients who had more severe conditions: Often when the treatment was working, and their problems went away, people suffering from severe mental illnesses would incorrectly assume that they didn't need the treatment anymore.

However, while mental illness itself is not a huge red flag, we would strongly recommend caution when considering a long-term relationship with anyone who identifies strongly with one. Some people like to make mental illness a major aspect of their self-identities. This can be a big problem because it means they are likely to use their mental illness as an excuse for bad behavior and see a request to improve bad behavior as an attack on their identity. A mental illness is never an excuse for failing to realize your goals for an ideal self; mental illness is just another small roadblock, and we all have roadblocks.

Partners Suffering from Addictions

While we strongly caution against relationships with individuals who have addictions to hard drugs that frequently lead to thievery and other violent acts, we often see individuals leave partners for lower-order drugs and habits that do not significantly affect their lives outside of shortening their personal lifespans. Nicotine, pot, video games, and even alcohol can be fairly innocuous, yet are often cited as red flags.

We are not encouraging you to marry a drunk (someone who allows being intoxicated to interfere with their career and relationships), but there is a huge difference between an alcoholic and a drunk. Marrying an alcoholic is OK; marrying a drunk is highly ill-advised. It is possible to drink way too much alcohol (Winston Churchill, for example) while still not allowing it to negatively impact your life in a way that makes lofty goals or a successful relationship all that difficult to achieve. The same holds for other lower-order drugs. So long as they do not completely control a partner's life, self-identity, or behavior, they do not warrant, per our calculations, the termination of a relationship based on them alone—though they are certainly a negative.

You may argue that someone who drinks a lot but doesn't allow it to affect their life is not an alcoholic. We would argue anyone who clearly has an addiction to the consumption of alcohol is an alcoholic. This is a semantic differentiation people use to not address their failings.

You also may argue that Churchill was not an alcoholic; we would point you to the historical record, which shows he drank 1.5 bottles of champagne or wine daily along with five to six ounces of whiskey or brandy. It is very possible to be addicted to alcohol or any other drug without it having a massive negative impact on one's potential; do not use this as a free pass to ignore the health effects of an addiction.

All that said, it is a huge and immediate red flag if a partner ever blames behavior on an addiction. Saying, "I only did this because I was drunk/high," and believing that such an excuse clears one from responsibility for the behavior should be a huge red flag. Such a person can easily justify any behavior.

Partners with Controlling Behavior

Controlling behavior, such as advice that you dump your current friend group and limits on when you may leave the house to go "partying," is often contextualized as being a red flag or toxic. In some cases, this is textbook abusive behavior, but in many cases this behavior can be quite healthy. Behavior that would be described as controlling is common within most Pygmalion relationships and often plays a necessary role in permitting another individual to work with you to improve yourself. If you decide you want to improve your life with the help of your partner, you must be willing to accept controlling behavior from a partner who is willing to act as your coach.

Why are the strict regimes Olympic trainers set for the athletes they train not categorized as abuse? The athletes consent. The discomfort caused by these regimes is a product of a strategic, thoughtful effort in pursuit of a shared goal. Having a partner who pushes you hard to improve yourself in ways you want to improve can "appear" like extreme controlling behavior. **The difference lies in consent and a shared vision for who you want to become.**

Partners Who Do Not Conform to Societal Ideals

Do not let general societal hang-ups—which may have nothing to do with your personal needs or preferences—dictate which partners are and are not viable. In many cases, relationship types that are seen as suboptimal by society may be highly optimal for *you*.

Examples of this include:
- Long-distance relationships
- Relationships in which you and your partner sleep in separate bedrooms
- A relationship without sex
- Relationships in which your partner is permitted to have sex outside the relationship, but you are not
- A relationship in which you only interact in a virtual environment

The fact that society may have a strong negative reaction to your relationship does not mean the relationship itself is inherently negative or toxic. So long as your relationship has an internal, logical consistency to its rules and those rules work to the ultimate benefit of both parties, we would consider it to be good.

Notes from the Research:
- One in four couples sleep in separate beds.
- Some research shows sleeping in separate beds may help with sleep.

Relationships in Which One Partner Voluntarily Surrenders Power to Another Partner

There appears to be a weird—one might even argue unnatural—fetishization of power in Western society.

Even groups that celebrate the fact that people want different things from a relationship express discomfort with the idea that some individuals enjoy surrendering power or operating under others within a dominance hierarchy. For example, polyamorous communities frequently belittle the concept of someone "belonging" to someone else. This discomfort even appears in the BDSM communities of all places, which often go on and on about how the sub is *really* the one with the power (a sub is the subordinate partner in a dominant-submissive coupling).

Power is not intrinsically good or bad. In fact, there are many logical—even enlightened—reasons why a person may decide they would prefer to not have power. Power is inversely proportional to responsibility. If you have power and you fail at something, then it is *your* fault. If, however, someone has power over you and you fail, then it is *their* fault.

Even if society stigmatizes the choice to relinquish power to another, many people possess the mental maturity and self-awareness required to admit to themselves that they would rather surrender power than risk having to take responsibility for failure to achieve their goals— either over their entire life or specific portions of it (such as their career, their kids, their style, etc.). This manifests not only in relationships, but also in careers: Many people who have the skills, opportunity, and resources to start their own companies or climb higher in their careers choose to remain in a comfortable position within other organizations, leaving bigger problems and more responsibility to the professionals above them in the ranks.

In addition to granting one a "get out of responsibility free" card to a certain extent, the surrender of power allows you to turn off some taxing and unpleasant aspects of your cognition, which in turn unlocks new tiers of emotional states not available to individuals who choose to assume power in life.

The idea that all humans everywhere are always better off being their own masters seems to have originated in the Western cultural tradition and come into being fairly recently. This bias certainly did not yet exist at the time of The Great Chain Of Being, a belief that all beings existed in a hierarchy (God -> King -> Nobles -> . . . -> father -> mother ->child -> animal) common throughout all Western cultures only a few hundred years ago. Favoritism of self-determination also does not seem to have been appropriated from Eastern traditions or indigenous populations during the time of colonialism.

Society's present phobia around the surrender of power appears to be tied to the emergence of capitalism in the

West and an association between power and wealth. This general phobia of power relinquishment could also be a reaction to chattel slavery, but we doubt this, as the ideas spread aligns more with the spread of capitalism than with chattel slavery.

Humans evolved to thrive in a world of servants and masters, serfs, and lords. It is likely that to some extent our cognition has mechanisms in place that are meant to help the serfs, servants, and conquered people survive and breed. The selective pressures on these cognitive mechanisms were likely stronger than the mechanisms meant to assist the cognition of rulers and conquering people (especially considering that throughout history, there have always been far more servants than masters—and a servant messing up is more likely to cull them from the gene pool than a master messing up). Even in present-day situations with strict dominance hierarchies, the only way to gain a position of dominance is through becoming skilled at holding a subservient position (think of military hierarchies, for example). This would further increase the pressure on humans being more cognitively optimized to be servants than masters.

In other words, the mental state a human enters when they are able to accept a position of servitude may be more cognitively optimized and "natural" to the human condition than the power-hungry mental state Western society forces on us. This would also explain why both men and women prefer to be submissive in some surveys of dom/sub kink participants (but not all)—this is something we discuss in detail in *The Pragmatist's Guide* to Sexuality where we frame it as a question of whether or not humans should be thought of as a "slave race".

Personal diatribes aside: A relationship in which one individual unconditionally submits themselves to another in every aspect of their existence because they judge the other to be worthy of that submission is not necessarily bad.

Right now, such relationships are relegated to small kink niches such as the Goreans, Taken in Hand, and 24/7 Total Power Exchange.

Partners with Strange Kinks

So your partner is into weird stuff... Like *really* weird stuff. This must be a sign of psychological damage, right? A giant red flag?

In *The Pragmatist's Guide to Sexuality,* we conducted a fairly large study, among other things, we checked for a correlation between unusual arousal patterns and abusive behavior. This relationship simply didn't appear in the data. What turns a person on is for the most part not their choice.

Limiting your partner pool to only those with vanilla sexual interests will significantly limit your options without improving the average quality of your now-more-limited pool of candidates. Filtering out those with strange kinks only makes sense if you have a specific religious motivation for doing so or if a partner insists on living out their strange sexual fantasies with you, and that is not something you want to make a part of your life.

HURTING PEOPLE IN RELATIONSHIPS

Getting good at relationships and keeping a partner happy is like getting good at anything else: We will all fail a lot initially and learn from those failures. Failing in a relationship usually involves hurting someone—even when doing everything right and bending over backward in an attempt to not cause harm.

This does not mean we shouldn't try to minimize the damage we do while on our sexual and romantic escapades—if not for others' sake, for our own. Not only may a hurt partner try to retaliate in some way, but most humans who lack the good fortune of being born as psychopaths feel tremendous pain when they realize they have hurt someone. That pain can linger for years, emerging every time something triggers reflection on the incident.

How To Avoid Hurting Relationship Partners

We could write volumes about the various precautions one can take to avoid hurting a long-term partner. Rather than waste precious minutes regurgitating common sense into readers' mouths like a mother bird, we will share three tips that are considered by our friends to be less obvious.

First, compliment partners when they achieve things **they value** (e.g., get good grades, break a personal record while exercising, exert emotional control, etc.). Only complimenting a partner on things you value can come off as self-interested and may not create the same emotional reward in them as being complimented for something they value. Relationship satisfaction improves on all sides through consistent and frequent deployment of gestures that improve a partner's mood. That said, this tactic will not work among those who use a Dominance Lure to secure a partner, as regular compliments and attempts to do nice things for your partner will undermine the lopsided balance of power that makes the relationship appealing to the target.

Second, if emotional investment or attention from a partner is important, request it clearly and directly. To subtly signal needs to a partner is to demand that they always monitor and analyze even the slightest of mood fluctuations. This sets people up to be hurt when they mistakenly assume they are being ignored (when in reality a cue is too subtle to be noticed, or the partner expected to pick up certain signals is too busy with their own problems to notice it one day), Such behavior ultimately leaves one partner hurt and the other confused.

Finally, it is easy to get into a pattern of romantic gestures that ultimately feel routine and hollow. Romantic gestures can sometimes begin to be more a sign of your financial success or leisure time than a celebration of your partner's dreams. An easy way to remedy this is to note major milestones related to a partner's goals and reward each milestone that is achieved.

How To Avoid Hurting Sexual Partners

Just as you will inevitably hurt people with whom you have longer-term relationships, it is almost surprisingly easy to hurt someone through a short-term sexual encounter. Let's review a few ways this can happen and discuss how such damage can be avoided.

If someone comes off as emotionally unstable, especially if they have extreme political, social, or religious views, avoid sex with them no matter how eager they are. Anecdotally, we have observed that these people often have a habit of finding ways to convince themselves that someone else hurt them because victimhood reinforces their understanding of how the world works. In many cases, social, political, and religious extremists can raise their social status within their extremist communities' dominance hierarchies by claiming that an outsider hurt them. Their convincing themselves that you did something that hurt them can cause almost as much pain as you actually hurting them. Do not give such people ammunition to shoot themselves in the foot.

Assuming that a guy has not indicated that he *likes* being humiliated, it is best to always pretend that his penis is on the larger side vis a vis those of **your past sexual partners**—unless this would be an obvious lie. This way, even if he is a bit smaller than average, he can still think he has the largest penis of men with whom you have been intimate (assuming that is believable—otherwise just don't draw attention to it). Remember that for most guys, sex is as much about validating their own sense of virility as it is about any actual pleasure gained from the encounter. Sexually inexperienced women sometimes try to brag about the large penis size of previous male sexual conquests in an attempt to raise their own perceived value through an association with higher-value men, which will needlessly hurt their present male partners.

On a related note, those not actively trying to humiliate a partner for sexual reasons (some partners clearly request humiliation, explaining it yields sexual gratification) should not comment on any part of a partner's body being abnormal after they are naked. If someone has taken off their clothes, they have let their guard down. Judgmental comments in this context will *not* aid a dominance-based sexual strategy. For those attempting to implement a Dominance Lure: Do not "neg" someone after they have consented to sexual interaction—it will cause them to feel unsafe making themselves vulnerable in the future and will not help odds of enjoyable or future sexual encounters.

When using dating websites, ask to connect with targets on another image-heavy social media platform before meeting them in person (especially a platform like Facebook where *other people* can post and tag photos of this person, which may be more realistic)—this makes it far easier to weed out cases of catfishing. This method is only part of a complete screening investigation, as someone can have many photos of themselves online and still look entirely different (and categorically worse) in person, but it still weeds out a non-trivial percentage of cases.

Not all catfishing happens intentionally. Sometimes people simply think they look best in photos that didn't show how physically unfortunate they may happen to be. Ultimately cutting a date short after it comes out that one (or both partners) mislead each other about their physical or social realities can really hurt all parties involved, so don't skimp on diligence, but also plan for a soft landing should, despite doing plenty of preemptive homework, the first date be a bust and require early termination. Meet in a public space and make first dates intentionally short and brief (with room for expansion should all be OK). Propose to meet over evening drinks and not dinner, late morning coffee and not lunch, and at locations close to public transport and other activities rather than remote places that might require a humiliating, long, lonely ride home.

Consensual sex that later comes to be regretted can cause as much emotional pain as some non-consensual sex. While this reality does not fit into the political agendas of some people, it is an apparent fact. Avoid casual sex with colleagues, employees, teammates, and those connected to important friends. High schoolers deciding to date early would be best served by avoiding sexual interaction with classmates entirely, sticking to their age group but focusing on isolated summer camp flings or students attending nearby—but not integrated—schools.

Finally, bear in mind that first-timers need (and by many measures deserve) more attention and caution (and should exercise far more caution themselves when selecting a first sexual partner). Avoid sex with virgins—especially virgin females—should there not be time or interest in investing in at least a few months of casual dating afterward.

Virgin females' brains react differently to sex than the brains of more experienced females and males. The studies we cited on oxytocin release declining in females after the first partner explain why this happens and how a female will experience an unusually high release of oxytocin with her first partner. Even a totally logical woman who really only wants sex has a high likelihood of developing an emotional attachment to her first sexual partner, especially if said partner makes an effort to make it a good experience for her (which, by the way, requires a bit of research; sleeping with a virgin requires different techniques). Sleeping with and summarily dumping a virgin female could hurt her in a manner that leaves a long-term impact on her life.

ABUSE

Abuse is one of many topics that society refuses to engage with honestly. What we are allowed to say about abuse (without suffering severe social consequences) is quite limited. For example, we are socially compelled to say that the only acceptable response to abuse is to leave a relationship.

This childish virtue signaling is extremely destructive when it happens on a societal level. The uncomfortable reality is that sometimes it is better to stay in an abusive relationship than it is to leave one. Someone living with an emotionally manipulative partner who threatens to kill their kids should the relationship end—and may just be unstable enough to follow through on that threat—is better off maintaining the relationship and enduring abuse long enough to set up protections for their kids before terminating the toxic relationship.

The platitude stating "the correct answer is always to leave" helps no one but the person saying it, who feels good about the fact that they live in a fair world with easy answers. Sometimes people really do follow through on their threats. Real people *really die* because virtue-signalers want to feel good about themselves and give these victims thoughtless, politically correct advice. Leaving a highly abusive relationship is risky and a lot of work, especially if the abused partner is financially dependent on the abuser, if the abuser has power in society, and/or if kids are involved.

The world isn't a kind place. Many abused people look at the dangers of leaving versus staying in an abusive relationship and recognize that each alternative is fraught with danger. Pragmatists accept that sometimes life involves a choice between two bad options with no clear answer.

Optional Thought Experiment: *A good case to look into if you want to think deeper on this is Dina Ali Lasloom. What action would you have pressured her to take?*

Politically correct, societally condoned views of abuse can leave people trapped in abusive relationships for longer-than-necessary periods of time. If you think you *might* be in an abusive relationship, but everyone to whom you turn for help insists that you immediately leave your partner, how can you move forward? By reflexively giving victims the same answer without thinking through their unique situation or internalizing the long-term damage the advice may cause victims, many sources of potential help inadvertently train victims to not seek assistance. We learned from one victim of abuse—who stayed in her abusive relationship for years—that many of the women's shelters to which she turned refused to take in abuse victims unless they promise to leave their abusive partners, (at least this was her personal experience and she blamed the length she stayed in the relationship partially on this). This policy, be it informal or formal, means these victims do not even get the sanctuary needed to think clearly about whether or not it is really worth the risk to leave their partners permanently, which, especially when kids are involved, is often a very real risk.

Talking with victims of abuse when writing this book really helped us better understand just what a tricky and nuanced situation, it can be to find oneself in an abusive relationship. Abuse is not like other relationship pitfalls and not something to which one can offer glib, one-size-fits-all solutions. That said, thinking on this topic and some of the one-size-fits-all answers presented in response to abuse cases inspired us to explore why people are abusive and investigate the prevailing narratives around the topic.

The Control Theory

The belief that abuse is about control—and specifically that people become abusive because they want more control—has attained significant purchase in popular consciousness.

We do not buy this theory at all. So far as we can see, there is just not much statistical evidence to back it up, and this theory around control feels like the kind of just-so story invented by someone attempting to explain a behavior they don't understand.

We agree that sometimes people are classically abusive with the goal of control, but we see no evidence that control correlates with abusive behavior any more than a myriad of behavioral patterns that correlate with hurting others in the name of self-service.

Classical abuse appears to fall into four broad categories:
    1) Learned/trained behavior patterns

2) Fetishistic behavior (See *The Pragmatist's Guide to Sexuality*)
3) Self-validation (the individual associates abuse with a character trait they want to embody, such as masculinity or power)
4) Intentional strategies to prevent a partner from leaving

We will focus on the fourth instigator of abuse, as it dovetails several concepts discussed in this book.

Abuse as a Relationship Strategy

Some adopt abusive behavior as an outright relationship strategy. Unpleasant as it may be to admit this, some forms of proto-abuse and abuse are effective at extracting certain elements of value from a relationship. Some people genuinely do not care whether their partner likes them—or at least they would rather be in a relationship with a partner who hates them than to be in no relationship at all.

Abusive relationship strategies typically fall into one of a few categories. The five core "game plans" common across most intentionally abusive relationships frequently involve:
1. Attempts to lower an individual's self-assessed market value
2. Attempts to lower an individual's actual market value
3. Attempts to introduce an externality to a breakup
4. Attempts to emotionally drain a partner
5. Attempts to prevent an individual from meeting or interacting with other potential partners

Let's explore each of these in turn.

Attempts to Lower a Partner's Perceived Market Value

A common strategy we have already addressed involves lowering a partner's perceived aggregate market value. Essentially, the abusive partner will attempt to make you feel as though other people would not want to date you were you to leave this abusive partner, suggesting that you are of lower value than you really are. If your partner ever suggests other people would not want you, be aware that this is not normal behavior: This person is willing to hurt you emotionally—not in order to improve you, but in order to reduce the odds that you will leave them. A partner demonstrating a willingness to hurt you in an attempt to keep you with them is an early and easy sign that much worse things are to come and that your feelings fundamentally do not matter to this person.

Attempts to Lower a Partner's Actual Market Value

Intentionally abusive partners may also increase the costs associated with leaving them through tactics that *actually* hurt your market value by ruining your looks, forcing you to quit your career, etc. This strategy can be harder to spot because often these tactics can have more innocent explanations (i.e., *you, independently,* let your own appearance slide, or you decided to quit your job to become a stay-at-home parent for the best interest of the kids). A good way to catch a partner leveraging this tactic is to look for instances in which your partner has hindered your attempts to quit a bad habit or cast off a vice. Consider an alcoholic trying to quit whose partner keeps asking if they want drinks. Imagine someone trying to lose weight whose partner keeps presenting them with unhealthy dishes. This is not normal behavior in relationships. This behavior is intentionally designed to cripple the victim and is most commonly performed by individuals with incredibly low self-esteem who find comfort in the idea of "bringing their partner down to their level."

Attempts to Introduce an Externality to a Breakup

It is easy to spot when a partner tries to introduce an externality to the act of leaving them. This means they try to increase the "cost" of leaving them through something, usually a threat. This threat can be self-focused, "I would see no reason to go on living if you left me," or externally focused, "I will ruin your life/beat you if you leave me." It is not normal for a person to say: If you leave me, I will do X. Even if X = something flattering, such as "never love another woman again," this partner is still trying to make any decision to leave them hurt you more. And this is the key to not separating out classical definitions of abuse from proto-abusive behaviors—if we ignore proto-abuse and only focus on "classical abuse" we may not raise the red flags when we hear "I will never love a woman again" that we would over phrases like "I will kill myself if you leave me" even though they are different levels of output of the exact same behavior pattern with the exact same intention, to make leaving them hurt you more.

Attempts to Emotionally Drain a Partner

Draining one's partner as a strategy is different from the others discussed here. Most abusive behaviors are primarily implemented to prevent a partner from leaving the abuser, while this one can actually just be to help the abuser "get off," win arguments more often, or in rare instances, just feel powerful.

Attempts to emotionally drain or demoralize a partner typically fall into two categories. The first is just straight up hurting a partner, either physically or emotionally, for the sake of the emotional impact hurting them will have—this one is pretty straightforward, so we won't wax on it. The second involves getting the victim to begin to question their sanity and the validity of their emotions. The most common technique used here is gaslighting, getting a person to question their own memory by systematically disputing its validity but can extend to other areas that are not as commonly labeled as red flags such as systematic sleep deprivation.

Attempts to Block a Partner from Meeting or Socializing With Others

Attempting to prevent a partner from meeting other potential partners can manifest in many ways. Such attempts may involve either directly exerting editorial control over a partner's friends removing any that are too attractive or the wrong gender, but may also involve spying on their email, monitoring how they spend money or demanding access to their phone—all with the intention of "catching them" interacting with people "they shouldn't be with."

The intent behind this kind of intentional abuse is to either prevent a partner from realizing that there might be other options, prevent a partner from interacting with temptations due to a complete lack of faith in even a basic level of impulse control, or intent to prevent a partner from discovering their partner is not "that great."

Still, there is a big difference between a partner who says: "I don't like that a friend keeps giving you meth and therefore if you want to date me, you can't hang out with them" and saying: "You can't hang out with a friend because they are too attractive," or even just a blanket demand that you not spend time alone with the gender you find attractive. Don't confuse a partner's attempts to improve your life with a partner's attempts to prevent you from meeting with perceived competition.

The key takeaway regarding these intentionally abusive strategies is that, while they may be implemented by someone who loves you, they will never be implemented by someone who cares about your personal wellbeing, and that is what makes these behaviors such important tells.

LYING IN RELATIONSHIPS

People lie in relationships and when dating—a lot. Most partners lie for convenience, to inflate their perceived value in the eyes of a target, or to convince a prospective partner that they are in a different market than they are. Statistics show us that lying differs across genders: Women lie more about their weight, age, and interest in long-term relationships, whereas men lie about their height, income, and interest in casual sex.

Intentional Misrepresentation in Relationships

Almost everyone tries to put forward their best foot early in a relationship. Does it really matter if a prospective partner knows that you had fairly serious cosmetic surgery? Should a prospective partner really be informed that you do not share their religious beliefs? Is now really the right time to tell a target that you used to work as a prostitute? How important is it that a potential partner knows you are already in a polyamorous relationship on a first date? Is it really unethical to not tell a partner that you enjoy masturbating to yourself while crossdressing?

Misrepresentation is totally normal, and a tool used in the following dating strategies:
- Misrepresentation because you are primarily looking for sex

- Misrepresentation because you plan to tell your partner later
- Misrepresentation because you plan to maintain the lie indefinitely
- Misrepresentation of intended relationship lifespan

Misrepresentation Because You Are Primarily Looking For Sex

If both you and your partner are both primarily looking for sex, outside of disclosing sexually transmittable diseases and infections, misrepresentation is the norm and is unlikely to lead to significant negative consequences unless you make an enormous misjudgment about your target's values. Misrepresentation is less benign if you are looking for sex and your target is looking for a relationship, but given how ineffective this strategy is, it is not terribly relevant, because a person looking primarily for a relationship will take significantly more time, money, and emotional investment when contrasted to someone looking for sex—relationship seekers are not worth the time of a Pragmatist looking primarily for sex.

Misrepresentation of facts presented to short-term sexual partners can yield enormous negative consequences in rare circumstances—specifically, circumstances in which something you think is insignificant is identity-shattering to your target.

Misrepresentation Because You Plan To Tell Your Partner Later

This strategy entails increasing your individual desirability in the eyes of your target by waiting to increase the emotional cost of leaving you before you drop bombs that you expect will negatively affect your desirability. While we would not recommend this strategy for more than a few secrets, it is fairly common and normal. In fact, we encourage anyone who has been with their present partner for less than three months to expect there are at least two significant individual-desirability-modulating personal details that this person is intentionally occluding.

This strategy is only stupid if you wait for a huge individual desirability increaser—like getting married or having children together—before you reveal something that could drastically affect your value in your partner's eyes. Waiting until after you are married to tell your spouse that you do not want to have kids, or waiting until after you are pregnant to tell a partner that you never really enjoyed sex with them, is beyond idiotic. Such unpleasant reveals decrease each partner's individual desirability.

When you tell a partner that you deceved them, there is a possibility that their opinion of you will decline significantly. Should that happen, this partner may come to regret ever meeting you. It is possible for both of you to hate each other and still have individual desirability to each other above your differential aggregate desirability and thus have a "good relationship," but certainly not a good life (this can happen through something like having kids together). We would never encourage someone to build a long-term relationship on false pretenses by withholding potentially damaging personal details for more than a few weeks.

Misrepresentation Because You Plan To Maintain The Lie Indefinitely

While deciding to hide a personally damning detail permanently is less patently stupid than waiting until after you are married or expecting children to reveal whatever it is you are hiding, we would not call this an optimal strategy. While living a lie is not the worst thing in the world (certainly not as bad as Western society likes to pretend), doing so is not something worth opting into without very good reasons, and there are few legitimate justifications for such drastic measures.

The one exception here is anything that makes you non-viable as a partner in your society or any personal detail which would be dangerous for you to disclose. For example, if you get aroused when watching people die, you should probably keep that to yourself (not as uncommon as you would think; see *The Pragmatist's Guide to Sexuality* for more info on this). Even in this scenario, you are still strictly better off if your partner knows this about you and accepts it.

Misrepresentation of Intended Relationship Lifespan

In this strategy, one partner misleads another to believe that a relationship will last longer than planned. The classic example is the young trophy wife whose husband intends to discard her for a new model as soon as she is no longer physically attractive. This form of misrepresentation is easy to circumvent; simply avoid relationships in which you are of a much higher individual desirability to your partner *earlier* in your relationship contrasted with *later* in the relationship. In other words, do not marry someone who primarily values your looks, youth, physical fitness, or fertility unless you have a strong reason to believe they will stay with you once these things inevitably fade.

Unintentional Misrepresentation in Relationships Due to Unanticipated Changes

It is entirely possible to represent yourself as a certain type of partner, absolutely believe you will always be that type of partner, and be completely committed to being that type of partner all your life, only to be hit by unexpected circumstances later in life that completely change you as a person and break the representation you had originally made to a partner.

A person may genuinely be emotionally available during one period of their lives only to, through no fault of their own, experience an extended period of clinical depression after marriage and lose this availability. A person may lose their sex drive as they get older while their partner does not. A person may even have a deep sexual or personal awakening and come out as gay after years of marriage.

Such situations are inconvenient and require a reevaluation of the relationship when they arise. Changes may need to be made to ensure all partners still benefit from the relationship. In some cases, the relationship will need to be dissolved entirely.

Fortunately, it is typically easy to update the (often implied) contracts that define our relationships to ensure that all parties still benefit. For example, a person who loses their sex drive may be willing to consider opening a previously closed marriage to ensure the marriage is still beneficial to their partner. Through these contract renegotiations and adjustments, you may even find yourself in a much better relationship than you would have had otherwise, without any life changes forcing such renegotiation.

Unintentional misrepresentation of your characteristics as a partner is more problematic if unexpected changes are at least partially your fault. If, for example, you decide to stop eating in moderation and exercising after getting married and subsequently become overweight, breaking a representation you had previously made to a partner to always be as attractive and fit as you can be, you should have warned your partner you might not always work hard to maintain your health and appearance. The same goes for those with addictive tendencies they thought they had under control and neglected to mention (e.g., a shopping or gambling addiction), and those who cannot resist sex with an attractive, willing third party outside of the rules of the relationship.

If your misrepresentation in a relationship stems from a failure of self-control, you should have warned your partner that you had reason to expect future changes related to this lack of impulse control. People fail at self-control all the time. Most overweight people do not want to be overweight, and very few smokers want to be smokers. Those who succumb to suboptimal temptations are largely at the mercy of their partners and how they decide to react to this failure.

While "semi-unintentional" situations are still potentially remediable through contract renegotiation, they build significantly more resentment than totally unintentional changes. This is because they demonstrate to your partner your willingness to act in bad faith, something they now have to expect during contract renegotiation. In these circumstances, it is also extremely common for the partner who lost self-control to take a pre-emptive offensive stance to avoid having to address their personal failure. This will lead to them being unfairly aggressive in contract negotiations, pushing for a contract even more in their favor than it had been before, and attacking their partner with perceived slights to remove personal accountability for their failure.

The most optimal resolution to such situations involves the offending partner accepting complete responsibility for their offense. Any relationship that survives a negative change without the offending party taking responsibility for their failure is likely to become a miserable affair.

Defense Against Misrepresentation

As a social species, we are designed to detect lying. You will therefore likely catch most liars through small social tells. Still, it helps to know what you have in your "anti-deception" arsenal.

You may circumvent most lying entirely by teaching your partners that they do not need to lie to you. If a partner has decided to lie about looking for a long-term relationship instead of just sex, they are more likely to drop the charade if they believe you would be just as happy with either scenario. Should you exercise emotional control and do not blow up (either with anger or sadness) when a partner fesses up to mistakes and personal shortcomings, you will not train them to withhold such confessions out of fear there will be an emotional explosion. Obviously, this is easier said than done; even if you are able to completely control your emotional reactions, you will still likely want to demonstrate to your partners that bad behavior yields consequences. Even if you don't explode at a partner for going on an unsanctioned spending spree, you will still have to lock their card, return what can be returned, and have them walk through with you how they will prevent this from happening again, and alas, these consequences which give them a reason to lie about such actions.

You may also compromise your partner's cognition. Lying is much harder to maintain in a compromised condition. The human default is to tell the truth; lying requires suppressing that instinct then performing the cognitively taxing task of coming up with a believable story in its place. Anything that exhausts inhibition is going to make someone less likely to lie and lie more sloppily.

Lies can also be detected through contradictions in a partner's narratives. If, for example, you suspect your partner does not actually want a long-term relationship despite having expressed such desires, ask them questions about where they see themselves in ten years. Doing so will create a situation in which they find it difficult to model a fictional set of desires based on a proposed path (the long-term relationship) that they never intended to walk down. They may either visibly mentally stumble or describe their actual intended future, which has nothing to do with you.

By getting your partner to make decisions that are costly if they are lying, you may also detect lies. An example of this might be asking someone who says they plan to stay with you forever to marry you. Such a decision bears little cost if they are telling the truth and a high cost if they are not. That said, this tactic often backfires: Consider all the people out there who have the names of their ex-partners tattooed on their bodies.

Should you have access to them, you might also interview a partner's exes. We frankly do not understand why this practice is not more common. This is an entirely logical way to determine how a person will act in a relationship. Besides, the practice is common in the professional world, in which prospective employers ask for references all the time so they might evaluate the potential value of relationships with far lower stakes. If someone has mostly negative relationships with their previous partners, you can safely assume there is something wrong with them—even if they will not admit it to themselves. If reading this makes you defensive, if it leads you to think: "It's not my fault all my exes hate me!" then please try to picture the most incredulous-looking face your imagination can conjure—that is the face you should imagine us giving you right now.

ATTACHMENT STYLES

Humans have a strong impulse to sort themselves and others into categories. The world just feels more "right" when people fall into neat little boxes. This is likely because social class played a much bigger role in early societies than it does today. If you were a butcher from a family of butchers, that particular classification and status impacted not only the relations you were expected to have with other types of people, but also the personality you were meant to exhibit. By meeting societal expectations for "your kind," you could increase your group's support of you. Thus, humans have a natural inclination to both want to determine their "type" and the expectations of behavior patterns from that "type."

There is presently a discrepancy between what may be an inbred desire to see the world through a group and class-based lens, and our current society in which there are stigmas against sorting people into groups and classes, be they be based on race, wealth, education, religion, occupation, or social class. These stigmas, combined with our vestigial longing to belong in clear groups with "natural" positions in the world, have given birth to a myriad of products and services that sell us stories about who we are and where we belong.

Clever entrepreneurs have invented totally new arbitrary categories into which their voracious customers may be comfortably nestled. We can find our places in the world by consulting astrologers, discussing our blood types (common in Asia), taking out an online quiz to find out what [Insert Show/Movie/Book/Whatever] character we are, or finding our Myers Briggs profiles.

The world of relationship psychology has even come up with its own special set of categories called "attachment styles," which it lifted from early childhood research. This fact gives it the added bonus of being one of the many concepts in pop psychology that allows you to take no responsibility for your own failings and blame your parents.

Obviously if you give someone a quiz to test their attachment style, you will find that it correlates to certain behaviors, but the suggestion that someone who answers that they feel very protective of their partner will show higher mate-guarding behavior is hardly revolutionary. The attachment style school of thought also serves the underwhelming finding that certain behaviors cluster— that someone who is a bit of an inconsiderate jerk in one category is likely to be an inconsiderate jerk in others as well. We are especially amused that many assume their reported attachment style grants them permission to deflect their own failures of character onto their parents (though we can see why such claims make a concept more convenient to market).

Despite our obvious disdain toward this way of categorizing people, the popularity of attachment theory necessitates some discussion in this book. Basically, attachment theory divides people into four categories based on self-esteem (thoughts about self) and sociability (thoughts about others): Secure, Anxious-Preoccupied, Dismissive-Avoidant, and Fearful-Avoidant.

Secure

Those with a secure attachment style have high self-esteem and high sociability and hence are comfortable with both intimacy and independence. They agree with statements like: "It is relatively easy for me to become emotionally close to others," "I am comfortable depending on others and having others depend on me," and "I don't worry about being alone or others not accepting me."

Basically, those with "secure" attachment styles are normal, healthy adults—the type of people anyone could choose to be. Alas, because bad behavior is normalized through frameworks like this (which do not even hold true cross-culturally), we have to deal with the three other types of people.

Anxious-Preoccupied

Those with anxious-preoccupied attachment styles have poor self-esteem and positive sociality. They agree with statements like: "I want to be completely emotionally intimate with others, but I often find that others are reluctant to get as close as I would like," and "I am uncomfortable being without close relationships, but I sometimes worry that others don't value me as much as I value them."

Basically, these are people who try to secure emotional validation from their partners, and instead of just attempting a new strategy when that fails, they keep attempting the same strategy with higher levels of desperation. Look, if you are going to use your partner as a field from which to harvest validation, intentionally build your relationship with that goal in mind and clearly communicate the importance of your validation needs to your partner.

Dismissive-Avoidant

Those with dismissive-avoidant attachment styles have positive self-esteem and negative sociability. They identify with statements such as: "I am comfortable without close emotional relationships," "It is important to me to feel independent and self-sufficient," and "I prefer not to depend on others or have others depend on me."

Basically, this category exists so people trying to sell this model can still market their services to people who are happy not being in relationships—because clearly those people are *broken*. We love how the literature on this group often notes how defensive they act in the face of the relationship psychologists who built the model and were apparently mentally unable to accept that someone could be happy and fulfilled without a relationship. People in this category also tend to be better at controlling their emotional states because they rely less than any other attachment style on other people for validation, but don't worry: People trying to sell this model have found a way to spin this as a bad thing.

Fearful-Avoidant

These are people with both low self-esteem and low socialization. They agree with statements like, "I want emotionally close relationships, but I find it difficult to trust others completely, or to depend on them" and "I sometimes worry that I will be hurt if I allow myself to become too close to other people."

Like the anxious-preoccupied group, these guys are desperate for validation and have a low opinion of themselves. Unlike the anxious-preoccupied group, they accept that they won't get the validation they crave easily through relationships with others and that relationships with others might not be worth the effort or emotional risk. Of course, this is not seen as a sign of emotional intelligence and maturity, as a sane person would see it, but of trauma and abuse within this model.

A More Effective Way to Approach Attachment Styles

Instead of leaning on classifications, we recommend focusing on what, specifically, you need and how you will ensure that need is satisfied. If you think that you need more validation, spend less time classifying yourself and more time putting together a sound strategy for receiving that validation you so sorely need.

There are all sorts of ways to achieve emotional validation—many of which do not require other people. Humans appear to be born with different sensitivities to the validation others grant. One person may receive far more emotional output from the same validating statement than another, and this variance in response need not necessarily be the result of childhood trauma.

If feeling validated and achieving emotional actualization is important to you, focus on easy-to-secure sources of validation that yield a large and lasting emotional impact. Organize your life and relationships in such a way that you receive validating stimuli regularly. Identify a vein of emotional validation, then harvest that source as sustainably as possible. Of course, you could also decide that luxuriating in another person's validation is just a subjective state of mind and that this state of mind may not be that important in the grand scheme of things. Ironically, accepting the latter significantly lowers most non-clinical anxiety—sadly, it also involves accepting that what other people think of you genuinely doesn't matter, which is both difficult and objectively not always true.

There is one small useful piece of relationship strategy that can be gleaned from the attachment model: **If your partner is relying on interactions with you as a source of personal validation, grant them the validation they so desperately desire when they come to you looking to harvest that resource.** Why? If you are not forthcoming with validation when partners request it, one of two things will happen: Your validation-craving partner will find another source of validation to harvest (likely ending in their cheating on you and/or breaking up with you), or their mental condition will deteriorate, making them less effective as a partner, and generally annoying.

Conversely, if you rely on your partner for validation when you are otherwise emotionally compromised, take measures to ensure that (1) your partner knows this is part of the role they are signing up for in the relationship, (2) you clearly signal to your partner when you need validation (no subtle bids for attention), and (3) you have mutually recognized and perfected interactions that will provide you with this validation. For example, you may feel a very consistent flush of happiness when a partner compliments you on your cooking. If this is the case, communicate to your partner that those compliments are important to you, make a point of cooking some meals your partner can enjoy, and make a point of improving your culinary skills.

Keep in mind that building controls to ensure consistent delivery of desired validation among partners is not the only solution for dealing with anxiety or a desire for validation. This is merely the only solution that attachment theory recognizes. When one of us (Simone or Malcolm) is feeling like we need validation or are anxious, instead of seeking validation from the other, we articulate this illogical desire while noting its lack of utility and request help being talked down from our emotional state, having our anxiety put in context by a more sober mind, and being reminded how the person we want to be would react (with grace, dignity, and calm) to the same environmental stimuli.

Because we are emotionally attached to each other, our gut desire is not to highlight the illogical nature of certain feelings and divert attention from indulging in them. Like most humans, we feel an innate desire to comfort someone when they express vulnerability. That said, we understand that taking the emotionally indulgent path is not in anyone's long-term best interest.

By not rewarding pleas for validation and moments of anxiety, we can actually decrease instances of both overall.

With practice on both sides, you and your partner can arrive at a place where you understand that emotional indulgence is not in anyone's long-term best interest. By not rewarding pleas for validation and moments of anxiety—and instead showing support for each other by bringing focus back to your values and logical solutions—you can actually decrease hunger for validation and waves of anxiety overall.

Bear in mind this approach does not involve partners emotionally shutting each other down and preventing each other from expressing vulnerability. Quite to the contrary, this approach requires greater vulnerability and emotional honesty than any attachment-theory-based solution. It takes a huge amount of intimacy, love, and trust for partners to not only acknowledge each other's anxieties and discomforts (and their own), but also help them ride those emotional waves in a manner that serves their personal values and logical long-term best interests.

We have said it before and will say it again: Behavioral research makes it clear that indulging in an emotional state (e.g., punching a punching bag to "let out" anger) usually heightens that emotional state, increases the expression of that state in the future, and makes it more difficult to control. This is well backed in the literature. While suppressing emotional states compromises an individual's cognition in the short term (like suppressing any idea does), doing so decreases expression of that emotion overall. If it were true that suppressing/redirecting an emotional impulse made it stronger, then counting to ten when you are angry would make you much angrier and yet we all anecdotally know of the "count to ten" method as an effective tool for lowering a negative emotional output. When you encourage negative emotions and indulge in them, you train yourself to express those emotions more (in adults at least; this is not quite as clear cut in children).

Beware that suppressing the outward expression of an emotion is different from successfully choosing not to indulge in an emotion. Merely suppressing the outward expression of an emotion can cause a physiological stress response, which may be damaging over time, as has been found in longitudinal studies of professions where this is a common requirement (such as elementary school teachers who must often mask their anger with a smile). In general, there is a large body of research around this—don't suppress the expression of an emotion, learn to suppress the experience of it. If you need help with your emotions, read the third chapter of our first book, *The Pragmatists Guide to Life*, which focuses on this topic.

Wait . . .

Hey, reader, what are you doing here? Did you actually read the whole appendix? The book was not supposed to be read that way . . . what a slog that must have been.

If you are indeed a true completionist and you'd like to make our day, please drop us a review on Amazon and Goodreads. We do not take money from these and are motivated by the validation those reviews provide us.

Made in the USA
Columbia, SC
21 October 2024

19fdbf72-aefc-4d6e-9ab3-94fb6448d7a9R01